Universal Traceability

A Comprehensive, Generic, Technology-Independent, and Semantically Rich Approach

Hannes Schwarz

Oktober 2011

Vom Promotionsausschuss des Fachbereichs 4: Informatik der Universität Koblenz–Landau zur Verleihung des akademischen Grades *Doktor der Naturwissenschaften (Dr. rer. nat.)* genehmigte Dissertation.

Vorsitzender des Promotionsausschusses: Prof. Dr. Rüdiger Grimm
Berichterstatter: Prof. Dr. Jürgen Ebert
   Prof. Dr. Uwe Aßmann

Datum der wissenschaftlichen Aussprache: 1. Februar 2012

Veröffentlicht als Dissertation an der Universität Koblenz-Landau.

Bibliografische Information der Deutschen Nationalbibliothek

Die Deutsche Nationalbibliothek verzeichnet diese Publikation in der Deutschen Nationalbibliografie; detaillierte bibliografische Daten sind im Internet über http://dnb.d-nb.de abrufbar.

ISBN 978-3-8325-3114-0

Logos Verlag Berlin GmbH
Comeniushof, Gubener Str. 47,
10243 Berlin
Tel.: +49 (0)30 42 85 10 90
Fax: +49 (0)30 42 85 10 92
INTERNET: http://www.logos-verlag.de

Acknowledgments

In the following, I would like to thank all those people who supported me in writing this thesis.

First of all, I want to express my sincere gratitude to Prof. Dr. Jürgen Ebert, who made it possible for me to work in his working group. With his invaluable advice, tireless support, and attention to detail, he kept me on the right track and allowed me to finally complete this thesis.

I also thank Prof. Dr. Uwe Aßmann for agreeing to examine my thesis. He and the whole MOST team, including my regular travel companions from Koblenz – Dr. Tobias Walter, Dr. Fernando Silva Parreiras, and Gerd Gröner – provided an excellent environment for presenting my work. The arising discussions yielded helpful input and led to new ideas.

Especially in the initial stages, Prof. Dr. Andreas Winter gave me advice on how to properly publish my results. For that, and for a lot of other useful comments, I am grateful.

To Kristina Heckelmann, I owe my thanks for her effort in developing extensions to the JGraLab library, based on some of my ideas.

Last but not least, I would like to thank Daniel Bildhauer and Tassilo Horn, with whom I shared the office. Together with Dr. Volker Riediger, they not only gave occasion to fruitful discussions, but also provided many diverting and entertaining moments that created an easy working atmosphere. In fact, I have to thank all current and former members of the Working Group Ebert, including the student assistants, for making the last five years a really enjoyable time.

Abstract

In software engineering, traceability describes the ability of stakeholders to understand and follow relationships between artifacts that play some role in software development, such as requirements, architecture components, and source code fragments. Traceability is essential for many development tasks, e.g., quality assurance, requirements management, or software maintenance. Nevertheless, traceability research still faces many obstacles. Research activities usually focus on narrowly defined problems for which they provide specifically tailored solutions, which in general depend on different, particularly suitable technologies. This makes the integration of several solutions in a comprehensive approach challenging. Furthermore, the solutions are seldom generic, i.e., customizable to specific environments. Finally, a lack of formalization of traceability relationship semantics hampers the automation of traceability tasks.

To overcome these deficiencies, this work presents a universal approach that describes required features of traceability solutions. In detail, a technology-independent, generic template for the definition of semantically rich traceability relationship types is conceived. This template also offers support for traceability-related activities such as the identification and maintenance of relationships. Furthermore, technology-independent patterns for the retrieval of traceability information are elaborated, reflecting generic problems common to traceability applications. These concepts are implemented on the basis of two concrete technologies which facilitate comprehensive traceability: the TGraph approach and OWL ontologies. The applicability of the universal approach is shown by three case studies dealing with the reuse of software artifacts, process model refinement, and requirements management, respectively.

Zusammenfassung

Im Bereich der Softwaretechnik bezeichnet Traceability das Vermögen der an einem Softwareentwicklungsprojekt beteiligten Stakeholder, Beziehungen zwischen Artefakten, wie etwa Anforderungen, Architekturkomponenten oder Quellcodefragmente, zu verstehen und nachzuverfolgen. Traceability ist für zahlreiche Aufgaben in der Softwareentwicklung unentbehrlich, z.B. Qualitätssicherung, Anforderungsmanagement oder Wartung. Dennoch steht die Forschung im Bereich Traceability weiterhin vor zahlreichen Hindernissen. So behandeln die meisten Forschungsarbeiten eng definierte Problembereiche, für die sie speziell angepasste Lösungen bieten, die zudem auf verschiedenen, jeweils besonders geeigneten Technologien aufbauen. Dadurch wird die Integration verschiedener Teillösungen in einen übergreifenden Ansatz erschwert. Die Lösungen sind nur selten generisch, d.h. an die Umgebungen verschiedener Organisationen oder Projekte anpassbar. Darüber hinaus wird die Automatisierung der von Traceability abhängigen Aktivitäten durch die mangelnde Formalisierung der Semantik von Traceability-Beziehungen erschwert.

Um einen Beitrag zur Beseitigung dieser Mängel zu leisten, stellt diese Arbeit einen universellen Ansatz vor, der die Erfordernisse bei der Umsetzung einer Traceability-Lösung beschreibt. Dazu wird ein technologieunabhängiges, generisches Template zur Definition von Traceability-Beziehungstypen mit einer formalisierten Semantik konzipiert, die zudem Traceability-Aktivitäten wie etwa die Identifikation und Wartung von Traceability-Beziehungen unterstützen. Weiterhin werden technologieunabhängige Muster entwickelt, die häufig wiederkehrende Problemstellungen bei der Anfrage von Traceability-Informationen auf eine generische Art und Weise beschreiben. Diese Konzepte werden auf der Basis zweier konkreter, für übergreifende Traceability-Ansätze geeigneter Technologien implementiert: dem TGraphen-Ansatz und OWL-Ontologien. Die Anwendbarkeit des universellen Ansatzes wird anhand dreier Fallstudien aus den Bereichen Wiederverwendung, Verfeinerung von Prozessmodellen und Anforderungsmanagement gezeigt.

Contents

1 Introduction

This chapter gives an outline of the context – traceability – and the goals of this work, followed by an overview of its structure. In detail, Section 1.1 describes traceability as a discipline of software engineering in practice and research. Based on this overview, Section 1.2 highlights existent shortcomings of the current state of the art that motivated this work and briefly sketches the derived research goals. Finally, Section 1.3 explains the structure of this book.

1.1 Context

This work is embedded in the context of *traceability*. In general, traceability refers to the ability to comprehend the interrelationships between "things" in a process, e.g., between finished products, their parts, and other utilized resources in production, or between goods and their locations in a logistics chain. Applied to the area of software engineering, traceability describes the ability of stakeholders to understand and follow relationships between artifacts which are part of a software system or which play some role in a system's development. To this end, these traceability relationships are usually physically recorded using suitable technologies. The breadth of entities that may be interconnected by traceability relationships ranges from the stakeholders issuing requirements, to the requirements themselves, to architecture components, and finally to source code. Cross-cutting concerns such as project plans, documentation, or test cases can also be important subjects of traceability.

Establishing traceability in a software development project is associated with different activities. These include the definition of which artifacts shall be traced and which kinds of relationships are to be used, the identification of actual relationships between artifacts, or the retrieval of pieces of traceability information required for a specific application, for instance. Traceability research efforts can mostly be categorized on the basis of these traceability-related activities. Examples are the definition of meta models proposing structures for traceability information, the development of techniques for the automatic identification of relationships, or the specification of special query languages for the targeted retrieval of relevant pieces of traceability information.

Once traceability has been established successfully, it can be employed for various fields of application associated with software development, such as quality assurance, requirements management, or software maintenance. Concerning quality assurance, traceability enables to check if there exists a test case for each requirement, for example. In requirements management, traceability allows for the handling of relationships between individual requirements, denoting dependencies, conflicts, or refinements. With the help of traceability relationships that capture dependencies between the different parts of a software system, especially on the source code level, software maintainers can comprehend the structure and functionality of the system. Thus, they are able to better estimate the effects of modifications to specific artifacts on other parts of the system.

Traceability played an important role in the two EU-funded projects *ReDSeeDS*[1] and *MOST*[2]. They provided the case studies used to show the applicability of the concepts developed in this work.

ReDSeeDS, short for *Requirements-Driven Software Development System* advocates a model-driven approach to software development: an initial set of manually specified requirements is automatically transformed to architecture components, design elements, and source code artifacts. Traceability relationships that connect source and target elements of the applied model transformations are automatically created in the course of transformation execution. All information, i.e., the requirements and the artifacts that result from applying the transformations, together with interconnecting traceability relationships, is retained in a repository. The requirements of some future development project can then be compared with the requirements stored in the repository. If similarities are discovered, following the traceability relationships yields artifacts that are possibly reusable in that project [Śmi06, Amb08].

MOST, short for *Marrying Ontologies and Software Technology*, involved the conception and development of various approaches for bridging ontology and software technology. Here, the term "bridging" refers to the combination of concepts and languages of both worlds to make the services and tools of one world usable in the other one [Ebe11]. As its main application, the project envisioned the development of an ontology-driven software development guidance system. Such a system uses ontology reasoning techniques to support developers with suggestions on further actions, relying on a formalized process model and on information on the state of development-related artifacts. Traceability is required to capture relationships between artifacts as well as between artifacts and process steps that influence the provided guidance. The guidance system is, among others, employed in a business process model refinement scenario, where traceability also serves to check the consistency of interconnected models. The MOST

---

[1]http://www.redseeds.eu
[2]http://www.most-project.eu

project also investigated the usability of ontology technology for requirements management and requirements traceability. The resulting *Eclipse-based*[3] tool allows for handling traceability relationships among requirements and other artifacts of the software development life cycle.

1.2 Motivation

Considering the existing body of literature on traceability, it becomes apparent that research activities are usually centered on special, narrowly defined problems for which they intend to provide specifically tailored solutions. While a given solution may effectively deal with a single issue, the whole picture is mostly neglected. In other words, it is unclear how, and even if, the underlying concepts can be combined with those of different state-of-the-art solutions for other traceability problems. The conception of a *comprehensive* approach for traceability, i.e., encompassing all traceability-related activities, has not become an important subject of traceability research yet.

Furthermore, existing solutions to traceability problems often make premature assumptions on the nature of the artifacts and the significant relationships between them that are to be considered by traceability. This is most notably reflected by the predefinition of a set of types of traceability relationships by many traceability approaches. There exist only few *generic* approaches which allow for user-definable, custom relationship types. Such approaches are highly adaptable to specific organizations or projects with their individual landscape of artifacts and relevant relationships.

In addition to the conceptual obstacles to the combination of different traceability solutions mentioned at the beginning, existing solutions generally make use of different technologies that are particularly suitable for the intended tasks. Thus, the integration of several solutions in a common approach may become even more complicated due to technological incompatibilities. Moreover, it is possible that organizational or economic necessities constrain the choice of technologies that are eligible for implementing traceability in a particular software development project. Literature lacks *technology-independent* descriptions of desirable characteristics of traceability implementations as well as recommendations on the choice of suitable technologies.

A general drawback of existing generic approaches is that they do not offer state-of-the-art features for the formalization of the semantics of traceability relationships. Instead, they rely on mere natural language descriptions of relationship purposes, augmented by a limited selection of formal concepts only. However, *semantically rich* traceability

---

[3]http://www.eclipse.org

relationships are essential for the automation of common tasks associated with traceability, such as automatically modifying artifacts which are affected by changes to other
artifacts or checking the consistency of the network of recorded traceability relationships itself.

To overcome the deficiencies of the current state of the art mentioned above, this work
aims at the development of an *universal*, i.e., *comprehensive, generic, technology-independent*, and *semantically rich* approach that describes required features of traceability solutions, especially considering the properties of traceability relationships. Subsequently, existing technologies are to be investigated for their suitability for implementing
traceability on the basis of these concepts. If certain aspects of traceability are not well-
supported, the technologies are to be adequately extended. Two technologies are taken
as examples in this work: the TGraph approach [Ebe08], featuring expressive graph
structures and providing querying and transformation mechanisms, and the Web Ontology Language [Mot09b] together with some complementing languages and concepts, a well-established standard for describing ontologies in the Semantic Web.

1.3 Structure

Following this introductory chapter, Part I lays out the foundations for being able to
understand the notion of traceability in research and practice. Chapter 2 introduces the
required terminology, including a definition for the term "traceability" itself and other,
related concepts. Chapter 3 presents the current state of the art in the field of traceability,
categorized on the basis of activities that are commonly performed in association with
traceability. In Chapter 4, the usage of traceability in practice is discussed, covering
possible fields of application, the features of existing commercial tools, and various
obstacles for the establishment of adequate traceability infrastructures in companies
and other organizations.

Building on the foundations in Part I, Part II derives comprehensive, generic, technology-independent, and semantically rich concepts that describe required features of traceability solutions. First, based on the identified deficiencies of the state of the art and
existing commercial tools, Chapter 5 contemplates the objectives of this work and formulates the research questions that are to be pursued. Underpinned by requirements
gathered in the MOST project, Chapter 6 conceives a generic, technology-independent,
template for the definition of semantically rich traceability relationship types that offer
support for different traceability-related activities. In Chapter 7, elementary traceability
tasks are identified and lead to the specification of patterns for the retrieval of traceability information. They reflect generic problems which are common to a wide range of

traceability applications. Consequently, to support all these applications, traceability implementations ought to facilitate retrieval conforming to the patterns.

Part III is concerned with the implementation of the technology-independent concepts on the basis of concrete, suitable technologies. Chapter 8 introduces the technologies that are employed as examples in this work: TGraphs and the Web Ontology Language (OWL), each one together with related languages and concepts. In Chapters 9 and 10, the suitability of TGraphs and OWL for implementing comprehensive, generic, and semantically rich traceability is investigated, respectively. Extensions to the technologies which were specifically developed in the context of this work are highlighted.

Part IV presents three case studies that illustrate the successful application of the previously elaborated traceability concepts and implementations. Chapter 11 describes their usage in the context of reuse as advocated by the ReDSeeDS project: based on an initial set of reusable requirements, traceability is employed to find potentially reusable software artifacts on lower levels of abstraction, e.g., architectural components, detailed design elements, or source code fragments. Based on a MOST project case study, Chapter 12 shows how the consistency between individual business process models in model refinement chains can be preserved with the help of suitable traceability information. The integration of traceability concepts in the *Eclipse* development environment, making use of an ontology for requirements management developed in MOST, is explained in Chapter 13.

Finally, Chapter 14 concludes this work by summarizing the achievements, discussing their contribution to the state of the art, and giving an outlook on possible future work.

Part I

Foundation

2 Terminology

This chapter is concerned with the origins and the general meaning of the term "traceability". It has a look at the subjects of traceability and at various categorizations used in literature.

In detail, Section 2.1 investigates the history of traceability in the context of computer science and especially software development, discusses popular definitions, and coins a new definition suiting the purposes of this work. In Section 2.2, some related terms are introduced. Finally, Section 2.3 examines different categorizations, called *dimensions*, of traceability.

2.1 The Notion of "Traceability"

In computer science, the history of the term "traceability" can be dated back to at least 1975: in [Wil75], it is used by Williams to relate the functions of a software system to the corresponding requirements. Later works, such as [Alf77], [Got94], [Döm98], and [Ram01], also treat requirements as the central subject of traceability. Frequently, as it can be observed in [Cle06], for instance, the term *requirements traceability* was and is still not clearly distinguished from "general" *traceability* without particular focus on requirements. Hence, the two terms are often used synonymously.

In recent years, researchers outside the requirements engineering community started to more extensively explore traceability of entities of the software development process other than requirements, e.g., source code and design models [Mur95] or documentation [Ant02]. In [Str02, Asu07], traceability is understood as a comprehensive concept encompassing the whole development process, without putting special emphasis on requirements. For that use, Spanoudakis and Zisman coin the term *software traceability* [Spa05].

Ramesh et al. and Pohl point out that traceability should not only consider "tangible" artifacts such as requirements, models, or code fragments, but also has to take into account the decisions which lead to their development, together with associated arguments and alternatives [Ram95, Poh96b].

The importance of traceability has also been recognized in the field of model-driven software development, where models are transformed to other models or source code and the relations between transformation source and transformation target have to be maintained [Aiz06]. Winkler and von Pilgrim argue that research activities on traceability in the requirements engineering and in the model-driven development communities are undertaken rather independently from each other, leading to the danger of "not reaching a common understanding and of reinventing the wheel" [Win10].

Section 2.1.1 gives common definitions for traceability taken from literature and discusses their various shortcomings. Subsequently, an alternative, more adequate definition is introduced in Section 2.1.2.

2.1.1 Existing Definitions for Traceability

Looking for a definition of traceability suiting the goals of this work, a survey on the existing body of literature reveals various candidates. The apparently most cited definition was introduced by Gotel and Finkelstein in [Got94]:

> "Requirements traceability refers to the ability to describe and follow the life of a requirement, in both a forwards and backwards direction (i.e., from its origins, through its development and specification, to its subsequent deployment and use, and through all periods of on-going refinement and iteration in any of these phases)."

Obviously, this definition is focused on requirements traceability and therefore is too narrow for a more generic conception of traceability potentially encompassing the entire development process, as advocated by this work.

The earliest definition known to the author goes back to an article by Greenspan and McGowan from 1978 [Gre78]:

> "Traceability is a property of a system description technique that allows changes in one of the three system descriptions – requirements, specifications, implementation – to be traced to the corresponding portions of the other descriptions. The correspondence should be maintained through the lifetime of the systems."

This definition does not center on requirements only, but ignores "descriptions" other than the three mentioned ones, e.g., test cases or documentation.

The term *software traceability* introduced by Spanoudakis and Zisman [Spa05] is more general:

> "[Software traceability] is the ability to relate artefacts created during the development of a software system to describe the system from different perspectives and levels of abstraction with each other, the stakeholders that have contributed to the creation of the artefacts, and the rationale that explains the form of the artefacts."

Similarly universal is the definition given by Aizenbud-Reshef et al. in [Aiz06]:

> "[Traceability is] any relationship that exists between artifacts involved in the software-engineering life cycle."

Traceability is also included in the *Standard Glossary of Software Engineering Terminology* by the *Institute of Electrical and Electronics Engineers (IEEE)* [Ins90]:

> "The degree to which a relationship can be established between two or more products of the development process, especially products having a predecessor-successor or master-subordinate relationship to one another; for example, the degree to which the requirements and design of a given software component match."

The three last-cited definitions consider traceability within the scope of the whole development process. However, neither Spanoudakis and Zisman nor Aizenbud-Reshef et al. nor the IEEE provide definitions for "artifacts" or "products", which are their proposed subjects of traceability. Following the author's intuitive conception of an artifact or product as some structure of the size of a document or a model, for example, which is possibly composed of smaller elements, e.g., paragraphs or model elements, these definitions only allow for traceability on a rather coarse level of granularity. Concerning the IEEE standard, this view is fostered by a second definition for traceability stemming from [Ins90]:

> "The degree to which each element in a software development product establishes its reason for existing; [...]"

Consequently, products are not atomic, but can be composed of other elements. But since the relationship between the two IEEE definitions is not clear, and since stakeholders, decisions and rationales to be traced can hardly be categorized as "products of the development process", the rather inappropriate terms "artefact" and "product" should be replaced by a more fitting one. This is considered in the next section which elaborates a new guiding definition of traceability for usage throughout this book.

2.1.2 Elaboration of an Alternative Definition

Based on the insights gained by the analysis of existing definitions for traceability, Definition 1 shall be used as guideline in this work. It resembles the definition for traceability formulated in the *MOST* project[1] [Sch09c] and avoids focusing on a particular aspect of the development process, such as the requirements specification.

DEFINITION 1 (TRACEABILITY)

Traceability refers to the ability of stakeholders to understand and follow relationships between entities being part of a software system or playing some role in its development.

In order to denominate the subject of traceability, the very general term *entity* is employed. While this term has its origins in philosophy, it is also used in computer science. An entity refers to a uniquely identifiable, but otherwise unspecified "thing" [Che76], which somehow occurs in or is connected to a software system or its development process. Examples for entities are stakeholders, individual requirements, the whole system architecture, or single lines of code.

2.2 Related Terms

To allow for a clear and unequivocal discourse on the subject matter, definitions for central concepts associated with *traceability* are introduced in the following.

Definition 1 in Section 2.1.2 used the term "entity" to denote the subjects of traceability, without specifying its meaning further than stating that it is related to "a software system or its development". A more precise definition of "entity" is provided by Definition 2.

DEFINITION 2 (TRACED/TRACEABLE ENTITY)

A **traced entity** or **traceable entity** is a uniquely identifiable, otherwise unspecified "thing" which is created, used, or in some other way involved in a software system or a software development project and which may be a subject of traceability.

---

[1] http://www.most-project.eu

The preceding attributes "traced" and "traceable" indicate whether the entity referred to currently participates in one or more *traceability relationship*s or whether it is only a candidate for such a participation. Traceability relationships are defined in Definition 3.

DEFINITION 3 (TRACEABILITY RELATIONSHIP)

A **traceability relationship** is a connection between two or more traced entities that serves traceability purposes.

If the context is clear, "traceable/traced" or "traceability" are omitted and only "entity" or "relationship" is used, respectively.

To refer to the combination of both, traced entities and traceability relationships, the concepts of "traceability model" and "traceability information" are introduced by Definitions 4 and 5, respectively. While *traceability model* emphasizes the network-like structure formed by *all* existing entities and relationships, *traceability information* is used to simply refer to *some* of the entities and relationships comprised by a traceability model if their underlying structures or interconnections are unimportant. For example, the traceability information returned by a query to a traceability model may be structured in a list, a set, or a table.

DEFINITION 4 (TRACEABILITY MODEL)

A **traceability model** denotes the network formed by all traced entities and traceability relationships which are comprised by a project-specific traceability solution.

The usage of *traceability model* shall not imply that these entities and relationships are necessarily represented on the basis of some modeling technologies such as the *Meta Object Facility* [Obj06] or the *TGraph approach* [Ebe08]. A set of documents with cross references between each other can also be viewed as a "network" of entities and relationships.

> **DEFINITION 5 (TRACEABILITY INFORMATION)**
>
> **Traceability information** refers to some of the traced entities and traceability relationships which are comprised by a traceability model, without making any assumptions on their underlying structure.

2.3 Dimensions of Traceability

Various terms for structuring different notions and views of traceability have been coined in literature:

- *forward* and *backward traceability*,
- *implicit* and *explicit traceability*,
- *intra-level* and *inter-level traceability*,
- *material* and *immaterial traceability*,
- *pre-RS* and *post-RS traceability*, and
- *version traceability*.

These concepts can be visualized as *dimensions* of a frame of reference formed by the *abstraction levels* of the software development life cycle. Abstraction levels are used to structure the set of traceable entities occurring in the life cycle according to their structure, purpose, or level of detail. Examples for such levels are the requirements specification, the architecture, the source code, the documentation, or the existing test cases. Note, that to a certain degree, the granularities and boundaries of abstraction levels cannot be fixed universally. For instance, the requirements specification could be split into a set of more abstract user requirements and more specific system requirements, depending on the necessary level of detail.

The above-mentioned dimensions are illustrated in Figure 2.1. It takes the resources and stakeholders which are the origins of a software system's requirements, the requirements themselves, the resulting design, and finally the system's implementation as exemplary abstraction levels.

Detailed explanations of the various dimensions are given in Sections 2.3.1 to 2.3.6. Since the research community often uses the associated terms in an inconsistent way,

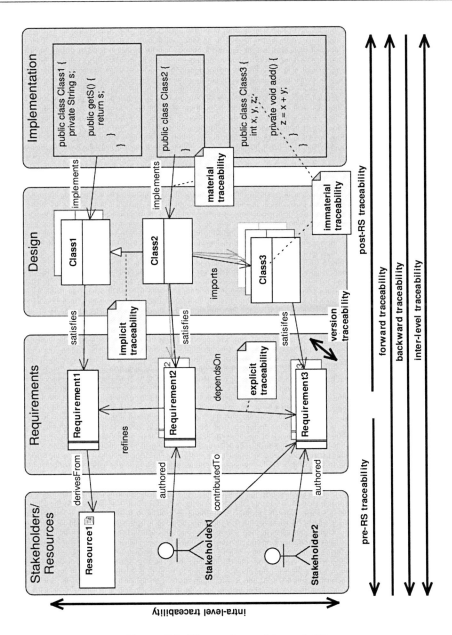

Figure 2.1: Dimensions of traceability

i.e., the same term is used for different dimensions or different dimensions are denominated by the same term, a consistent terminology is introduced where required.

2.3.1 Forward and Backward Traceability

Originally, *forward* and *backward traceability* specified the availability of relationships linking requirements forward to derived entities such as design models or source code and backward to their sources, respectively [ANS84]. Later, Ramesh and Edwards have generalized the concepts to denote the direction of traceability relationships with respect to a system's abstraction levels [Ram93]: while forward traceability identifies the ability to follow relationships from entities on more abstract to entities on more specific abstraction levels, backward traceability refers to the reverse direction.

Ramesh and Edwards emphasize that traceability relationships should be inherently bidirectional, thus able to be followed in both directions [Ram93]. Although this conception is based on the assumption that traceability relationships always exist between two entities only, it can be generalized to n-ary relationships: starting from any traced entity participating in a given relationship, it shall be possible to trace to all other entities connected by that relationship, thus rendering the distinction between forward and backward traceability meaningless.

Considering Figure 2.1, forward traceability is established by the possibility of traversing the depicted traceability relationships from left to right, while traversal from right to left corresponds to backward traceability.

2.3.2 Implicit and Explicit Traceability

Looking at the relevant literature, it is discernible that there is no common understanding of the terms *implicit* and *explicit traceability* and their relation to each other. In [Lin94], Lindvall defines implicit traceability to refer to non-materialized relationships, i.e., relationships that are not physically present, such as the implicit relationship between two entities having the same name. On the other hand, explicit traceability includes materialized relationships only. Paige et al. essentially concur with Lindvall's notion of explicit traceability, but have a different conception of implicit traceability, influenced by their focus on traceability in model-driven contexts: "implicit traceability involves trace links that are created and manipulated by application of MDE operations" [Pai08].

Von Knethen and Paech [Kne02] as well as Mäder et al. [Mäd07] argue that implicit traceability involves, on the one hand, non-materialized relationships and, on the other hand, materialized relationships which were originally established for other reasons than traceability. Examples for the latter are messages between elements in *UML interaction diagrams* or compositions in *UML class diagrams* [Obj10c], expressing whole-part relationships. By claiming that explicit traceability refers to relationships which were set up for traceability purposes exclusively, both publications also exhibit a similar comprehension of explicit traceability.

To a large extent, this work adopts the conception of von Knethen and Paech and Mäder et al. However, implicit traceability is considered to only subsume materialized relationships which did not originally serve traceability purposes. Immaterial relationships are treated by the distinction between *material* and *immaterial traceability*, explained in Section 2.3.4.

An example of an implicit traceability relationship is the generalization connecting Class1 and Class2 in Figure 2.1. The dependsOn relationship from Requirement2 to Requirement3 denotes an explicit relationship.

2.3.3 Intra-Level and Inter-Level Traceability

The dimensions of *vertical* and *horizontal traceability* introduced by Bohner describe whether a traceability relationship only involves entities on the same or on different abstraction levels, respectively [Boh91]. Other authors, e.g., Ramesh and Edwards in [Ram93], use the two terms inversely. Focusing on requirements traceability, Pinheiro distinguishes between *inter-requirements traceability* and *extra-requirements traceability* to refer to relationships connecting only requirements or requirements to other entities, respectively [Pin03].

In order to maintain a consistent terminology, the terms *intra-level traceability* and *inter-level traceability* shall be used henceforth [Bil07]. While intra-level traceability considers relationships on one abstraction level, inter-level traceability refers to the connections between entities on different levels. In [Anq08], Anquetil et al. introduce similar terms: *intra traceability* and *inter traceability*.

In Figure 2.1, refines and imports are intra-level traceability relationships on the requirements or the design level, respectively. Examples for inter-level relationships include the satisfies and implements relationships.

2.3.4 Material and Immaterial Traceability

The terms *material* and *immaterial traceability* cannot be found in literature, but are based on the idea of implicit and explicit traceability as understood by Lindvall [Lin94]. Material traceability involves only relationships which are physically existing in the traceability model. This includes cross references in texts, hyperlinks, or connections between model elements, for instance. In contrast, immaterial traceability considers relationships which are not physically present, but can be derived from other information, e.g., by choosing the same identifiers for an architecture component and its implementing class. In general, it is difficult to benefit from immaterial traceability relationships, for they cannot be handled directly by query languages or other technologies that are suitable for accessing material relationships. To overcome this limitation, immaterial relationships may be *materialized*.

While Figure 2.1 only visualizes material traceability relationships as arrows. An immaterial relationship could be imagined between the Class3 on the design level and Class3 on the implementation level: since both classes have the same identifier, it is likely that the implementation class implements the design class. Another candidate for an immaterial traceability relationship is an imports relationship between Class2 and Class3 on the implementation level , for there is an imports relationship between the respective classes on the design level.

2.3.5 Pre-RS and Post-RS Traceability

The dimensions of *pre-RS* and *post-RS traceability*, with *RS* standing for *requirements specification*, go back to Gotel and Finkelstein [Got94] and are obviously closely related to the notion of requirements traceability. Another pair of terms for the same concepts, *pre-traceability* and *post-traceability*, is used by Pohl in [Poh96a]. The requirements specification constitutes their pivotal point: pre-RS traceability considers traceability between requirements and their sources or between the sources themselves. Analogously, post-RS traceability refers to the entities derived from the requirements specification.

Pre-RS and post-RS traceability are not used in the following chapters because they entail a requirements-centric view of traceability which does not match the generic conception pursued by this work.

With respect to Figure 2.1, authored or derivesFrom represent pre-RS traceability relationships, while the satisfies as well as the imports relationships contribute to post-RS traceability.

2.3.6 Version Traceability

In [Gor02], Gorschek and Tejle use the term *version traceability* to refer to traceability between different versions of requirements.

For different reasons, other terms which can be found for this notion in literature turn out to be problematic. Corriveau speaks of *horizontal traceability* [Cor96], obviously colliding with the notions of horizontal traceability promoted by Bohner [Boh91] and Ramesh and Edwards [Ram93]. Anquetil et al. call traceability relationships between versions *evolution traceability links* [Anq08]. However, the notion of *evolution* in the context of traceability is also ambiguous, for Ramesh and Jarke employ it in the sense of inter-level traceability, denoting the evolution of an entity across different abstraction levels [Ram01]. Finally, the term *traceability by history* coined by Ramamoorthy et al. [Ram90] can be misleading, too. Readers could assume that it refers to an identification technique for traceability relationships, based on analyzing the version history of entities.

In Figure 2.1, version traceability is indicated by placing older versions of a given entity behind the current version.

3 State of the Art of Traceability-Related Activities

In this chapter, the state of the art of traceability research is presented, structured on the basis of six traceability-related activities that are derived in the following.

In [Pin96a], Pinheiro introduces three activities he associated with traceability: *trace definition*, *trace production*, and *trace extraction*. The first activity, trace definition, is concerned with determining the types of traceable entities and traceability relationships required for a specific application. Trace production refers to the identification and recording of relationships between entities. Finally, trace extraction deals with the retrieval of recorded traceability information. With the maintenance of traceability relationships, von Knethen and Paech propose a fourth activity [Kne02]. However, in a later publication, Pinheiro himself attributes maintenance to the activity of trace production which is described as the "perception, registration, and maintenance" of traceability relationships [Pin03].

Winkler and von Pilgrim name four traceability-related activities: *planning and preparing*, *recording*, *using*, and *maintaining* [Win10]. Planning and preparing includes the determination of traceable entity and traceability relationship types and also considers managerial aspects, such as the selection of appropriate methods and tools. Recording subsumes the identification and storage of traceability relationships. The activity of using covers the pure retrieval of traceability information as well as its further processing for various applications, such as impact analysis or quality management. Maintenance according to Winkler and von Pilgrim not only refers to the update of traceability relationships, but also to the examination and possible adaptation of the employed methods and tools.

To classify different aspects of traceability and to structure the state of the art, this chapter introduces an own scheme of traceability-related activities, based on Pinheiro's work. The scope of this scheme is situated between the previously presented ones: while it considers the further usage of retrieved traceability information, managerial and organizational aspects, such as included by Winkler and von Pilgrim, are ignored, as they transcend the more technical view on traceability adopted by this work.

In detail, Pinheiro's activity of *definition* is adopted without changes. Extraction is renamed to *retrieval* to avoid confusion with the identification of relationships, which is also called extraction in some publications (see [Che10], for instance). The activity of trace production is split into its three subactivities which are named *identification, recording,* and *maintenance*. Furthermore, utilization is added as another activity, involving the usage of retrieved traceability information for given applications. This may comprise the presentation of the traceability model or parts thereof to the users. Summing up, the six traceability-related activities relied on in this work are:

- *definition* – the determination of traceable entity and traceability relationship types relevant for a given application,

- *identification* – the manual or automatic discovery or computation of traceability relationships,

- *recording* – the physical representation of identified traceability information in a data structure,

- *retrieval* – the localization and gathering of recorded traceability information answering a specific purpose,

- *utilization* – the usage and processing of retrieved traceability information, possibly including the visualization of parts of the traceability model, and

- *maintenance* – the manual or automatic updating of recorded traceability relationships with respect to modifications of entities or other relationships.

Table 3.1 directly juxtaposes the discussed traceability-related activity schemes in order to compare their scope.

Pinheiro [Pin03]	This work	Winkler and von Pilgrim [Win10]
		Planning and preparing
Trace definition	Definition	
Trace production	Identification	Recording
	Recording	
Trace extraction	Retrieval	Using
	Utilization	
Trace production	Maintenance	Maintaining

Table 3.1: Comparison of different traceability-related activity schemes.

Activity	Subcategory/Technique		Publications
Definition	Structuring traceability information	Relationship types	Car01, Dah03, Esp06, Ram93, Spa05, Try97
		Meta models	Ama08, Anq10, Dut01, Ebn02, Gli08, Gok11, Gra10, Jir09, Let02, Moo07, Old06, Obj10b, Obj10c, Pai08, Poh96b, Pot88, Ram01, Sch10c, Sou08
		Generic approaches	Dri08, Esp06, Esp11, Sch10b, Wal06
	Traceability relationship semantics	Informal	Ebn02, Esp06, Mir11, Obj10c, Ram01, Try97
		Attributes	Dic02, Dri08, Esp11, Ram01, Sch10b
		Constraints	Dri08, Poh96b, Sch10b
		Logics and Math.	Car01, Dah03, Dic02
		Rules	Aiz05, Gok11, Hov09, Jir09, Lam11, Sch10b Wal06
	N-ary relationships		Dri08, Mal05, Mun05, Obj10b, Obj10c, Sch10b
Identification	Text-based techniques	NL processing	Kai99, Yos09
		Text mining	Wit07
		Information retrieval	Ant02, Che10, Cle07a, DeL06a, DeL06b, DeL08, DeL09, DeL11, Huf06, Lin06, Mar05a, Oli10 Set04
	Rules		Ale08, Cle03b, Cys08, Esp06, Gok11, Jir09, Rie11, Sch10b, She03, Spa04
	Model transformations		Jou05, Ols07, Pil08, Sch10c, Yie09
	Program analysis		Aze11, Egy01, Gre07, Qus10
	Differencing		Ant01, Ric03, Wen07, Yil11
	Other		Ass11, Buc11, Poh96b, Pfe10, Sha11
Recording	Internal		Kai93, Ram01, Obj10c, Son98, Wie95
	External (fact repositories)	Relational databases	Poh96a, Son98
		XML technology	Klo11, Mal05, Spa04
		Ontologies	Wit07
		EMF	Rie11
		Graph technology	Sch10c
		Other	Con95, She03
	External (other)		Bar07, Hal11, Kol06
Retrieval	Retrieval patterns		Sch10c
	Query languages		Mäd10, Mal09, Sch10a, Sch10c, Wit07
	User interfaces		Pin96b, Poh96b, She03
Utilization (visualization)	Matrices		Dua06
	Hyperlinks		Kai93, Ngu03, Ols02, Pin96b
	Diagrams		Che10, Con95, Pil08, Pin96b, Poh96b
	Other		Cle07b, Mar05b, Wen07
Maintenance	Text-based techniques		Por11
	Rules		Aiz05, Cle03a, Cos07, Dri10, Gok11, Mäd08b, Mur08, Sch10b
	Model transformations		Sei10
	Constraints		Dri08, Sch10b

Table 3.2: Overview of related work.

The activities are ordered logically, i.e., in general an activity can only be performed if the preceding activity has been accomplished at least once. The exceptions are utilization and maintenance. For approaches basing on immaterial traceability, traceability information is utilized directly, because it is not recorded and retrieved. Maintenance only relies on the existence of already recorded traceability relationships.

This ordering shall not imply some waterfall process model where it is not possible to revert to an activity which has been accomplished. On the contrary, it is essential to constantly identify, record, and maintain traceability information as a software development project evolves.

Subsequently, Sections 3.1 to 3.6, each dedicated to one traceability-related activity, provide a survey of related work in the field of traceability research. Table 3.2 gives an overview of the cited publications.

3.1 Definition

The activity of *definition* is concerned with the determination of types of traceable entities and potentially interconnecting traceability relationships which are suitable for a given application or environment.

Existing literature on this activity can be roughly assigned to one of two categories. Publications falling into the first category try to structure traceability information by distinguishing between types of traceability relationships or by introducing meta models for traceability, for instance. These approaches often rely on informal descriptions of the meaning of relationship types, i.e., in the form of natural language descriptions or even only as implied by the types' names. To facilitate the automation of tasks relying on traceability information, the second category of publications elaborates on the formalization of the semantics of traceability relationships.

In the following, Sections 3.1.1 and 3.1.2 examine these two categories in detail. Finally, Section 3.1.3 briefly highlights some publications which do not treat traceability relationships as binary links, as most approaches do, but allow for the connection of more than two entities by a single relationship.

3.1.1 Structuring Traceability Information

Literature belonging to this category can again be classified into three groups. While in the first group of publications, mere enumerations of different relationship types can be found, works in the second group conceive traceability meta models prescribing which entities may be connected by which relationships. While some of these meta models are explicitly declared as being *reference* meta models, others are labeled as *domain-specific language (DSL)*. Reference (meta) models shall be adaptable to specific applications or act as template for the design of specific models [Win00]. Domain-specific languages are languages developed for a specific application [Mer05]. The third group includes more generic languages and templates that specify the properties an entity or relationship type should possess, thus aiding in the development of application-specific meta models. Below, each group of publications is discussed separately.

Note, that works primarily dealing with another traceability-related activity, e.g., the identification of relationships, often introduce meta models which serve as basis for exemplifying the respective concepts. However, due to the exemplary nature of these meta models, such publications are not regarded as related work here.

Traceability Relationship Types

Focusing on requirements traceability, Carlshamre et al. [Car01] and Dahlstedt and Persson [Dah03] introduce various relationship types for interconnecting requirements without embedding them in a meta model. In [Try97], Tryggeseth and Nytrø take a more holistic view of the development process and describe relationship types between requirements, design elements, source code, test cases, and documentation. The surveys conducted by Spanoudakis and Zisman [Spa05] as well as by Espinoza et al. [Esp06] give an overview of several relationship types proposed by different authors and try to put them into broader categories that reflect their intended meaning.

Similar discussions on the choice of traceable entity types for specific applications, i.e., without putting them in the context of a meta model, can hardly be found. In essence, only general recommendations are offered. For example, Ramesh and Edwards believe that "a comprehensive scheme for maintaining traceability [...] requires that all system components (not just software), created at various stages of the development process, be linked to the requirements" [Ram93].

Meta Models

There is a multitude of proposals for traceability (reference) meta models in literature. However, most of them only capture specific parts of the whole development process, such as the requirements specification, or are geared towards particular development practices, e.g., product line engineering.

25

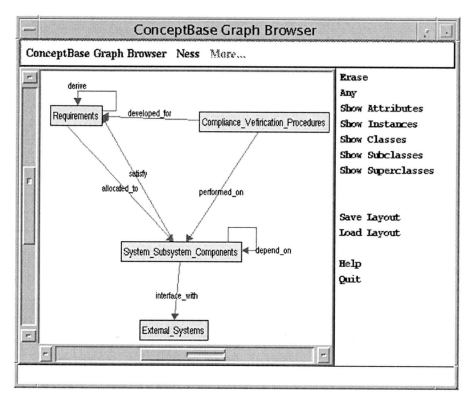

Figure 3.1: The low-end traceability reference meta model by Ramesh and Jarke. Taken from [Ram01].

In [Ram01], Ramesh and Jarke introduce two rather general reference meta models[1]. The models' focus lies on capturing traceability relationships between requirements together with associated decisions, arguments, change proposals, etc., but they also consider a system's architecture and "compliance verification procedures", such as inspections and test cases. The authors distinguish between a "low-end" reference meta model (see Figure 3.1) and a "high-end" meta model, with both of them being based on empirical studies conducted among 26 software development organizations. While the low-end model is very simple, consisting of only few entity and relationship types, the high-end model is much more complex.

---

[1]The authors of [Ram01] speak of a reference *model*. However, by the standards of this work, it is to be considered as a *meta model*.

The *Traceability Reference Schema* (*TRS*) by Schwarz et al. is a meta model that spans the whole development process and considers commonly occurring traceable entities on different abstraction levels, such as requirements, architecture elements, and code fragments [Sch10c]. The TRS has been applied in the *ReDSeeDS* project[2] for the creation of a specific traceability meta model in the context of requirements-based reuse of software artifacts (see Chapter 11).

The requirements engineering approach presented by Pohl in [Poh96b], supported by the *PRO-ART* tool, short for *Process and Repository-based Approach to Requirements Traceability*, features a complex model hierarchy comprising a traceability meta model. Pohl provides a multitude of different relationship types based on a survey of related work. In addition to the requirements themselves, entity types such as decisions and arguments are also included.

Other meta models focusing on requirements traceability are suggested by Ebner and Kaindl in [Ebn02] and by Goknil et al. in [Gok11]. Approaches specifically developed for tracing rationales and arguments supporting decisions are described by Potts and Bruns [Pot88] and Dutoit and Paech [Dut01].

The work of Moon et al. [Moo07] is concerned with tracing variability between product line requirements and architecture. To that end, the authors introduce an integrated meta model consisting of three different, yet interconnected submodels to represent the requirements, the system architecture, and the interconnecting traceability relationships, respectively. Jirapanthong and Zisman [Jir09] present an *XML*-based [Bra08] reference meta model for product line engineering. They distinguish between eight document types, among them feature models, process models, and class diagrams, and provide nine different traceability relationship types for interconnecting elements of those models. Another traceability meta model for software product line engineering can be found in [Sou08] by Sousa et al.

In [Anq10], Anquetil et al. are concerned with model-driven product line engineering and provide an appropriate meta model. Their approach is implemented by the *AMPLE Traceability Framework* (*ATF*), which is based on the *Eclipse* development environment[3]. In addition to ATF's distinction between intra-level, inter-level, and version traceability relationships, the framework introduces a fourth, product line-specific dimension of relationships: *variability*. Such relationships link product variants to their realizing artifacts or artifacts on the product engineering level to the corresponding reused artifacts on the domain engineering level. ATF provides basic features such as recording traceability information in a relational database or in XML format and an interface for posing simple queries. However, the framework is designed to accept further plug-ins

---

[2]http://www.redseeds.eu
[3]http://www.eclipse.org

which extend its functionality, for example for automatic identification, more sophisticated retrieval, and visualization of traceability information.

Meta models for usage in model-driven contexts are proposed by various authors, e.g., Oldevik and Neple [Old06], Amar et al. [Ama08], Glitia et al. [Gli08], Paige et al. [Pai08], and Grammel and Kastenholz [Gra10].

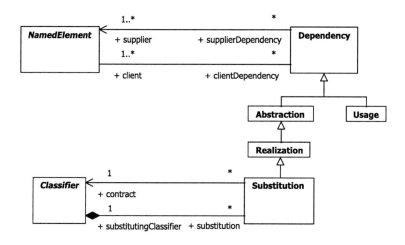

Figure 3.2: The UML Dependencies package. Adapted from [Obj10c].

By allowing to model *dependencies* between model elements, traceability concepts have also found their way into the well-known *UML (Unified Modeling Language)* [Obj10c]. The UML's traceability relationship type hierarchy is depicted in Figure 3.2. The hierarchy's topmost relationship type Dependency may connect any number of NamedElements, which subsume UML classes, attributes, and even associations, for instance. Specializations of Dependency are Usage, Abstraction, Realization, and Substitution. These types may be extended by applying UML stereotypes.

The UML-based *System Modeling Language (SysML)*, which is an Object Management Group (OMG) standard for modeling complex systems, introduces special concepts for representing requirements and associated traceability relationships [Obj10b]. In [Let02], Letelier uses UML profiles for extending the traceability capabilities of the UML meta model. To represent stakeholders, requirements, and rationales, for instance, he defines stereotypes for UML meta classes. Specializations of the UML stereotype Trace denote different traceability relationship types.

Generic Approaches

In [Esp06], Espinoza et al. present the so-called *Traceability Schema Specification (TS)* which specifies recommended characteristics of a traceability concept. Concerning the activity of definition, the significant constituents of the TS are the *Traceability Meta-type* and its instances forming the *Traceability Type Set*. Further features of the TS address management issues, security aspects, and metrics for traceability. The Traceability Meta-type has the following properties: *description*, given in natural language; *purpose*, providing a natural language explanation of the type's reason for existence; *objects to link*, restricting the kinds of traceable entities to be connected by instances of a type; *linkage rule*, referring to rules for automatically creating instances of a specific type; *sub-type classification*, specifying specializations of a type; *uses*, giving project-specific sample applications of the type; and *examples*, offering sample applications in other, more general contexts.

Drawing upon their previous work in [Esp06], Espinoza and Garbajosa introduce their *traceability metamodel (TmM)* [Esp11]. The TmM allows for user-definable relationship types, stakeholder roles with different rights concerning the manipulation of the traceability model, and linkage rules. As argued by the authors, these customization possibilities are required for supporting different development methodologies, including agile ones.

The approach by Walderhaug et al. in [Wal06] is based on three pillars. First, a *Traceability Metamodel* (see Figure 3.3) provides concepts for modeling TraceableArtefactTypes (i.e., traceable entity types), RelationTraceTypes (i.e., relationship types connecting two entity types), and ArtefactTraceTypes, which describe types of attachments to a single traceable entity type. The latter can be used for tagging traceable entities with version information, for instance. The second pillar is an archetypical *Traceability System* which provides a repository for concrete entities and relationships. Finally, *Traceability Services* specify the users' possible interactions with the traceability system, including the creation, querying, and usage of traceability information.

Based on the observation of recurring practices in the development of traceability meta models, Drivalos et al. propose the *Traceability Metamodelling Language (TML)* for creating such meta models (see Figure 3.4) [Dri08]. Relationship types defined with the TML, i.e., instances of the meta class TraceLink, are supposed to interconnect traceable entity types already specified by some existing *Ecore* [Ste08] meta models. Meta models designed with the TML can be transformed to Ecore meta models in order to implement them using the *Eclipse Modeling Framework* (*EMF*) [Ste08]. Explanations of the other TML concepts shown in Figure 3.4 are provided in Section 3.1.2.

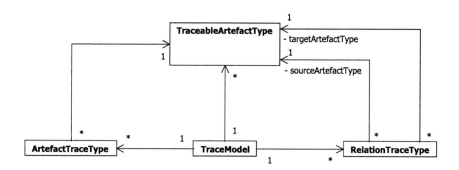

Figure 3.3: The *Traceability Metamodel* by Walderhaug et al. Adapted from illustrations in [Wal06].

In [Sch10b], Schwarz et al. present the *Traceability Relationship Type Template* (*TRTT*). Building upon traceability requirements collected in the MOST project and combining state-of-the-art approaches, the TRTT describes desirable properties of traceability relationship types in a generic and technology-independent way. The TRTT is supposed to be instantiated by specific *technological spaces* that are able to implement its defined properties. A technological space is a "working context with a set of associated concepts, body of knowledge, tools, required skills, and possibilities" [Kur02]. Note, that there is no standard or common agreement on the naming, categorization, or granularity of technological spaces. The term rather serves as an informal concept to ease communication. Examples for technological spaces are relational databases, markup languages such as XML, or semantic technologies including *RDF* [Kly04] and *OWL* [Mot09b]. The TRTT constitutes one of the central concepts of this work and is further elaborated on in Chapter 6.

3.1.2 Traceability Relationship Semantics

As already mentioned, many approaches define the semantics of traceability relationships in an *informal* way. This ranges from completely anonymous relationships, to the

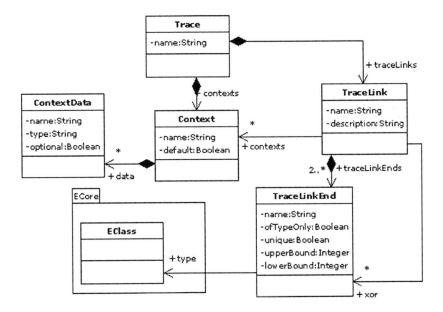

Figure 3.4: The *Traceability Metamodelling Language* by Drivalos et al. Taken from [Dri08].

distinction between different relationship types whose semantics shall be reflected by the types' names, and finally to natural language explanations of the types' semantics. Examples can be found in [Try97, Ram01, Ebn02, Esp06, Obj10c, Mir11].

Several approaches allow for the attachment of additional information to traceability relationships by using some form of *attributes*. The formalization of relationship semantics may rely on various concepts and techniques, including *constraints*, *logical and mathematical expressions*, and *rules*. Relevant publications are discussed in the following.

Attributes

Some approaches predefine specific attributes for traceability relationships. For relationships that express a dependency, Ramesh and Jarke propose to attach the "strength of dependency" as a value between 1 and 10 [Ram01]. Similarly, the traceability metamodel TmM by Espinoza and Garbajosa [Esp11] defines a special attribute called *link weight* that indicates the "dependency level" between related entities. The *rich traceability* approach by Dick [Dic02] complements relationships by textual rationales. See Figure 3.5 for an example taken from Dick's work.

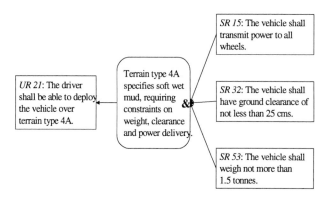

Figure 3.5: Example of rich traceability as proposed by Dick. Taken from [Dic02].

In contrast, another group of approaches allow users to assign their own attributes to relationship types. One example is the Traceability Metamodelling Language by Driva-los et al. [Dri08] (see Figure 3.4), where the classes Context and ContextData represent multivalued attributes of boolean, integer, or string type. Another such approach is the Traceability Relationship Type Template by Schwarz et al. [Sch10b]. See Chapter 6 for more information on the TRTT.

Constraints

In [Poh96b], Pohl employs a constraint language to define integrity constraints. The TML by Drivalos et al. [Dri08] features a set of attributes for relationship types which allow to enforce a predefined set of such constraints. For example, the unique attribute of the class TraceLinkEnd specifies whether more than one relationship of the respective type can be connected to a given entity. If ofTypeOnly is set to true, instances of subtypes of the referred-to EClass may not participate in the respective TraceLink instance.

The Traceability Relationship Type Template by Schwarz et al. (see Chapter 6) also aug-ments relationships with constraints. In [Sch10b], they are formulated using the graph query language *GReQL* [Ebe10].

Logical and Mathematical Expressions

Another approach towards formalization is taken by Carlshamre et al. [Car01] and Dick [Dic02], who associate traceability relationships with logical operators. Carlsham-re et al. in fact merely derive link types from logical operators. For example, an AND relationship indicates that the two interconnected requirements depend on each other and thus, both need to fulfilled. The rich traceability approach by Dick uses logical operators to complement relationships that express the refinement of a rather abstract requirement by more specific ones. In Figure 3.5, a traceability relationship designated as conjunction indicates that three system requirements have to be met in order to satisfy a user requirement.

Dahlstedt and Persson [Dah03] take up relationship types by other authors to build a relationship type hierarchy. Part of this hierarchy are so-called *cost/value interdependencies*. They express positive or negative effects of the realization of some requirement on the cost or value of another requirement's realization.

Rules

Aizenbud-Reshef et al. [Aiz05] augment traceability relationships in UML by *event-condition-action* rules. According to the authors, events refer to the creation, update, or deletion of a model element, conditions can be formulated using the *Object Constraint Language (OCL)* [Obj10a], and actions can be described on the basis of the semantics of the UML *action* modeling concept. The authors differ between *preventative* actions, which essentially inhibit the event to actually take effect, and *reactive* actions, which result in a modification of the traceability model. Walderhaug et al. [Wal06] envision a similar approach. However, they only consider creation events and do not make any statement on which language or technology to use for the specification of conditions and actions. The reference meta model by Jirapanthong and Zisman is complemented by a set of condition-action rules which specify how to automatically identify relationships of a given type [Jir09] (see also Section 3.2.2).

Goknil et al. [Gok11] use first-order logic to describe the semantics of the relationship types in their meta model. Based on logic formulae together with relational properties for relationship types, e.g., symmetry or transitivity, they derive integrity constraints and rules for determining entities which are potentially impacted by particular changes to the traceability model. Their approach is prototypically implemented by the *Tool for Requirements Inferencing and Consistency Checking (TRIC)*. In [Hov09], ten Hove et al. apply a similar approach to formalize the traceability relationship types provided by the OMG's SysML.

In [Lam11], Lamb et al. define three types of associations between nine different relationship types: *implication*, *weak implication*, and *derivation*. Implication refers to the inference of a relationship between two entities from the existence of another relationship that connects the same two entities. For example, the existence of a *containment* relationship implies a *dependency* relationship. Weak implication means that a given relationship does not necessarily imply some other relationship, but that this implication depends on some other conditions, such as the types of the related entities. Finally, derivation addresses the inference of relationships from patterns of several relationships.

The technology-independent TRTT by Schwarz et al. [Sch10b] allows for the specification of so-called *impact designators* to handle changes, i.e., "impacts", to the traceability model automatically. Many technologies that can be used to represent TRTT-conforming traceability relationships implement impact designators as rules. Chapter 6 of this book describes the TRTT and impact designators in more detail.

3.1.3 N-Ary Relationships

Many of the cited approaches treat traceability relationships as binary links, which connect exactly two different entities or one entity to itself. Exceptions which support n-ary relationships possibly referring to more than two entities are the UML and SysML, as well as the rich traceability concept by Dick [Dic02], the TML by Drivalos et al. [Dri08], the TRTT by Schwarz et al. [Sch10b], and the approaches by Maletic et al. [Mal05] and Munson and Nguyen [Mun05], for instance. While Maletic et al. describe an XML-based concept for enabling traceability between models, Munson and Nguyen report on the *Software Concordance Editor*, which supports traceability between Java source code and XML documents.

3.2 Identification

Identification refers to the discovery, computation, or generation of previously unknown traceability relationships conforming to the defined relationship types. Since *manual* identification is costly and error-prone [Aiz06], much research has been devoted on *semi-automatic* and *automatic* identification. Semi-automatic approaches depend on the existence of some relationships that were already identified manually. Fully automated identification does not require any user interaction before or during relationship identification. However, depending on the employed technique, automatically identified relationships vary in precision, so that a subsequent review by the software developers may be reasonable. Since the case studies used for evaluating these techniques differ, if an evaluation is conducted at all, an objective comparison between them is hardly possible.

The following sections discuss various semi-automatic and automatic identification approaches which can be found in literature. To compute traceability relationships, most of them employ *text-based techniques*, different kinds of *rules*, *model transformations*, *program analysis*, or *differencing* techniques. These approaches are described in Sections 3.2.1 to 3.2.5, respectively. Finally, Section 3.2.6 discusses some approaches which do not fit in the other five categories.

3.2.1 Text-Based Techniques

Naturally, identification approaches which rely on text-based techniques, including *natural language processing*, *text mining*, and *information retrieval*, can only be applied for interconnecting entities such as requirements, documentation parts, or source code fragments.

Natural Language Processing

An approach employing natural language processing is pursued by Kaindl in [Kai99]: based on the comparison of terms in textual entities and glossaries, hyperlinks to the glossaries are established. This approach involves techniques such as matching synonyms or reducing plural word forms to singular. An Eclipse-based tool by Yoshikawa et al. relates natural language sentences, e.g., requirements, to methods in the source code which realize the specified functionality [Yos09]. Besides taking the call graph of the program and comparing it with ontologies modeling the domain of the analyzed software, it also uses *stemming*, i.e., the normalization of the word form, to analyze the given sentences.

Text Mining

In [Wit07], Witte et al. identify relationships between source code and documentation. Their approach first parses the source code to build a corresponding ontology. Subsequently, text mining techniques, such as are applied to find passages in the documentation which are related to concepts in the source code ontology.

Information Retrieval

Despite the aforementioned works that use natural language processing and text mining, most text-based relationship identification approaches rely on *information retrieval*.

While information retrieval is generally concerned with representing, storing, organizing and accessing information [Bae10], its most important aspect for traceability is the finding of natural language documents matching a given query. The form of the query depends on the employed retrieval technique. Common techniques used for traceability relationship identification are the *vector space model*, the *probabilistic model*, and *latent semantic indexing* [Bae10].

Antoniol et al. have compared the suitability of the vector space and the probabilistic model for the discovery of relationships between documentation and code [Ant02]. Basically, the approach operates by querying the documentation with identifiers extracted from the source code. According to the authors, the results regarding precision and recall are "satisfactory" for both models. In [Set04], Settimi et al. evaluate the performance of different variants of the vector space model for identifying relationships between requirements, *UML* models [Obj10c], and source code. The authors state that even though precision is low at a high level of recall, the application of their approach still constitutes an improvement compared to purely manual identification. With respect to the probabilistic model, Cleland-Huang et al. achieve similar results [Cle07a]. Lin et al. have developed a research prototype tool – *Poirot* – which employs the probabilistic model to identify relationships between various software development entities, e.g., requirements and UML diagrams [Lin06].

Latent semantic indexing offers some advantages compared to the other techniques, such as the recognition of synonyms. However, the results of the experiments conducted by various researchers are somewhat ambivalent. While Marcus et al. observe a better performance for detecting relationships [Mar05a], De Lucia et al. report results similar to or worse than the vector space model for particular case studies [DeL06b]. Oliveto et al. claim that most identification approaches based on information retrieval yield similar results [Oli10]. An exception is *Latent Dirichlet Allocation (LDA)* [Ble03], a specific probabilistic model that, albeit less accurate, discovers traceability relationships which are not captured by the other techniques.

In [DeL11], De Lucia et al. successfully adapt the notion of *smoothing filters*, known from the field of digital image processing, to improve the results of relationship identification on the basis of the vector space model and latent semantic indexing.

The *Advanced Artefact Management System (ADAMS)*, which is described by De Lucia et al. in [DeL06a], is a web-based system for supporting software project management. It captures entities such as plain files as well as more fine-grained requirements, document sections, or system components together with traceability relationships between them. Besides the manual identification, recording, and visualization of traceability relationships between these entities, ADAMS offers a special component dedicated to automatic relationship identification based on latent semantic indexing: *ADAMS Re-Trace* [DeL08]. This component continuously computes candidate relationships in defined intervals if entities are added or deleted. It allows users to select source and target entities for which potential relationships shall be displayed if their likelihood is above a given threshold. The user can then choose to either store or discard single relationships. A controlled experiment indicates that compared to manual identification, ADAMS Re-Trace improves both efficiency and relationship accuracy [DeL09].

RETRO by Huffman Hayes et al. [Huf06], short for *REquirements TRacing On-target*, is a tool for identifying relationships between requirements, using a variant of the vector space model and latent semantic indexing. In addition, the algorithms consider user feedback on the accuracy of previously determined relationships to improve performance.

In [Che10], Chen combines information retrieval with text mining techniques, claiming to achieve an improvement compared to the application of information retrieval or text mining alone. An Eclipse-based prototype implementation is able to identify relationships between Java classes and PDF documents representing test cases, manuals, or other documentation.

3.2.2 Rules

Rule-based identification approaches can take many different forms, ranging from the detection of predefined patterns in the traceability model from which new relationships are derived, to complex, user-definable *event-condition-action* rules. A representative of the former group can be found in [She03] by Sherba et al. Their *TraceM* system recognizes specific chains of traceability relationships so that new relationships can be introduced between the source entity of the first relationship in the chain and the target entity of the last relationship. The *TRACES* prototype by Aleksy et al. [Ale08], situated in a model-driven context, takes a similar approach.

The approach by Cleland-Huang and Schmelzer [Cle03b] for identifying traceability relationships between non-functional requirements and implementations of *design patterns* [Gam94] is based on the existence of manually identified relationships between the requirements and class clusters which contain the classes responsible for the realization of the design patterns. Using techniques to automatically identify the sets of classes that implement design patterns, more fine grained relationships directly connecting the requirements to the right classes and their methods can be established.

The inference of relationships between design model elements and source code is pursued by Cysneiros and Zisman [Cys08]. Since their approach allows users to specify rules for identification in a special language based on the *XML* query language *XQuery* [Boa07] extended by functions implemented in Java, it is required that the artifacts containing the traceable entities are represented in XML [Bra08]. An example rule would be to create a traceability relationship between a design element and a code entity whose names are synonyms.

In [Spa04], Spanoudakis et al. show how condition-action rules can be used to identify relationships between requirement statements, use case documents, and class diagrams. They distinguish between two kinds of rules, with both of them formulated in an XML-based syntax. The first type of rules is responsible for connecting requirements and use case documents to class diagrams by directly analyzing the contents of the entities. Rules of the second type check for specific patterns of already existing relationships and link requirements and use cases to each other. Jirapanthong and Zisman refine the former approach for usage in the context of product line engineering [Jir09]. They support more traced entity types, including feature and process models, and allow for more general rules which are now formulated in an XQuery dialect. They implemented the *XTraQue* prototype to show the feasibility of their approach. Another tool that supports XML-based rules is *EMFTrace*, described by Riebisch et al. [Rie11].

The Traceability Meta-type by Espinoza et al. envisions relationship types to carry so-called linkage rules, which specify how to automate the identification of respective instances [Esp06].

Based on their traceability relationship semantics relying on first-order logic, Goknil et al. use logical implications to denote that new traceability relationships are to be inferred from specific combinations of existing ones [Gok11].

The *impact designators* proposed by the technology-independent *Traceability Relationship Type Template* by Schwarz et al. [Sch10b], which are usually implemented as rules, allow for the automatic handling of changes to the traceability model. See Chapter 6 for a detailed description of the TRTT.

3.2.3 Model Transformations

The usage of model transformation techniques in model-driven development allows to automatically convert a given model to another model, with both models possibly conforming to different meta models. The exact mapping of model elements is encoded in the transformation rule. Naturally, there exists a relationship between the corresponding elements of source and target models which can be exploited for traceability-related applications.

According to the survey by Czarnecki and Helsen [Cza06], contemporary model transformation technologies can be divided into two groups concerning their traceability support. While technologies belonging to the first group require users to manually en-code the generation of traceability relationships in the transformation rule, members of the second group allow for automatic recording.

The *ATLAS Transformation Language* (*ATL*) [Jou06] does not provide dedicated support for recording. To remedy this problem, Jouault explains how to automatically trans-form ATL transformation rules, which are models themselves, to rules incorporating the generation of traceability relationships [Jou05]. Another solution is proposed by Yie and Wagelaar in [Yie09]: they modify the bytecode of transformations to externally record the mappings between source and target elements in a separate model.

Dealing with model-to-text transformation, Olsen and Oldevik [Ols07] describe how traceability relationships are recorded in a separated traceability model by *MOFScript*, a tool for transforming *EMF* models [Ste08] to arbitrary textual representations, e.g., source code. References to text are stored in special attributes which point to the posi-tion in the respective file.

Von Pilgrim et al. have extended the *Unified Transformation Infrastructure* [Van07], a tool for modeling and executing model transformation chains, by a feature to identify and record traceability relationships between source and target model elements [Pil08]. These relationships are recorded in dedicated models which conform to a specialized traceability meta model.

In [Sch10c], Schwarz et al. show the transformation of requirements, specified using the *Requirements Specification Language* (*RSL*) [Wol09], to architectural and detailed design artifacts and finally to source code. In the course of the model transformations, inter-connecting traceability relationships are generated. The approach is implemented by the *ReDSeeDS Engine* [Rei08] on the basis of *TGraphs* [Ebe95] as recording technology and *MOLA* [Kal04] as transformation language. See Chapter 11 for more details.

3.2.4 Program Analysis

In general, program analysis subsumes various techniques for computing particular properties of programs or other associated entities. Qusef et al. apply *data flow analysis* to identify relationships between unit tests and the tested classes [Qus10]. Based on the source code, their approach determines the definitions of all variables which may affect the parameters of the last assertion within every method of a unit test class. The classes used in the definitions, minus standard classes such as String, Integer, or classes belonging to the test framework, are candidates for being tested by a particular unit test.

In contrast to a *static* program analysis approach as applied by Qusef et al., which mostly relies on performing computations on the source code, *dynamic* program analysis addresses the usage of information collected during program runs. Egyed suggests to use *program execution logs* to identify traceability relationships between model elements, test cases, and source code [Egy01]. An analysis of the execution logs together with a limited number of manually identified relationships between model elements and code and between test cases and code yield a so-called *footprint graph*. One of the properties of this graph is to reflect the overlap of test cases with regard to the code parts they execute. By performing certain operations on the footprint graph, further traceability relationships can be derived. For example, if a given test case executes the same code part as another test case which is linked to some model element, it is derived that the first test case must be related to that model element, too. In [Aze11], Azevedo Vianna Ferreira and de Oliveira Barros use the *XDebug* profiling tool[4] to derive relationships between test cases and tested source code fragments.

The identification of relationships between use case diagrams and source code is the subject of the work by Grechanik et al. [Gre07]. They also employ the analysis of information gathered during a program's runtime, but combine it with *machine learning*. The approach is implemented by the Eclipse plug-in *LeanArt*, which is short for *Learning and Analyzing Requirements Traceability*. Based on identifier comparison and already existing relationships, the tool matches use case diagram elements with variables and types in the source code to identify candidate relationships. As the users confirm and reject these relationships, the tool receives feedback in order to improve its accuracy.

3.2.5 Differencing

Differencing refers to the computation of (dis)similarities between software artifacts. There exist various approaches and algorithms for different kinds of artifacts, such as textual documents, images, or models. In [Ant01], Antoniol et al. infer relationships between releases of object-oriented software systems, i.e., between interrelated portions of source code originating from different releases. Their approach, prototypically implemented for C++ programs, is based on computing the similarity of classes using *edit distance* [Gus97] and mapping them to each other using a *maximum match algorithm* [Cor01]. Edit distance together with linear programming is used by the *API Compliance and Analysis Report Tool (ACART)* tool presented by Yilmaz and Kent [Yil11]. The tool computes traceability relationships between API specifications and their implementations.

---

[4]http://xdebug.org

In [Wen07], Wenzel et al. describe an Eclipse plug-in which aims at identifying relationships between different versions of models, e.g., in UML or some other domain-specific language. To achieve this, the authors employ a graph-based similarity computation algorithm called *SiDiff* [Tre07].

Richardson and Green suggest a concept for discovering traceability relationships by comparing the results of applying the same transformation to two similar source entities [Ric03]. The source entities are nearly identical with only one atomic difference, i.e., a modification which can be made in a single step. The differing entities in the transformation result can then be considered to be related to the source entity to which the modification was applied. The authors explain how their approach can be automated and illustrate it on the basis of text-to-text transformations, such as a compiler's transformation of source code to object code. However, it is thinkable to apply it for model-to-model or model-to-text transformations, as well.

3.2.6 Other Techniques

There exist further approaches for the identification of traceability relationships, which are based on various technologies and ideas.

In [Poh96b], Pohl describes a tool which integrates relationship identification with the development process. More precisely, the tool takes note of performed steps in the process model and entities related to this steps. If new entities are created as result of a specific sequence of steps, suitable relationships can be established based on the previous observations. The *LISA* approach (short for *Language for Integrated Software Architecture*) by Buchgeher and Weinreich allows for the semiautomatic generation of traceability relationships between recorded design decisions and architectural or implementation entities [Buc11]. Before manipulating and editing these entities, developers first have to select the decision they like to work on. The developers' activities are automatically logged. After finishing the work, the handled entities are suggested to be linked to the decision. Subsequent to a review by the developers, the actual relationships are generated.

In [Pfe10], Pfeiffer and Wąsowski present *Tengja*, an extension to Eclipse whose purpose is to identify relationships between the abstract syntax of models, i.e., the object network conforming to a meta model constituting the modeling language, and the serialization syntax which is used to persist models. In Eclipse, models are serialized using an XML-based format. Tengja uses aspects to integrate with the Eclipse model traversing mechanism. As Eclipse traverses a model in order to serialize it, the tool produces the desired mapping between the processed model elements and their XML representation.

Sharif and Kagdi advocate the recording of the behavior of developers when inspecting models or source code with the help of eye trackers [Sha11]. Based on studies that analyze how UML models and source code are perceived by humans (such as published in [Yus07]), it could be possible to identify relationships between respective entities, for instance.

The *multiperspective requirements traceability* (*MUPRET*) framework by Assawamekin et al. [Ass11] combines three different techniques to facilitate the identification of traceability relationships between sets of textual requirements for a single system, but issued by different stakeholders. These requirements are characterized by the usage of different vocabularies, which makes it difficult to detect potential overlaps. First, the requirements of a given set are analyzed with the help of natural language processing techniques and broken down into individual parts of speech. Second, an ontology is constructed from the processed requirements. For example, nouns in requirements are represented as specializations of the concept object in the ontology, while verbs result in specializations of relationship. Using the *S-Match* ontology matching framework[5] together with differencing techniques, the ontologies resulting from the requirement sets of two different stakeholders are then compared, finally resulting in the identification of overlapping relationships.

3.3 Recording

Recording denotes the physical representation, i.e., materialization, of traceability information in the form of data structures. Whether this traceability information only includes identified relationships or also encompasses traced entities depends on the specific recording approach. Basically, there exist two variants: *internal* and *external* recording, depending on whether traceability relationships are recorded inside or outside the artifacts that contain the traced entities [Kol06].

With respect to external recording, it can be observed that early approaches advocate the creation of traceability matrices in a spreadsheet. In such a matrix, each cell entry corresponds to a traceability relationship between the traceable entities represented by the respective row and column. While traceability matrices are easily to understand by users [Wie95], they are suitable for small projects or at a very coarse level of granularity only, i.e., where the number of traceable entities is rather small.

More sophisticated and better-scaling approaches for external recording are based on *fact repositories*, where all traceability information is stored in dedicated data structures [Bil08]. Compared to internal recording, this necessitates the creation of prox-

---

[5]http://s-match.org

ies for traceable entities. The original entities are usually kept in an artifact repository such as *Subversion*[6]. They are accessed by so-called *fact extraction* tools that extract the relevant data for creating traceable entities in the fact repository. An additional challenge imposed by the fact repository concept is to keep the original entities and their abstractions properly synchronized. A rather simple approach is to regenerate the whole fact repository in predefined time intervals. However, there also exist incremental approaches that only replace those traceable entities whose originals have changed [Kam98]. This issue gets even more complicated if changes to the abstractions in the fact repository have to be applied to the original entities.

In Section 3.3.1, publications that address internal recording are discussed. External recording using fact repositories is covered in Section 3.3.2. Section 3.3.3 treats other external recording approaches.

3.3.1 Internal Recording

Possible forms of traceability relationships internally recorded in text documents are cross references, such as discussed by Wieringa [Wie95] and introduced in the *STAR-Track* requirements traceability system by Song et al. [Son98], or hyperlinks as proposed by Kaindl [Kai93] for the *RETH* tool, which is short for *Requirements Engineering Through Hypertext*. Concerning models, suitable model elements such as associations and links can be employed, for example as envisaged by the meta models of Ramesh and Jarke [Ram01] or by the *UML* [Obj10c].

However, as pointed out by some authors, internal recording can be problematic. First, creating relationships between entities of different, incompatible technologies or tools may be difficult: tools which employ internal recording are mainly specialized on specific kinds of traceable entities using homogeneous forms of representation, e.g., requirements in textual form. Some tools allow to trace to other entities by linking to the respective files, but more fine-grained traceability, especially between entities managed by tools of different vendors, is usually not possible [Win10]. A second problem of internal recording is the *"pollution"* caused by the addition of traceability relationships to artifacts that contain traceable entities. Clarity and understandability may be impaired by the extra burden of distinguishing between traceability relationships and original information [Kol06].

---

[6]http://subversion.apache.org

3.3.2 External Recording Using Fact Repositories

A literature survey reveals the usage of various technologies for the implementation of fact repositories. Among others, these technologies include *relational databases*, *XML technology*, *ontologies*, the *Eclipse Modeling Framework* [Ste08], and *graph technology*.

Note, that recording approaches based on fact repositories usually require the previous definition of the structure of the traceability model, e.g., in the form of database schemas or meta models, depending on the specific technology. Furthermore, the usage of one of the technologies mentioned above not necessarily implies external recording. If entities natively represented in an ontology shall be traced, for instance, it might be reasonable to extend the given ontology with the needed traceability relationships, effectively leading to an internal recording concept.

Relational Databases

Pohl uses a relational database to store traceability information recorded in his requirements management environment *PRO-ART* [Poh96a]. The *STAR-Track* system by Song et al. [Son98] also makes use of a relational database to cache the traceability information which is originally stored internally (see also Section 3.3.1). Thus, effective retrieval and browsing of recorded traceability information is facilitated. Actually, Ramesh and Jarke report that many traceability tools rely on relational database systems [Ram01].

XML Technology

For their approach to enable traceability between different models in software development, Maletic et al. [Mal05] represent traceability relationships as well as traceable entities using *XML* [Bra08] and the related languages *XPath* [Ber07] and *XLink* [DeR10] for referring to specific entities in the XML representation and for storing the traceability relationships themselves, respectively. Since many modeling tools feature the serialization of models in XML format, the population of the repository with traced entities is straightforward. By introducing a technique to embed source code constructs in XML, the authors even allow for tracing a software system's implementation. A similar, XML-based approach for recording traceability relationships between requirements documents, use case documents and UML diagrams is pursued by Spanoudakis et al. [Spa04]. The *Traceclipse* Eclipse plug-in by Klock et al. stores traceability relationships between implementation entities, including packages, classes, and methods, in an XML file, too [Klo11].

Ontologies

Witte et al. show how to populate ontologies with entities parsed from source code and related documentation in order to subsequently establish traceability relationships between them [Wit07].

The Eclipse Modeling Framework

A fact repository based on *EMF* is *EMFTrace* by Riebisch et al. [Rie11]. By providing Ecore[7] meta models for various languages, including UML, *BPMN* [Obj11], and *OWL* [Mot09b], EMFTrace is prepared to retain entities from different abstraction levels. The repository is populated with the help of the XML export facilities of language-specific modeling tools. To import the XML representations of such models into EMF-Trace, however, they first have to be transformed to an EMFTrace-specific XML format.

Graph Technology

Schwarz et al. describe the usage of graph technology – the *TGraph approach* [Ebe08] – for creating a fact repository for traceability information [Sch10c]. Refer to Section 8.1 and Chapter 9 for an introduction to the technology and its application for traceability purposes, respectively.

Other Technologies

Further notable publications concerned with repositories for traceability information include the works of Constantopoulos et al. [Con95] and of Sherba et al. [She03] for representing traceability information between heterogeneous entities of a software development project. While the *Software Information Base (SIB)* of the former group of authors is based on the early object-oriented knowledge representation language *Telos* [Myl90], the latter's tool *TraceM* relies on *open hypermedia* [Whi97], which treats links as first-class objects and stores them separately from the linked entities.

---

[7]the meta-meta model on which EMF is based

3.3.3 Other External Recording Approaches

In [Kol06], Kolovos et al. present an approach for externally recording traceability relationships between elements of EMF or MOF [Obj06] models or of XML documents. More precisely, they create a separate traceability model which only adopts entities which are connected by traceability relationships. On demand, this traceability model can be *merged* with the original models containing the traced entities, thus providing a composite model which comprises the traceability information together with other entities and non-traceability relationships. In [Bar07], Barbero et al. propose a similar approach.

A rather novel approach to traceability is to use *tagging*, as suggested by Hale et al. in [Hal11]. The integrated development environment *SEREBRO* allows for the attachment of textual tags to different artifacts. Artifacts with the same tag are considered to be related.

3.4 Retrieval

To be able to utilize recorded traceability information, it has to be *retrieved*. This activity involves the finding and gathering of that piece of information which is relevant for a specific application. An examination of existing traceability literature shows that little research has been conducted on the activity of retrieval up to now. This observation is seconded by Winkler and von Pilgrim [Win10], who make the same claim about the closely related activities of *querying* and *navigating* traceability information.

It can be distinguished between two different notions of retrieval. First, using suitable query languages, traceability information has to be extracted from the data structures used for recording. While it is thinkable that end-users of traceability tools directly access traceability information with user-friendly query languages, the second notion of retrieval addresses the encapsulation of these rather low-level technologies by more convenient user interfaces. Relevant publications that belong to these two categories are shortly discussed in Sections 3.4.1 and 3.4.2, respectively.

With [Sch10c], Schwarz et al. published a retrieval-relevant article that cannot be assigned to one of the two notions. They introduce the three *traceability retrieval patterns Existence, Reachable Entities*, and *Slice*. Basically, these are abstractions of common traceability retrieval problems and can be treated as requirements for technologies that are intended to implement traceability. Chapter 7 of this book explains the three patterns and their derivation in more detail.

3.4.1 Query Languages

Naturally, the choice of techniques and languages for directly accessing recorded traceability information depends on the employed recording approach. For instance, information recorded in relational databases is retrieved with *SQL* [Cha74], while ontologies can be queried using the *World Wide Web Consortium (W3C)* standard query language *SPARQL* [Pru08] or *nRQL* [Haa04]. The latter is employed by Witte et al. for querying their ontology-based traceability repository [Wit07].

In [Mal09], Maletic and Collard specify a dedicated *Trace Query Language (TQL)*. Based on *XPath* [Ber07], TQL is designed to query traceability information recorded using *XML* [Bra08]. For instance, the language provides concepts to detect if two entities are, possibly indirectly, connected by relationships, or to find all entities participating in relationships of a given type.

Schwarz et al. show how to implement their traceability retrieval patterns on the basis of the graph query language *GReQL* [Sch10c]. A detailed description is provided in Section 9.4. In [Sch10a], Schwarz and Ebert transform GReQL queries to SPARQL queries in order to retrieve traceability information recorded in *OWL* ontologies [Mot09b]. Since in GReQL, the structure of traceability information can be expressed more concisely than in SPARQL, their approach promises to ease users' work with ontology-based traceability implementations.

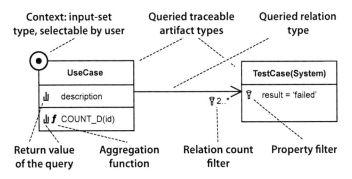

Figure 3.6: A *VTML* query. Taken from [Mäd10].

The *Visual Trace Modeling Language (VTML)*, advocated by Mäder and Cleland-Huang in [Mäd10], is a visual query language for traceability information. Under the assumption that there exists a *UML*-based [Obj10c] traceability meta model, a VTML query is itself represented by a stereotyped UML class diagram. The stereotypes, depicted as symbols, serve to mark model elements as query context, return values, or query constraints. Furthermore, aggregation functions may be used. Figure 3.6 shows an example VTML query. It returns the descriptions and the overall number of UseCases that are linked to two or more TestCases which have failed. Marking the UseCase class as query context shall allow users to provide a specific set of UseCases on which the query is to be performed, instead of taking all UseCases as input. Prototypically, VTML queries are transformed to SQL for execution.

3.4.2 User Interfaces

To support retrieval of traceability information by end-users, Pohl's *PRO-ART* environment features a query form where properties of sought-for relationships, such as their type or connected entities, can be specified [Poh96b]. A similar approach is pursued by Sherba et al. in [She03] for their tool *TraceM*. In their requirements traceability tool *TOOR*, short for *Traceability of Object-Oriented Requirements*, Pinheiro and Goguen allow for the usage of regular expressions to describe specific structures in the traceability model [Pin96b].

Note, that certain retrieval approaches for end-users and the graphical visualization of traceability information, which falls into the activity of utilization, cannot be clearly separated. For example, there exist browsers for traceability information showing all traced entities directly connected by some traceability relationships to a currently focused entity. Clicking on one of those entities shifts the focus to that entity. Such approaches are discussed in Section 3.5.

3.5 Utilization

Utilization addresses the usage and further processing of retrieved traceability information for specific applications, such as impact analysis, project management, or reuse of software artifacts. Although this activity constitutes an important step in the "life cycle" of traceability information, it is not a subject of traceability research in a narrower sense. For this reason, and due to the multitude of different applications for traceability information, a discussion of related work is not within the scope of this work. Please refer to Section 4.1 for an overview of important fields of application for traceability. However, these applications require the presentation of retrieved traceability information to the user, demanding suitable means of *visualization*.

Various publications deal with the visualization of traceability information. As shown in Sections 3.5.1 to 3.5.3, many authors employ *matrices*, *hyperlinks*, or different forms of *diagrams* for displaying traceability relationships to the users. Section 3.5.4 describes approaches that rely on other techniques.

3.5.1 Visualization by Matrices

A rather simple idea for visualizing traceability information is a matrix. Such an approach is especially suitable if the traceability information is already recorded in a similar form, e.g., in a spreadsheet. In their basic form, traceability matrices represent entities as rows and columns and relationships as marks in the appropriate cells. Enhanced variants of traceability matrices, e.g., employing color to denote certain properties, are realized by the *VisMatrix* tool presented by Duan and Cleland-Huang [Dua06], for instance. Figure 3.7 shows a screenshot of VisMatrix. While the shading of the cells depicts the probability of candidate relationships computed by some external tool, the check marks represent relationships which were identified as definitely existing.

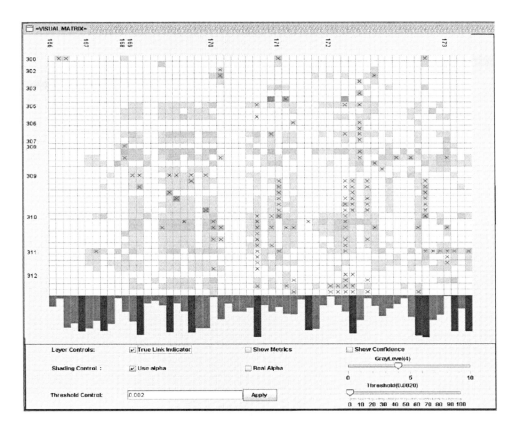

Figure 3.7: Screenshot of the *VisMatrix* visualization tool. Taken from [Dua06].

3.5.2 Visualization by Hyperlinks

Several authors visualize traceability relationships by hyperlinks. While Kaindl directly stores textual requirements in hypertext form [Kai93], other approaches preprocess otherwise recorded traceability information in order to present it this way. Examples are the requirements traceability tool *TOOR* by Pinheiro and Goguen [Pin96b], the tool described by Olsson and Grundy [Ols02], and the approach by Ngyuen and Munson [Ngu03]. These tools allow for using a common web browser to navigate through the traceability model.

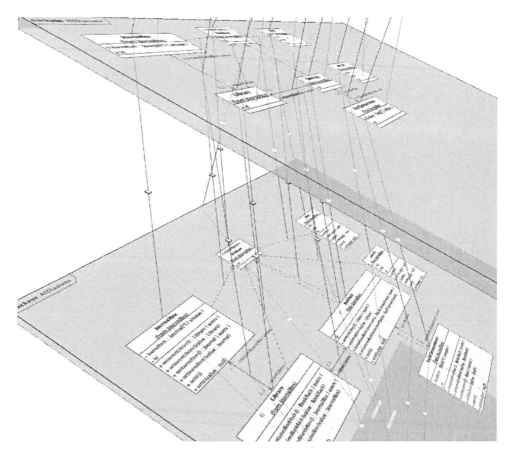

Figure 3.8: Screenshot detail of the 3D visualization tool presented by von Pilgrim et al. Taken from [Pil08].

3.5.3 Visualization by Diagrams

Visualization in diagrammatic form stands to reason if *UML* [Obj10c], *SysML* [Obj10b], or elements of some other modeling language with a graphical concrete syntax shall be traced and the traceability relationships are directly recorded within the models. Since there already exist many tools that are able to display such diagrams, traceability tools can be integrated with those and do not need to provide their own visualization component. But even before the advent of UML, requirements traceability tools employed diagrams as a means of visualization, e.g., *TOOR* by Pinheiro and Goguen [Pin96b], *SIB* by Constantopoulos et al. [Con95], and *PRO-ART* described by Pohl in [Poh96b]. All of them offer a graph-based view of the traceability model, with requirements and other entities displayed as vertices and relationships represented as edges. The Eclipse-based tool described by Chen in [Che10] features a graph-based representation of traceability information, involving Java classes and PDF documents. Here, the vertices represent the classes and the documents as well as contained methods and headings, respectively.

Von Pilgrim et al. experiment with a 3D visualization of traceability relationships of model transformation chains as recorded by their extension of the *Unified Information Infrastructure* (see Section 3.2.3). In their approach, all models in such a chain can be displayed simultaneously as each model's diagram constitutes a plane in a 3D view [Pil08]. Thus, traceability relationships interconnecting elements of different models can be clearly distinguished from interconnections within a single diagram. Figure 3.8 shows an example screenshot detail of a tool implementing the approach.

3.5.4 Other Visualization Approaches

Concerning version traceability of models, an Eclipse plug-in developed by Wenzel et al. [Wen07] visualizes revisions of models as rectangles. These rectangles contain circles which correspond to individual model elements (see Figure 3.9). The tool supports various analysis functions which may fill the circles with different colors. For example, the "global track analysis" highlights all occurrences of a selected model element in the recorded model revisions.

Marcus et al. [Mar05b] have developed *TraceViz*, a traceability relationship visualization plug-in for Eclipse. In essence, a special view is integrated with the Eclipse workbench, depicted in the lower right part of the screenshot in Figure 3.10. Each box in the middle section represents a traceability relationship connected to the selected source entity. While the labels above the boxes indicate the targets of the relationships, the larger boxes group the relationships according to the packages the targets belong to. The colors of the boxes denote the status of relationships, e.g., "normal" or "false positive".

51

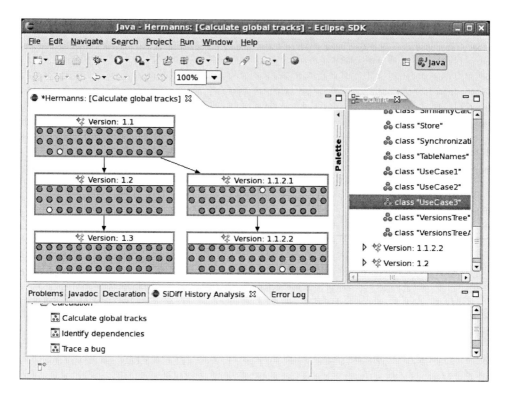

Figure 3.9: Screenshot of the version traceability visualization tool by Wenzel et al. Taken from [Wen07].

In [Cle07b], Cleland-Huang and Habrat elaborate on a set of approaches to complement the automatic relationship identification tool *Poirot* with the visualization of various relationship properties, such as the precision of identified relationships. The employed techniques range from icons to distinguish relationship types, to tag clouds, and to diagrammatic tree structures.

3.6 Maintenance

Maintenance deals with keeping traceability relationships up to date, including their deletion, as traced entities and other relationships are modified. Since manual maintenance of possibly many relationships is tedious and error-prone [Dri10], some research devoted to its automation has been conducted. Basically, similar techniques as for the

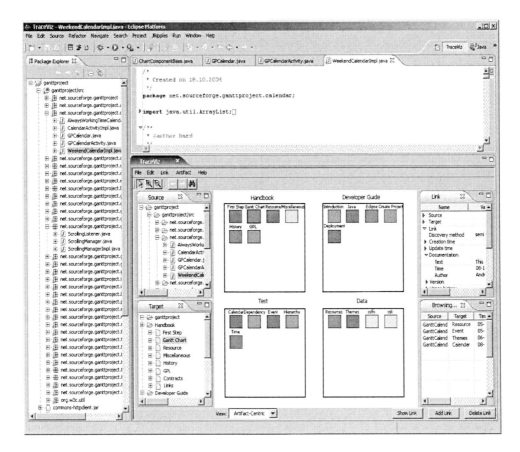

Figure 3.10: Screenshot of the *TraceViz* visualization tool. Taken from [Mar05b].

identification of traceability relationships are employed: *text-based techniques*, *rules*, and *model transformations*. In addition, some semiautomatic approaches rely on *constraints*. In the following, Sections 3.6.1 to 3.6.4 discuss respective publications.

3.6.1 Text-Based Techniques

Concerning text-based techniques, Port et al. advocate the usage of text mining to validate existing traceability relationships between functional and non-functional requirements [Por11]. In principle, they compute similarities between pairs of requirements and compare the results with already recorded relationships. Two requirements which are similar but not already linked as well as linked pairs of requirements that are not similar are candidates for further investigation by the developers.

3.6.2 Rules

Most maintenance approaches rely on rules to facilitate a higher degree of automation. In an extension to their Traceability Metamodelling Language, Drivalos et al. allow to attach so-called *maintenance data* to the ends of their traceability relationship types [Dri10]. The maintenance data features an expression which may access the traced entity at the respective end to derive a specific value. If that value changes due to some modification to the entity, the relationship is considered to require updating. To this end, a maintenance script uses the given expression to automatically calculate the values of other entities to find candidates for attachment to that relationship end. If no exact match is found, additionally specified fuzzy matching algorithms are used to determine the most similar entities. If more than one entity is found, the user is notified in order to make a decision.

The approach by Aizenbud-Reshef et al. envisions to complement *UML* traceability relationships [Obj10c] with *event-condition-action* rules [Aiz05]. The actions of such rules could be used for updating relationships. Goknil et al. derive rules from the logic-based formalization of the semantics of traceability relationships [Gok11]. On the basis of these rules, the consistency of the traceability model can be checked. The *impact designators* featured by the Traceability Relationship Type Template by Schwarz et al., which are implemented as rules by many technologies, also serve traceability relationship maintenance [Sch10b] (see Chapter 6).

Cleland-Huang et al. propose to register traced entities at a so-called *event server* which monitors them for changes [Cle03a]. Depending on the kind of a change, different event notifications are created and sent to the *subscriber manager* which initiates subsequent actions. While the publication explicitly mentions the provision of guidance to developers, thus helping them to manually apply the update, a fully automated handling is also thinkable.

In [Mäd08b], Mäder et al. describe *traceMAINTAINER*, a traceability maintenance tool which is to be integrated with third-party UML modeling tools. The traceability tool recognizes specific sequences of user interactions when modifying UML models and invokes a proper reaction by automatically updating traceability relationships. The rules that specify the triggering events and the actions to be performed are formulated in *XML* [Bra08]. Figure 3.11 shows an example of an invocation of traceMAINTAINER.

54

Steps 1 to 5 involve user manipulations to the depicted UML model. In Step 6, trace-MAINTAINER automatically generates a traceability relationship from the AudioSystem class to the Create Order use case.

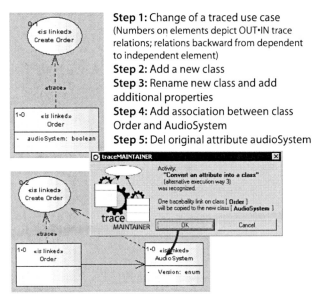

Step 1: Change of a traced use case
(Numbers on elements depict OUT·IN trace relations; relations backward from dependent to independent element)
Step 2: Add a new class
Step 3: Rename new class and add additional properties
Step 4: Add association between class Order and AudioSystem
Step 5: Del original attribute audioSystem

Step 6: Traceability links have been updated automatically
(2 incoming links on use case, 1 outgoing link on each class)

Figure 3.11: Example invocation of the *traceMAINTAINER* tool. Taken from [Mäd08a].

Costa and da Silva [Cos07] and Murta et al. [Mur08] propose further rule-based approaches that rely on the monitoring of entities managed by third-party tools. The approach by the latter group of authors, intended to maintain traceability relationships between architectural and source code entities, is realized by the *ArchTrace* tool. Using suitable adapter components, it has to be integrated with architectural design and configuration management tools. For a prototypical implementation, connections to the *xADL 2.0* architecture description language [Das01] and to Subversion have been established. The relationships are recorded internally by tagging the architecture descriptions. ArchTrace listens for events in the connected tools, such as the creation of new versions of architecture components or source code files. Upon the occurrence of events, so-called policies can be triggered. Policies can be either constraints, which may prevent the modification associated with a certain event from actually being applied, or rules, which automatically update the traceability model. Taking the example of creating a new version of an architecture component, a predefined policy of ArchTrace is to inherit the old version's relationships.

3.6.3 Model Transformations

Seibel et al. [Sei10] promote an approach for maintaining traceability relationships between *EMF* model elements [Ste08] which depends on running a maintenance process autonomously in specific intervals or as demanded by the user. The process checks if the observed models have changed and applies in-place model transformations to update the relationships. By providing a generic *task* concept, other techniques than transformations could be employed. The approach is prototypically implemented on the Eclipse platform.

3.6.4 Constraints

One group of maintenance approaches is based on constraints imposed on the traceability model. If a modification to the traceability model causes some constraint to be violated, the user is informed so that he can properly react in order to restore the model's integrity. Obviously, such approaches do not aim at full automation, but at assisting users with manual maintenance. An example is the *Traceability Metamodelling Language (TML)* by Drivalos et al., which provides special attributes for enabling or disabling a number of predefined constraints [Dri08]. The technology-independent *Traceability Relationship Type Template* by Schwarz et al. also envisions traceability relationships to carry constraints [Sch10b] (see Chapter 6).

4 Traceability in Practice

This chapter intends to give an impression of traceability application and realization in practice. To this end, Section 4.1 describes fields of application which rely on the presence of traceability or where traceability can lead to an increased efficiency when performing associated tasks. In Section 4.2, an overview of existing commercial traceability tools for application in industry is given. Finally, Section 4.3 discusses the extent of traceability application in industry.

4.1 Fields of Application

Compilations of applications of traceability can be found in the publications of Antoniol et al. [Ant02], von Knethen and Paech [Kne02], Dahlstedt and Persson [Dah03], Brcina and Riebisch [Brc08], or Winkler and von Pilgrim [Win10], for instance. The following sections draw upon these works to give a condensed overview of fields which benefit from or even require traceability. Where information from other publications is used, they are explicitly referenced.

Note, that as it is often not possible to unambiguously assign a particular activity to a single field of application, the fields cannot be clearly divided. Furthermore, fields may overlap, such as maintenance and reverse engineering. For these reasons, the fields of application identified in the following sections should not be regarded as definitive, but as a rather non-binding classification used for illustrative purposes.

4.1.1 Change Management

Basically, *change management* involves the determination of the effects of changing a specific entity on other entities. This is facilitated by the recording of adequate traceability relationships between entities. For example, a change to a requirement demands that its implementing source code fragments are determined so that they can be adapted accordingly. Conversely, a modified code fragment has to be traced back to the requirements in order to be able to ensure that they are still properly realized [Sch08]. Concerning intra-level traceability, consider a change to a Java package which is imported by another package. This calls for the examination of the importing package in order to identify necessary modifications. Another example is the automatic propagation of model changes to their documentation [Bar09].

Change management also benefits from the recording of decisions, alternatives, and rationales, which help to understand why a specific entity was created or changed.

4.1.2 Configuration Management

In *configuration management*, version traceability (see Section 2.3.6) can be employed to keep track of the various versions of a traced entity. Since fine-grained relationships between elements of different versions of non-textual entities cannot be recovered using common tools such as SVN, special traceability identification approaches, such as proposed by Wenzel et al. for different versions of models [Wen07], may offer support here.

4.1.3 Maintenance

Maintenance of software systems requires their proper understanding. This involves the identification of dependencies and other connections between the entities composing the various parts of a system – not only on the source code level, whose examination and understanding is commonly known as *program comprehension*, but also considering the system's environment, which is captured by its requirements and documentation, for instance . This is referred to as *application comprehension*. The relevant connections between the various parts and artifacts may be captured by traceability relationships.

Subsequent to the understanding of the structure and functioning of a system, maintenance also comprises its modification. This leads to change management (see Section 4.1.1), which also benefits from traceability.

4.1.4 Project Management

With regard to *project management*, traceability information helps to keep track of the progress of development projects by connecting requirements to their realizing entities. Consequently, project managers are able to find out which requirements have already been realized or which project parts lag behind and will probably cause delay. In connection with change management (see Section 4.1.1), it is also possible to assess the costs of applying changes.

In addition, provided that stakeholders and project members are treated as traceable entities, other entities could be related to the persons responsible for their creation or maintenance, thus facilitating accountability.

4.1.5 Quality Assurance

Concerning *quality assurance*, traceability relationships can aid in validating a software system, i.e., investigating whether the system is suited for its intended application. Inter-level relationships are of particular importance here. For instance, if a requirement is traceable to one or more source code fragments, this could imply that the ready system fulfills that requirement. Conversely, such relationships also assist in avoiding gold plating, i.e., the creation of system features not corresponding to any requirement [Jar98].

Other possible applications include the recording of relationships between test cases and entities to be tested to determine test coverage, the calculation of certain metrics which depend on traceability information, or the debugging of model transformations in the context of model-driven development.

4.1.6 Release Planning

Release planning involves the selection of requirements to be implemented in a software system's next release. Here, the presence of intra-level traceability relationships in the system's requirements specification helps in understanding conflicts and dependencies between requirements.

With respect to product line engineering, traceability is also employed to link features to software components, so that new products can be efficiently constructed and delivered [Anq10].

4.1.7 Requirements Management

The representation of various types of interconnections between requirements, such as conflicts, dependencies, or refinements, for example, as traceability relationships allows to preserve a requirements specification's coherence. Furthermore, traceability in requirements management also serves to keep track of stakeholders and other sources of requirements, as well as of associated decisions, rationales, or risks.

4.1.8 Reuse

Having identified reusable entities from accomplished software development projects, ranging from small code fragments to whole subsystems, following existing traceability relationships which capture dependencies or other interconnections allows to determine further potential *reuse* candidates.

In [Poh96b], Pohl proposes a reuse approach for software components which is based on the availability of traceability relationships that connect requirements to these components. More precisely, during a software development project, requirements, software components, and interconnecting traceability relationships are recorded in a suitable repository. Later projects can then access this repository and compare their own requirements with those of the already accomplished projects. Provided that similarities are detected, the components fulfilling the respective requirements in the old project can be considered as candidates for reuse in the current project.

A similar approach was the central subject of research in the *ReDSeeDS* project [Śmi06]. This project deals with software development in a model-driven context, where the traceability relationships are automatically identified and recorded in the course of model transformations. More information on the ReDSeeDS project can be found in Chapter 11.

4.1.9 Reverse Engineering

Analogous to their usage for maintenance, inter-level traceability relationships are used in reverse engineering to understand the interconnections of source code fragments to entities on higher abstraction levels of a system, such as design and architecture models or the requirements specification. If entities on these higher levels are missing, existing intra-level relationships on the source code level allow developers to comprehend the dependencies between different parts of the system's code, thus aiding in the recovery of a system's architecture or even its requirements.

4.2 Commercial Tools

To give a glimpse of traceability support in commercial tools, the respective capabilities of the established [Gei07, Müh06] requirements management tools *DOORS* and *CaliberRM* as well as of the software modeling tools *Rational Software Architect* and *Enterprise Architect* are shortly discussed in Sections 4.2.1 to 4.2.4.

4.2.1 DOORS

IBM Rational DOORS[12] is an application for managing requirements and associated entities such as glossaries, issues, or test plans. The tool was known as Telelogic DOORS until the acquisition of Telelogic by IBM in 2008.

DOORS organizes requirements and other entities in a tree-like hierarchy, with structures such as *folders*, *projects*, and *modules* that act as containers. Using traceability relationships, called *links* in DOORS, cross references can be established. These standard links are untyped, but can carry attributes to record the creation date, the author, or the purpose of a link, for instance. Links connecting entities of two specific modules are grouped by so-called *link sets* which are again contained by a special *link module*.

Links of two special types – "implemented by" and "validated by" – serve to connect to entities maintained by change management and quality management tools offered by the same vendor. To connect to external artifacts, *URLs* can be attached to entities. Since DOORS entities can also be referred by a URL, users can insert an appropriate hyperlink back to DOORS into the respective artifact in order to get a relationship which is traversable in both directions.

The *identification* and *maintenance* of traceability links in DOORS is conducted manually. Some assistance is offered by marking links as "suspect" if a connected entity has been changed. Whether the modification of a specific entity attribute causes the incident links to be marked can be toggled by setting a special flag. With the help of this mechanism, users are hinted at which relationships are to be checked for validity.

Retrieval of traceability information is performed by interacting with the graphical user interface which visualizes the recorded information. Upon selection of an entity, its incident links are shown in a dedicated tab. This is illustrated in Figure 4.1, where the outgoing and incoming links of the selected requirement in the center ("The user shall be able store luggage internally.") are listed on the right of the screen. The left- and right-pointing triangles in the requirements window in the center of the screen indicate whether a requirement has incoming or outgoing links, respectively. Using a special traceability analysis wizard, indirect relationships between entities over a chain of links can be computed and displayed. A further *visualization* option is the creation of a traceability matrix for a specific link set.

---

[1]`http://www-01.ibm.com/software/awdtools/doors/`
[2]Product version used for evaluation: IBM® Rational® DOORS® Web Access 1.4.0.3 (Build 554), with additional information taken from product documentation

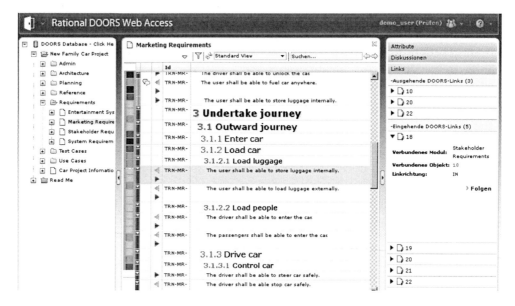

Figure 4.1: Screenshot detail of Rational DOORS Web Access.

4.2.2 CaliberRM

Another requirements management tool is CaliberRM[34] from Borland. Requirements are categorized according to user-definable types, e.g., business requirements, functional requirements, or constraints. As a requirement can contain other requirements, they form a tree-like structure.

Traceability relationships between requirements in CaliberRM are called *dependencies*. Dependencies are anonymous, i.e., they do not exhibit further semantics such as a type or attributes, for instance. If CaliberRM is integrated with other tools from Borland, dependencies to other entities, e.g., test cases or model elements, can be established, too. In addition to dependencies, *references* to external files or URLs can be attached to requirements.

The *identification* and *maintenance* of dependencies and references has to be performed manually. Similar to DOORS, dependencies are marked as *suspect* if a connected entity has changed.

---

[3]http://www.borland.com/us/products/caliber/index.aspx
[4]Product version used for evaluation: Borland® CaliberRM™ 2008 SP1 (Version 10.0)

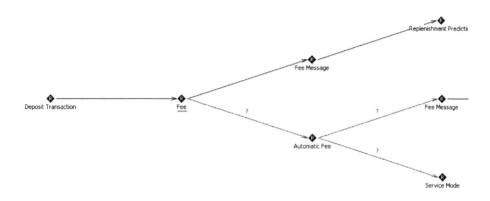

Figure 4.2: Screenshot detail of a CaliberRM dependency diagram.

Concerning *retrieval* and *visualization* of traceability information, lists of outgoing and incoming dependencies as well as of associated references can be displayed for each requirement, offering the possibility to navigate to the connected entity. A more sophisticated visualization option is a traceability matrix which can be configured to include only selected requirements and which also shows indirect dependencies. Furthermore, there is a graph-based illustration that shows all requirements which depend on a selected requirement and the selected requirement is dependent on. An example can be taken from Figure 4.2, showing such a dependency diagram for the requirement "Fee". Suspect dependencies are highlighted and annotated by a question mark.

4.2.3 Rational Software Architect

The Rational Software Architect[5][6] (*RSA*) is a modeling tool by IBM. Though the tool's focus lies on the design of *UML* models [Obj10c], it also supports the creation of pro-

---

[5]http://www-01.ibm.com/software/rational/products/swarchitect/

[6]Product version used for evaluation: IBM® Rational® Software Architect™ Standard Edition (Version 7.5.5.1, Build ID 2100323_1627)

cess models using the *Business Process Modeling Notation (BPMN)* [Obj11], another OMG standard. RSA is based on the Eclipse platform, thus providing the platform's full source code engineering functionality.

RSA makes use of the traceability relationship type hierarchy defined by the UML, presented in Section 3.1.1. Note, that while the UML specification defines instances of most its relationship types to be n-ary, RSA only supports binary relationships. In addition to UML-defined traceability relationships, URLs can be attached to model elements, linking to external resources.

The *identification* and *maintenance* of traceability relationships between model elements is conducted manually. However, source code entities which are the result of model-to-code transformations are automatically connected to their originating model elements via Abstraction relationships.

Besides the navigation from model element to model element via traceability relationships and other relationships such as UML associations and generalizations, RSA predefines some queries for the *retrieval* of traceability information: so-called *traceability* and *impact analysis* queries. The queries' results are *visualized* in special UML diagrams: . Traceability queries compute specifying or implementing entities of a selected entity, taking into account only Abstraction and its specializations Realization and Substitution. In contrast, impact analysis queries consider all Dependencys as well as other UML constructs such as associations and generalizations, which are treated as implicit traceability relationships in this case.

Figure 4.3 shows the result of an impact analysis query executed on a class Person. Person is considered to be part of a platform-independent model in a model-driven context. The query determined all direct and indirect clients of Person, i.e., all entities which are dependent on Person. Among these entities are specializations of Person, another class Person in a platform-specific model, as well as some Java classes that finally implement the UML classes.

4.2.4 Enterprise Architect

The Enterprise Architect[78] *(EA)* by Sparx Systems is a software modeling tool which is mainly suited for designing UML models, but which also offers support for modeling requirements, business processes based on BPMN, data flow diagrams, and others.

Similar to the Rational Software Architect, EA also incorporates the traceability concepts of the UML. However, it does not obey the OMG's UML specification as strictly.

---

[7]http://www.sparxsystems.com/products/ea/index.html
[8]Product version used for evaluation: Enterprise Architect 8.0 (Version 8.0.864, Build 864)

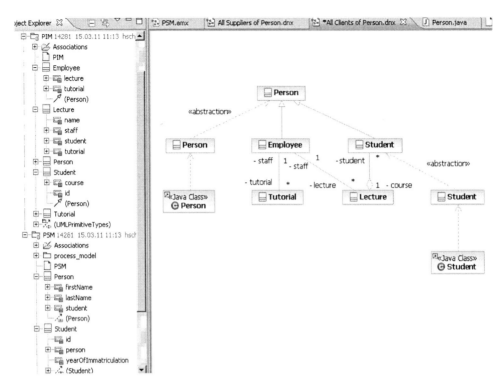

Figure 4.3: Screenshot detail of the Rational Software Architect impact analysis view.

For example, Abstraction and Usage are not individual relationship types, but can be applied to general Dependency relationships as stereotypes. EA allows to attach textual notes and tagged values to relationships and other model elements.

With respect to *identification* and *maintenance*, EA does not differ from the other tools examined above, as both activities have to be performed manually by the users. An exception is the automatic generation of traceability relationships in the course of model-to-code transformations.

In addition to *retrieval* by simply listing all incident relationships of a selected model element and allowing to navigate to connected elements, EA provides three different *visualization* options for traceability relationships. First, there are two lists showing all Dependencys and all Realizations in a selected package, respectively. Second, a tree-like hierarchical view allows for browsing through the traceability information of a given diagram and also includes other UML relationships such as associations and generalizations. Finally, a traceability matrix illustrates traceability relationships between model elements displayed in different diagrams. However, while the elements to be considered can be filtered rather precisely, only relationships of a single type can be displayed simultaneously. Figure 4.4 depicts the hierarchical view (on the left) and a traceability matrix (on the right).

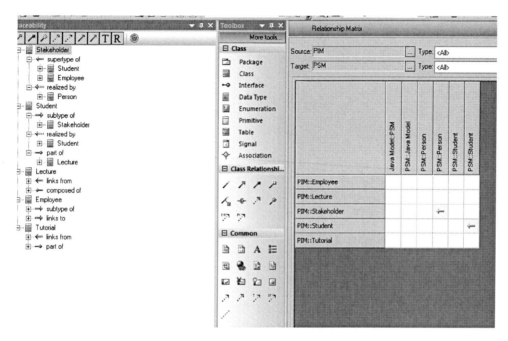

Figure 4.4: Screenshot detail of the Enterprise Architect traceability view and relationship matrix.

4.3 Role in Industry

In general, the application of traceability concepts in industrial practice is not very widespread [Aiz06] and is often limited to the requirements analysis phase [Ark05]. Only few organizations implement traceability practices because they realize the benefits. Others do it because they have to obey legal regulations or want to satisfy their customers' wishes [Win10]. This situation can be attributed to organizational, social, technical, and economical obstacles, as detailed in the following sections.

4.3.1 Organizational Obstacles

One of the main organizational reasons for the insufficient adoption of traceability in industry is the lack of a common agreement on a best practice for traceability, combined with a lack of a common terminology as well as of documented techniques and methods [Ant06]. Besides, the need for traceability is often insufficiently explained to developers, potentially leading to a lack of appreciation for the importance of traceability or to little motivation for performing associated tasks [Ark05].

In many cases, the required granularity of traceability information to be recorded is not clearly defined on an organization-wide level. Thus, individual developers may identify and record too few or too many traceability relationships [Got95, Ark02].

Development projects which are based on a cooperation between different organizations impose further obstacles to traceability. Due to corporate non-disclosure policies, usage of incompatible tools, or insufficient communication, the establishment of traceability relationships between entities belonging to the different parties frequently proves to be difficult. [Ark02]

4.3.2 Social Obstacles

Large software development projects heavily rely on division of work: people who initially develop a software system are not necessarily the ones which are responsible for quality assurance, release planning, or the system's subsequent maintenance. So, while those developers have the best knowledge of the interrelations between the various entities in a development project and are therefore best capable of identifying and recording traceability relationships, they do not directly benefit from traceability themselves. As a consequence, they may show little motivation for the extra burden involved with these tasks [Ark05].

In addition, the achieved accountability may be unwanted by some developers, as they do not like to create structures which allow to trace bugs, defective components, or other committed mistakes back to themselves [Jar98].

4.3.3 Technical Obstacles

Possible technical reasons for the limited application of traceability in industry are manifold. The foremost reason is the lack of adequate support for (semi)automatic relationship identification and maintenance offered by common traceability tools. Consequently, much effort has to be spent on manual identification and maintenance [Aiz06].

With respect to the definition activity, there is no complete and universal traceability meta model, leading to incomplete and insufficient recording of traceability relationships. However, it is argued that such a meta model does not exist because of the domain-specific nature of traceability information [Ant06] and because there is implicit knowledge which cannot be formalized [Win10].

Furthermore, the different traceability tools organizations tend to use are often difficult to integrate and to customize to specific organizations' environments [Kli09]. Traceability tools are also poorly integrated with tools used for the actual development of software. This requires additional effort as traced entities must be manually mapped to the traceability tools [Ark02].

Regarding scalability, it is claimed in that current traceability techniques, especially considering querying, navigation, and visualization, do not scale well for large amounts of entities to be traced [Ant06].

4.3.4 Economic Obstacles

The introduction of traceability in an organization requires an expensive training of employees. Therefore, organizations tend to only educate few developers to become proficient in applying the respective concepts and techniques, resulting in an uneven distribution of relevant knowledge [Ark02].

Generally, managements have a low awareness for the benefits of traceability [Ark05]. Since the costs of traceability, caused by training, tools, and the integration of a traceability concept into the existing workflow, are more obvious, this leads to a negatively perceived cost-value ratio.

Part II

Conception

5 Research Questions

Drawing from the presentation of the state of the art together with the considerations on traceability in practice in Part I, this chapter highlights significant shortcomings of the state of the art and commercial tools in order to formulate the central research questions that are investigated by this work.

In the following sections, the research questions are elaborated and categorized according to the traceability-related activities they address. However, instead of structuring the discussion along the logical ordering of the activities introduced in Chapter 3, the activities are classified according to common concepts and dependencies. Concerning definition, the available concepts for the definition of traceability relationships are dependent on the employed recording technology. Conversely, only defined concepts need to be recorded. Therefore, Section 5.1 discusses problems associated to definition and recording. Section 5.2 is concerned with identification and maintenance, which rely on similar techniques. In Section 5.3, research questions with respect to retrieval are formulated. Although retrieval leads to the further utilization of traceability information, the latter activity is not taken into account here, for it transcends the more technical scope of this work. Finally, Section 5.4 discusses issues related to comprehensive traceability that considers all activities.

The research questions can be divided into two groups, depending on whether they address the development of generic, technology-independent concepts or the implementation of these concepts on the basis of concrete technological spaces, respectively. Solutions for the former group, which comprises Research Questions 1, 3, and 5, are elaborated in the following two chapters of this part of the book. The latter group, including Research Questions 2, 4, 6, and 7, are treated by Part III.

5.1 Questions Relating to Definition and Recording

Considering the multitude of software development methods and techniques together with countless different domains of application, it is not possible to foresee and predefine all traceability relationship types which will ever be needed by different software development projects [Anq08]. This insight is not considered by many of the existing traceability relationship type hierarchies and traceability meta models presented in Section 3.1.1, e.g., [Try97,Car01,Ebn02,Dah03,Gok11]. They are tailored to a given scenario and are not per se envisioned to be adaptable to other domains and artifact landscapes. Furthermore, traceability meta models not only prescribe a set of relationship types, but also the traceable entity types and their granularity.

Besides focusing on specific domains of application, existing definition approaches are often explicitly based on specific technological environments, such as [Poh96b, Let02, Aiz05], for instance. But to be able to employ a traceability approach in a wide range of software development projects with possibly restrictive technological requirements, the ability to adapt the approach to different technological spaces is a desirable feature.

The traceability reference meta model by Ramesh and Jarke, which is explicitly intended to be adaptable to various environments, defines the semantics of most relationship types solely by giving a natural language description of their purpose [Ram01]. Such informal definitions are subject to the users' interpretation and can lead to misunderstandings due to imprecision or ambiguity. While this may be sufficient for a purely manual handling of traceability, an automation of tasks associated to relationship identification and maintenance such as checking the consistency of the traceability model or automatic change processing is hardly possible. Thus, in addition to natural language descriptions, other approaches use various techniques to formalize the semantics of traceability relationships. One example is the approach by Aizenbud-Reshef et al., who augment traceability relationships with event-condition-action rules that are able to automatically modify the traceability model [Aiz05].

Existing *generic* approaches, i.e., approaches that allow for defining customized traceability relationship types, have their shortcomings, too. If they provide some means of formalizing relationship semantics, they are usually restricted to specific formalization concepts. The Traceability Meta-type and the traceability metamodel TmM by Espinoza et al. are limited to linkage rules which specify how to automatically generate instances of a given relationship type [Esp06, Esp11]. The approach by Walderhaug et al. only supports event-condition-action rules where the single possible event is the creation of a relationship [Wal06]. The Ecore-based Traceability Metamodelling Language (TML) by Drivalos et al. supports the attachment of tagged values to relationships and offers a small set of predefined constraints, e.g., the restriction of the number of relationships of a specific type which are incident to instances of a given entity type or the declaration that a tagged value is optional. It is not possible for users to define their own constraints. More information on these three generic definition approaches can be found in Section 3.1.1.

Other techniques for formalizing traceability relationship semantics are usually treated individually and independent of the relationship hierarchies, meta models, and generic approaches discussed above. Thus, it remains unclear whether they can be properly integrated.

Regarding the commercial tools presented in Section 4.2, the possibilities to customize relationship types and specify their semantics are rather rudimentary. While the requirements management tools DOORS and CaliberRM basically do not distinguish between different relationship types at all, the Rational Software Architect RSA and Enterprise Architect rely on the type hierarchy of the *UML* [Obj10c] and its stereotyping mechanism for user-defined extensions. With the exception of CaliberRM, all other tools allow to add information to relationships with the help of attributes or tagged values.

Altogether, it seems that the two presented aspects of traceability research with respect to the activity of definition, i.e., providing a *generic, technology-independent* means of defining application-specific traceability relationship types on the one hand and formalized, *rich* relationship *semantics* on the other hand, have not been contemplated in combination yet. This forms the basis for Research Question 1.

RESEARCH QUESTION 1

How can a generic, technology-independent approach for the definition of custom traceability relationship types be combined with rich, formalized relationship semantics?

Provided that such a combined approach is feasible, traceability still has to be implemented on the basis of an adequate technological space. However, even publications that present technology-independent traceability approaches mostly do not discuss candidate technological spaces for implementation at all. Thus, it remains unclear which technological spaces are suitable for the definition of semantically rich traceability relationship types and the recording of corresponding traceability information. This issue is covered by Research Question 2.

RESEARCH QUESTION 2

How can existing technological spaces facilitate the customized definition of semantically rich traceability relationship types and the subsequent recording of traceability information?

5.2 Questions Relating to Identification and Maintenance

As stated in Section 3.2, the (semi)automatic identification and maintenance of traceability relationships is highly preferable to the manual handling of these activities. With the definition of rules for formalizing relationship semantics, as done in [Gok11, Jir09], automatic identification and maintenance can be associated to the traceability relationships themselves. However, in both publications, the available traceability relationship types are preset. This raises the question if and how relationships of user-defined types, as pursued by Research Question 1, are able to assist in the (semi)automatic identification and maintenance of new and existing relationships, respectively. This concern is captured by Research Question 3.

RESEARCH QUESTION 3

How can the (semi)automatic identification and maintenance of traceability relationships be supported by a generic, technology-independent approach for the definition of custom relationship types?

Furthermore, Section 3.2 indicates that the various techniques for (semi)automatic relationship identification and maintenance proposed in literature are highly specialized, i.e., they are suitable for specific types of traceable entities only, pose specific requirements to the development process, or depend on specific technological environments. For example, identification relying on information retrieval, such as can be found in [Ant02, Set04, Lin06], only works for text-intensive entities. Relationship identification based on model transformation, e.g., [Jou06, Ols07, Yie09], necessitates a development process which is at least partly model-driven. Rule-based identification techniques such as [She03, Cys08, Jir09] as well as the maintenance approaches presented in [Dri10, Mäd08b, Sei10] are only applicable if traceability models are represented in a specific technological space. This can be achieved by external recording of traceability information using a suitable repository.

Considering all these restrictions, it currently appears rather visionary to assume that these heterogeneous identification and maintenance approaches can be integrated into a common process or technological environment. However, literature even lacks an appraisal of the inherent features of existing technological spaces that can be used for supporting identification and maintenance, leading to Research Question 4.

> **RESEARCH QUESTION 4**
>
> How can existing technological spaces facilitate the (semi)automatic identification and maintenance of traceability relationships?

5.3 Questions Relating to Retrieval

The overview of related work in Section 3.4 together with the discussion of commercial tools in Section 4.2 shows that rather little research effort has been devoted to the actual retrieval of traceability information. While there are some publications that introduce languages specifically designed for querying traceability information, others are concerned with convenient interfaces for retrieval which can be employed by less proficient users.

To the author's best knowledge, there is no study of the requirements of traceability applications with respect to retrieval. The analysis of these requirements could result in an enumeration of *generic, technology-independent* traceability retrieval problems or even in a more formal categorization. This shortcoming is taken up by Research Question 5.

> **RESEARCH QUESTION 5**
>
> How can common problems of traceability retrieval be categorized in a generic, technology-independent way and how can these categories be formalized?

Under the assumption that such a categorization can be achieved, it has to be determined how existing technological spaces can solve the represented retrieval problems, resulting in Research Question 6.

> **RESEARCH QUESTION 6**
>
> How can existing technological spaces facilitate the retrieval of traceability information as defined by the generic categories?

5.4 Questions relating to Comprehensive Traceability

Given the overview of traceability literature in Chapter 3, it is discernible that most publications treat selected problems belonging to one or two traceability-related activities only. The approaches are examined rather isolated, i.e., assuming standard technological environments which are well understood but do not provide state-of-the-art solutions for other activities, or even without considering potential consequences to other activities at all. Furthermore, since the solutions are individually developed using the most suitable methods and technologies, it is not clear how well they can be combined with each other [Sch10c].

Current research activities do not involve a seamless integration of existing solutions for different problems based on a common, consistent conceptual and technological foundation. Similarly, the conception of comprehensive traceability approaches providing state-of-the-art solutions for all or at least most of the traceability-related activities has not been considered yet.

Given a generic and technology-independent approach for the definition of semantically rich traceability relationships (see Research Question 1) which supports automatic identification and maintenance (see Research Question 3), together with a generic approach to the categorization of traceability retrieval problems (see Research Question 5), it is of interest if existing technological spaces can integrate these individual issues into a comprehensive implementation. This challenge is taken up by Research Question 7. Basically, a positive answer to this research question depends on the provision of satisfactory solutions to Research Questions 2, 4 and 6 by individual technological spaces.

RESEARCH QUESTION 7

Can existing technological spaces facilitate a comprehensive traceability implementation?

---

6 Generic, Technology-Independent, Semantically Rich Definition

Research Questions 1 and 3 ask for a generic, technology-independent approach for the definition of semantically rich traceability relationship types that also offers support for (semi)automatic identification and maintenance. In response, this chapter presents the *Traceability Relationship Type Template (TRTT)*.

The TRTT allows for the definition of custom, application-specific relationship types and is intended to be instantiated for individual technological spaces as needed, thus permitting its applicability in a wide range of development projects with varying environments. In addition, the TRTT aims at the integration of various state-of-the-art means for specifying relationship semantics, including attributes, relational properties, constraints, and rules. With these features, traceability relationships can inherently offer support for (semi)automatic identification and maintenance.

In the following, Section 6.1 lists requirements for traceability relationships that were elicited in the *MOST* project[1]. Besides the requirements that are already expressed by the research questions, these requirements, collected in a "real" project, additionally underpin the relevance of the relationship type properties that are taken up by the TRTT. Section 6.2 describes the TRTT and offers a detailed explanation of its constituents.

6.1 Requirements for Traceability Relationships

The overall goal of the MOST project was to investigate how software engineering can be supported by ontology-based technologies. As its main tangible result, the project aimed at the development of an ontology-driven software development guidance system. Based on a formalized process model and on the availability of information on the state of development-related artifacts, the guidance system makes use of reasoning techniques to compute possible development activities which can be proposed to

---

[1] http://www.most-project.eu

No.	Description
REQ-1	The set of available traceability relationship types must be adaptable to the needs of specific projects and domains.
REQ-2	The purpose of traceability relationship types must be clearly understandable by users.
REQ-3	Traceability relationships must aid in the detection of inconsistencies between traced entities.
REQ-4	Traceability relationships must aid in the analysis of the impact of changes to traced entities.
REQ-5	Traceability relationships must allow for the recording of associated decisions and rationales.

Table 6.1: Requirements for traceability relationships gathered in the MOST project. Adapted from [Bar08] and [Sch09c].

the developers. Such a system is strongly dependent on the availability of traceability relationships between software artifacts as well as between software artifacts and associated development process steps.

The requirements of the guidance system for traceability relationships are summarized by Table 6.1. They are adapted from the description of use cases for the guidance system given in [Bar08] and from requirements for the whole MOST traceability concept presented in [Sch09c].

Since the guidance system is to be applied for a wide range of different projects and systems to be developed, the underlying traceability solution has to be generic. Thus, Requirement REQ-1 demands the possibility of defining custom, project- and domain-specific traceability relationship types. To allow developers to properly distinguish between the available relationship types, their purpose must be specified clearly and unambiguously, leading to Requirement REQ-2. Concerning requirements management, the guidance system must be able to detect inconsistencies between requirements in order to make according proposals to the users. Requirement REQ-3 extends this notion to all kinds of traced entities. To be able to provide guidance in response to the modification of some traced entity, Requirement REQ-4 specifies that traceability relationships must be able to support impact analysis, i.e., the detection of the effects of changing traced entities on other traced entities. To assist developers in assessing the consequences of modifications, it should be possible to remind them of their previous motivations to create or update some entity. Therefore, Requirement REQ-5 finally asks for the capturing of decisions and rationales.

6.2 The Traceability Relationship Type Template

Essentially, the TRTT acts as a guideline for the definition of traceability relationship types. It specifies a set of desired properties of traceability relationship types which should be implemented by a given technological space. Depending on the traceability requirements of a specific project or on the expressiveness of the technological space which instantiates the TRTT, some of its properties may be omitted. Also, some properties may not be needed by particular relationship types. Considering the requirements for traceability relationships introduced in Section 6.1, the conception of the TRTT itself already contributes to the fulfillment of Requirement REQ-1.

The TRTT belongs to the group of generic definition approaches, which also includes the *Traceability Meta-type* by Espinoza et al. [Esp06], the approach by Walderhaug et al. [Wal06], and the *Traceability Metamodelling Language* by Drivalos et al. [Dri08]. While the TRTT amalgamates the individual benefits of these three approaches, it also integrates other state-of-the-art techniques for the specification of rich traceability relationship semantics. These techniques include attributes, relational properties, constraints, and rules.

The usage of logical operators for the formalization of semantics, as proposed by Dick's *rich traceability* approach [Dic02] (see Section 3.1.2), is not taken up here. This concept is useful for specifying whether only one (disjunction) or all (conjunction) of the requirements connected by a single relationship must be fulfilled, for instance. However, it could be simulated by a special attribute. If required, the concerned requirements' fulfillment can be ensured by suitable constraints which check the traceability model for the existence of respective relationships.

Identification and maintenance are addressed by the possibility to define constraints and rules. Other approaches to (semi)automatic identification and maintenance, e.g., text-based techniques, model transformations, or differencing, cannot be inherently attributed to the traceability model itself and are highly dependent on the nature of the traceable entities and the employed technologies. Therefore, such approaches are not covered by the generic and technology-independent TRTT.

In the following, Sections 6.2.1 to 6.2.9 explain the properties of the Traceability Relationship Type Template in detail. Where some property contributes to the satisfaction of one of the MOST requirements given in Section 6.1, this is explicitly stated in the property's description. Table 6.2 gives an overview of the TRTT. Besides listing the properties and giving a short description, the table also features a *multiplicity* column, indicating how many instances of a specific property a relationship type may possess.

Property	Multiplicity	Description
Name	1	The traceability relationship type's unique identifier.
Description	1	An accurate description of the meaning and purpose of the traceability relationship type.
Supertypes	0..*	Any number of other traceability relationship types that are generalizations of the relationship type at hand.
Schema fragment	1	A schema excerpt specifying how instances of the traceability relationship type connect traceable entities to each other. The schema fragment also defines the arity of the instances.
Attributes	0..*	Any number of *identifier–domain* pairs that describe attributes of the traceability relationship type.
Relational properties (for binary traceability relationship types only)	0..*	Any feasible combination of relational properties, such as *reflexivity*, *symmetry*, or *transitivity*.
Constraints	0..*	Any number of constraints which must all hold true for an instance of the traceability relationship type to be valid.
Impact designators	0..*	Any number of specifications of how changes to recorded traceability relationships or traced entities affect other relationships or entities.
Examples	0..*	Any number of examples that illustrate the usage of the traceability relationship type.

Table 6.2: Overview of the TRTT.

6.2.1 Name

The identifier of the traceability relationship type. It should be well-chosen in order to allow users to quickly grasp the relationship type's purpose. Furthermore, the name should be unique, so that the relationship type at hand can be unambiguously distinguished from other types.

The definition of a meaningful, unique relationship type name contributes to the fulfillment of Requirement REQ-2.

6.2.2 Description

A natural language description of the purpose and the meaning of the traceability relationship type. The description should be precise enough to clearly distinguish the relationship at hand from other types, thus helping users in choosing the correct type for connecting a given set of traceable entities.

Similar to a relationship type's *name*, the description has a share on the fulfillment of Requirement REQ-2.

6.2.3 Supertypes

A set of other traceability relationship types that generalize the relationship type at hand. The semantics of generalization depend on the technological space that instantiates the TRTT. Typically, in spaces such as *MOF* [Obj06] or *EMF* [Ste08], a given type can be employed where one of its supertypes is requested. This mechanism results in a subtype to inherit its supertypes' attributes and in constraints and rules attached to a supertype to also refer to relationship instances of the type at hand.

This property does not derive from some requirement, but is introduced to benefit from the concept of generalization that is supported by many technological spaces.

6.2.4 Schema Fragment

An excerpt of the schema[2] which defines the traced entity types and traceability relationship types to be used for a specific traceability model. The excerpt only includes the relationship type at hand and its relevant surroundings, i.e., the entity types it connects and, if deemed necessary, other relationship and entity types which are referred to by some constraint or impact designator. Depending on the capabilities of the technological space instantiating the TRTT, traceability relationship types do not necessarily have to be modeled as, in many cases directed, binary connections, but may be represented by more complex structures. For example, in a technological space such as

---

[2]Here, the term "schema" acts as placeholder for the structure defining concepts together with their properties and interrelations to be used in a technological space for a specific domain or application. The exact terminology depends on the considered technological space. Examples are *meta model* for the MOF space, *database schema* for relational databases, or *TBox* for ontologies.

OWL [Mot09b], which only supports binary connections in the form of so-called object properties, an n-ary relationship type may be represented by a dedicated OWL class with multiple outgoing object properties that link to the entity types to be interrelated.

The arbitrary embedding of traceability relationship types in the schema as needed constitutes a substantial contribution to the fulfillment of Requirement REQ-1.

6.2.5 Attributes

A set of of identifier-domain pairs. Instances of the traceability relationship types assign a value taken from the domain to the identifier.

The inclusion of attributes by the TRTT derives from a more general interpretation of Requirement REQ-5. Using attributes, any data can be attached to relationships.

6.2.6 Relational Properties

A combination of relational properties such as reflexivity, irreflexivity, symmetry, anti-symmetry, or transitivity. The chosen combination must be feasible, e.g., an a relationship type must not be reflexive as well as irreflexive. Relational properties can only be defined for binary relationship types. Furthermore, the choice of relational properties is restricted if a binary relationship type does not have the same entity type as source and target. In that case, only suitable relational properties such as injectivity or surjectivity are permitted.

Relational properties could be viewed and formulated as *constraints*. The choice to treat them as an individual TRTT property is due to the features of some technological spaces to handle them separately in form of query extensions or by inference mechanisms (see Chapters 9 and 10).

6.2.7 Constraints

A set of invariants which must all hold true for an instance of the traceability relationship type at hand to be valid. Essentially, constraints ensure the integrity of the traceability model. Their specification may consider properties of traceability relationships as well as of the traced entities in the traceability model.

This TRTT property serves to fulfill of Requirement REQ-3. Since constraints capture the conditions which must be met for a relationship to be valid, they may also be used for maintenance purposes. For instance, relationships which violate some constraint could be reported to the developers who can then handle them appropriately.

6.2.8 Impact Designators

A set of specifications of how a change to an instance of the traceability relationship type at hand or to one of its incident entities impacts, i.e., affects, other relationships or entities. These specifications may involve the autonomous handling of the impact or some kind of guidance provided to the users. provision of Depending on the technological space instantiating the TRTT, impact designators are typically implemented as event-condition-action or condition-action rules.

The possibility to add impact designators to traceability relationship types directly satisfies Requirement REQ-4. By automatically creating or updating relationships, impact designators can also fulfill identification and maintenance purposes, respectively.

6.2.9 Examples

A set of example applications of the traceability relationship type that clarify its usage. The examples should be taken from the project or environment the relationship type is used in as well as from other, more general contexts.

Together with a relationship type's *name* and its *description*, examples serve to fulfill Requirement REQ-2.

7 Generic, Technology-Independent Retrieval

Research Question 5 demands the generic, technology-independent, yet formalized categorization of common traceability retrieval problems. To provide a solution, this Chapter first derives six elementary traceability tasks that abstract from concrete fields of application such as given in Section 4.1. Considering the retrieval-related aspects of these tasks, three *traceability retrieval patterns* are developed: *Existence, Reachable Entities*, and *Slice*. They represent generic, technology-independent descriptions of retrieval problems that are common to many traceability applications.

Section 7.1 introduces the six elementary traceability tasks. Subsequently, Section 7.2 describes the three patterns in detail.

7.1 Elementary Traceability Tasks

Based on a literature survey and on an analysis of the activities of the software life cycle conducted in the MOST project [Bar08], it is discernible that the basic traceability functionalities required by the various fields of application strongly overlap and, in most cases, can be reduced to a set of six elementary tasks: *consistency analysis, coverage analysis, dependency analysis, impact analysis, origin analysis*, and *result analysis*. These tasks, described in detail in the following sections, should be supported by traceability implementations in order to be usable for a wide range of applications.

7.1.1 Consistency Analysis

Consistency analysis refers to the detection of conflicts and inconsistencies between different entities. This is permitted by the presence of suitable traceability relationships interconnecting the entities in question.

For example, in change management, consistency analysis plays an important role for the detection of inconsistencies that were caused by some modification to the system, such as the introduction of naming conflicts or circular dependencies. Concerning release planning, especially with respect to product line development, this kind of analysis prevents the integration of conflicting features in a final product. Finally, consistency analysis can be used in requirements management for finding ambiguities in related requirements specifications.

7.1.2 Coverage Analysis

The purpose of coverage analysis is to check whether given entities are traceable to a specific set of other entities.

Coverage analysis is essential for quality assurance, where it is required to check if there is a test case for every requirement or for every system component, for instance. In the field of project management, when it comes to measuring a development project's progress, coverage analysis serves to determine yet unimplemented requirements.

7.1.3 Dependency Analysis

Dependency analysis deals with the discovery of entities a given entity is directly or indirectly dependent on, e.g., if the dependent entity makes use of some service or functionality supplied by other entities. Dependency is often represented by implicit traceability relationships, such as generalizations or whole-part relationships.

Typical fields of application for performing dependency analyses are maintenance and reverse engineering, as developers need to comprehend the dependencies between different parts of the source code or other software artifacts. With respect to release planning, dependencies between requirements need to be considered, as requirements that are selected for implementation in the next release of a system may require the implementation of other requirements.

7.1.4 Impact Analysis

Impact analysis refers to the detection of the consequences of changing entities. This includes the discovery of all entities which are impacted, i.e., affected, by the modification or deletion of a given entity. To account for the initial change, the impacted entities potentially have to be modified, too. Going beyond the determination and subsequent manual adaptation of impacted entities, it is desirable to automate the adaptation where possible.

Obvious fields of application of impact analysis are change management and maintenance. They involve the modification of various software artifacts and require the tracking of possible effects of these changes. Impact analysis is also used in project management for estimating the cost of changes. In requirements management, changing a requirement may require the revision of requirements which refine, are dependent on, or are other otherwise related to the changed requirement.

7.1.5 Origin Analysis

Origin analysis serves to detect all traced entities which played some role in the creation of a given entity.

In the context of change and requirements management, origin analysis may be used for the determination of stakeholders that were involved in the authoring of some requirement in order to discuss needed deviations. With respect to project management, origin analysis permits to identify the developers that are responsible for the creation or modification of software artifacts, thus facilitating accountability. In reverse engineering, origin analysis allows for finding the origins of source code artifacts on higher abstraction levels. Finally, configuration management often involves the tracing of the version history of software artifacts.

7.1.6 Result Analysis

As counterpart of origin analysis, result analysis is intended to find all traced entities which were created on the basis of or with the help of a given entity.

Result analysis is employed by the reuse approach pursued by the *ReDSeeDS* project[1]. The approach relies on the identification of requirements of already existing systems which are similar to "new" requirements of a system that is currently in development. Given a set of such similar "old" requirements, all artifacts that realize these requirements, such as architectural components, design models, and source code artifacts, constitute reuse candidates and are to be retrieved by performing result analyses.

7.2 Traceability Retrieval Patterns

In the following, the three traceability retrieval patterns Existence, Reachable Entities, and Slice are introduced, providing technology-independent, abstract descriptions of

---

[1]http://www.redseeds.eu

the retrieval problems posed by the elementary traceability tasks identified in Section 7.1. To facilitate proper support for these tasks, technological spaces implementing a traceability solution should be able to realize retrieval of traceability information conforming to the three patterns.

Prior to the detailed description of the three patterns in Sections 7.2.2 to 7.2.4, Section 7.2.1 introduces a template which serves to structure the pattern specifications.

7.2.1 Pattern Template

A complete description of a traceability retrieval pattern consists of the pattern's *name*, a *description* of the addressed problem, a prototypical *traceability model* depicting the context where the pattern is to be applied, a set of prototypical *queries* to retrieve the required traceability information, and finally an enumeration of potential areas of *application* of the pattern. In the following, these facets of a retrieval pattern are explained in more detail.

Pattern Name

The name of the traceability retrieval pattern. It should reflect the problem addressed by the pattern as well as the provided solution.

Problem Description

A natural language explanation of the problem addressed by the traceability retrieval pattern. The explanation is generic and does not refer to specific applications or domains.

Traceability Model

A prototypical traceability model that serves as context for visualizing the queries associated with the retrieval pattern.

In essence, the traceability model constitutes a graph where the vertices represent traceable entities and the edges denote traceability relationships. Two specific traceable entities may be connected by more than one relationship. Considering the *Traceability Relationship Type Template* introduced in Section 6.2, traceability relationships are often directed and are supposed to have a type and attribute values. Therefore, the prototypical traceability model corresponds to a directed multigraph with typed and attributed edges, as defined by Definition 6.

DEFINITION 6 (DIRECTED MULTIGRAPH WITH TYPED AND ATTRIBUTED EDGES)

Let

- *Vertex* be the *universe of vertices,*
- *Edge* be the *universe of edges,*
- *TypeID* be the *universe of type identifiers,*
- *AttrID* be the *universe of attribute identifiers,* and
- *Value* be the *universe of attribute values.*

A *directed multigraph with typed and attributed edges* G over the sets $V \subseteq$ *Vertex* and $E \subseteq$ *Edge* is a quintuple $G = (V, E, \Lambda, type, value)$ with the following properties:

- $\Lambda : V \to \mathbb{P}(E \times \{in, out\})$ is the vertices' *incidence mapping*, where
  $\forall e \in E : \exists !v, w \in V : ((e, out) \in \text{ran } \Lambda(v) \wedge (e, in) \in \text{ran } \Lambda(w))$,
  i.e., to each vertex, the set of incident edges with their respective direction is assigned.
- $type : E \to TypeID$ is a *typing* of the edges.
- $value : E \to (AttrID \nrightarrow value)$ is an *attribution* of the edges.

Explanations:

- ran R: the range of the binary relation R
- $X \nrightarrow Y$: a partial function from X to Y

In the following descriptions of the patterns, these graphs are represented using the usual visual notation. The edges are labeled with their types and attributes as depicted in Figure 7.1. Here, the traceability relationship r connects the traced entity e1 to the entity e2. T denotes the relationship's type and attr1 = 42 and attr2 = "myValue" are assignments of attribute values to attribute identifiers.

Naturally, "real" technological spaces for implementing traceability solutions may offer further modeling concepts, e.g., for specifying properties of traced entities.

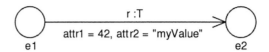

Figure 7.1: Traceability relationship notation example.

Queries

A list of prototypical queries based on the *traceability model* part, illustrating what information has to be retrieved to solve the problem addressed by the pattern.

The queries are precisely formulated in natural language. In addition, since the retrieval patterns rely on the specification of the structure of paths of traceability relationships between traced entities, a more formal description that employs *regular path expressions* (RPEs) on the traceability models is given.

The basic constituents of RPEs on directed multigraphs with typed and attributed edges are the *simple path descriptions* $\longrightarrow$ and $\longleftarrow$. They denote that a vertex has some outgoing or incoming edge, respectively. To refer to any edge regardless of its direction, $\longleftrightarrow$ is used. The set of eligible edges can be restricted by providing constraints on the edge type or attribute values to be taken into account, e.g., $\longrightarrow^T$ or $\longleftrightarrow_{attr1=42,attr2=2}$. Commas in the list of attribute values are to be read as *and*.

With the help of the regular expression operations concatenation, alternation, and iteration, these simple path descriptions may be combined to RPEs (see Definition 7).

DEFINITION 7 (RPES ON DIR. MULTIGRAPHS WITH TYP. AND ATTR. EDGES)

Let $\longrightarrow^{typeID}_{attrID_1=value_1,attrID_2=value_2,...}$, $\longleftarrow^{typeID}_{attrID_1=value_1,attrID_2=value_2,...}$ and

$\longleftrightarrow^{typeID}_{attrID_1=value_1,attrID_2=value_2,...}$

be RPEs with optional restrictions on types and attribute values.

Then

- given two RPEs rpe_1 and rpe_2, $(rpe_1\ rpe_2)$ is an RPE (concatenation),

- given two RPEs rpe_1 and rpe_2, $(rpe_1\ |\ rpe_2)$ is an RPE (alternation), and

- given an RPE rpe, rpe^* is an RPE (iteration).

For example, the regular path expression $\longrightarrow^* (\longleftarrow\longrightarrow^T | \longleftarrow^S_{attr1=42,attr2="myValue"})$ refers to a path consisting of any number of edges in outgoing direction, followed either by some edge of type T or by an incoming edge of type S with the attribute values attr1 = 42 and attr2 = "myValue".

Furthermore, given a regular path expression *rpe* and two vertices v and w,

- v *rpe* w corresponds to the boolean value *true* if w can be reached from v by a path conforming to *rpe*, otherwise to *false*,

- v *rpe* denotes the set of vertices that is reachable from v by following all paths that conform to *rpe*, and

- $\lhd(v, rpe)$ refers to the subgraph that consists of all vertices and edges lying on paths that start at v and conform to *rpe*.

If technological spaces that implement retrieval conforming to the patterns support additional querying concepts, e.g., for considering properties of traced entities, the queries should be extended appropriately.

Applications

A collection of possible applications for the retrieval pattern taken from the set of elementary traceability tasks given in Section 7.1, including some examples taken from specific contexts to foster comprehension of the purposes of the pattern.

7.2.2 Existence Pattern

Based on the traceability retrieval pattern template defined in Section 7.2.1, the *Existence* pattern is specified in the following.

Pattern Name

Existence

Problem Description

The Existence pattern deals with the question whether any traceable entity out of a set of traceable entities can be traced to some other entity included by a second set of entities. More formally, given two disjoint sets of traceable entities E_{source} and E_{target}, it is to be tested if there exist some $e_{source} \in E_{source}$ and $e_{target} \in E_{target}$ with e_{source} and e_{target} being connected by traceability relationships, either directly or indirectly by a sequence of traceability relationships with one or more intermediate traced entities. Instead of accepting any path between e_{source} and e_{target}, restrictions on the paths of traceability relationships may be imposed.

Traceability Model

The directed multigraph with typed and attributed edges in Figure 7.2 represents a prototypical traceability model which is sufficient to explain the idea behind the Existence pattern and its associated queries. The model consists of five traced entities e1 to e5 and six traceability relationships r1 to r6. While r1, r3, and r5 are instances of the traceability relationship type T, r2, r4, and r6 are instances of S.

Queries

Referring to the traceability model in Figure 7.2, the following queries illustrate how to retrieve traceability information in accordance to the Existence pattern.

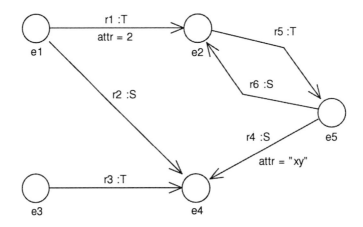

Figure 7.2: Structure of a prototypical traceability model.

1. Does there exist a single relationship of type T between e1 and e2?

   e1 $\longleftrightarrow^T$ e2

   Result: *true* – because of the path $(e1, r1, e2)$

2. Does there exist a single outgoing relationship with the attribute value attr $=$ "xy" from e4 to some other entity?

   $\exists i \in \{1, 2, 3, 5\} : e4 \longrightarrow_{attr="xy"} e_i$

   Result: *false*

3. Does there exist a path of relationships between some entity of the set $\{e2, e3\}$ and an entity of the set $\{e4, e5\}$ which starts with an outgoing relationship of type T or an incoming relationship of type S which is followed by a second outgoing relationship?

   $\exists i \in \{2, 3\}, j \in \{4, 5\} : e_i \, (\longrightarrow^T | \longleftarrow^S) \longrightarrow e_j$

   Result: *yes* – because of $(e2, r5, e5, r4, e4)$, for instance

Applications

The Existence pattern can be used for consistency analysis. Consider a traceability relationship of the type tests connecting a test case to a requirement it is supposed to test, for instance. Since the recording of such a relationship is only feasible if the requirement can actually be tested, i.e., the requirement is implemented, a constraint of tests may demand that there exists a path of suitable traceability relationships which connects the requirement to an implementing source code artifact.

Another application is coverage analysis, e.g., in the context of project management for examining if all requirements of a system have been implemented. This is the case if there exists a path of relationships from each requirement to some source code artifact. Conversely, investigating if every source code artifact can be traced back to a requirement avoids the implementation of unneeded features. Furthermore, every architecture component could be tested for the existence of a dedicated test case.

7.2.3 Reachable Entities Pattern

This section describes the *Reachable Entities* traceability retrieval pattern, using the template from Section 7.2.1.

Pattern Name

Reachable Entities

Problem Description

The Reachable Entities pattern involves the determination of traced entities that are traceable from any entity in a given set of entities. That is, given a set of traced entities E_{source}, the set $E_{reachable}$ of traced entities which are reachable from some $e \in E_{source}$ by traversing a path of traceability relationships is to be identified. Analogous to the Existence pattern, restrictions for constraining the eligible paths of traceability relationships may be specified.

Traceability Model

For this pattern, the same traceability model as for the Existence pattern can be used, depicted in Figure 7.2. Refer to Section 7.2.2 for a description of the model.

Queries

Referring to the traceability model in Figure 7.2, the following queries illustrate how to retrieve traceability information in accordance to the Reachable Entities pattern.

1. Which entities are reachable from e2 by any single incoming relationship?

   e2 $\longleftarrow$

   Result: $\{e1, e5\}$ – because of the paths $(e2, r1, e1)$, $(e2, r6, e5)$

2. Which entities are reachable from e4 by traversing paths consisting of an incoming relationship of type S followed by a sequence of outgoing relationships of type T of any length?

   e4 $\xleftarrow{\quad S\quad}\xrightarrow{\quad} T*$

   Result: $\{e1, e2, e5\}$ – because of $(e4, r2, e1)$, $(e4, r2, e1, r1, e2)$, $(e4, r4, e5)$, for instance

3. Which entities are reachable from the set of entities $\{e1, e3\}$ by traversing paths consisting of outgoing relationships of type T with a length of at least one?

$$e1 \longrightarrow^T \longrightarrow^{T*} \cup\ e3 \longrightarrow^T \longrightarrow^{T*}$$

Result: $\{e2, e4, e5\}$ – because of $(e1, r1, e2)$, $(e1, r1, e2, r5, e5)$, $(e3, r3, e4)$

Applications

The Reachable Entities pattern is applicable for various problems situated in the areas of dependency analysis, impact analysis, origin analysis, and result analysis.

An example of the usage of the Reachable Entities pattern for dependency analysis is the computation of import dependencies between Java classes. Given a specific class, a regular path expression using iteration can be used to reach all its imported classes so that they can be returned to the developer requesting this analysis.

Upon the change of a requirement, the Reachable Entities pattern could be used for performing an impact analysis. Thus, other requirements potentially affected by that change can be found in order to adapt them accordingly.

With respect to origin analysis, the developers who implemented a given source code artifact can be determined for sending bug reports, for instance.

A result analysis on the basis of the Reachable Entities pattern could be performed for finding source code artifacts implementing specific requirements in order to reuse them in another project with similar requirements.

7.2.4 Slice Pattern

In this section, the last of the three identified retrieval patterns – *Slice* – is specified. Again, the template from 7.2.1 serves to structure the description.

Pattern Name

Slice

Problem Description

The Slice pattern is similar to the Reachable Entities pattern in that it is concerned with the determination of all traced entities that are traceable from any entity in a given set of entities. More precisely, given a set of traced entities E_{source}, the traced entities which are reachable from some $e \in E_{source}$ by traversing paths of traceability relationships are determined. However, unlike the Reachable Entities pattern, all the entities and relationships *on* these paths are to be returned to the user. Essentially, such a slice constitutes a submodel of the queried traceability model. Analogous to the other patterns, restrictions on the traceability relationship paths to be considered may be imposed.

Traceability Model

For this pattern, the same traceability model as for the other patterns can be used, depicted in Figure 7.2. Refer to Section 7.2.2 for a description of the model.

Queries

Referring to the traceability model in Figure 7.2, the following queries illustrate how to retrieve traceability information in accordance to the Slice pattern.

1. Starting from e5, which slice results from following any single relationship?

   $\triangleleft(e5, \longrightarrow)$

   Result: see the subgraph marked in Figure 7.3

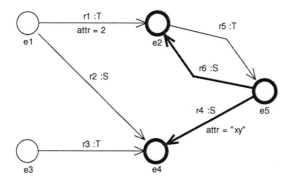

Figure 7.3: Result of Slice query 1.

2. Starting from e2, which slice results from following a path consisting of a relationship of type T followed by an outgoing relationship with the attribute value
attr = "xy"?

$$\lhd(e2, \longleftrightarrow^T \longleftarrow_{attr="xy"})$$

Result: see the subgraph marked in Figure 7.4

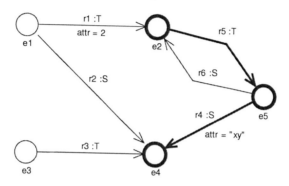

Figure 7.4: Result of Slice query 2.

3. Starting from the set of entities {e2, e4}, which slice results from following a path
consisting of a relationship of type S followed by a sequence of incoming relationships of any length (including a length of 0)?

$$\lhd(e2, \longleftrightarrow^S \longleftarrow^*) \cup \lhd(e4, \longleftrightarrow^S \longleftarrow^*)$$

Result: see the subgraph marked in Figure 7.5

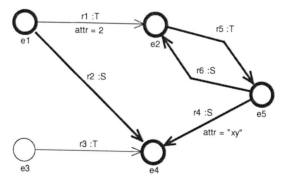

Figure 7.5: Result of Slice query 3.

97

Applications

Since possible applications of the Slice pattern come from dependency analysis, impact analysis, origin analysis, and result analysis, it apparently addresses the same areas of application as the Reachable Entities pattern. However, specific use cases that rely on a profound comprehension of the interrelationships between traced entities can benefit from the additional information on intermediate traced entities and interconnecting traceability relationships provided by the Slice pattern.

For example, dependency analyses for program understanding purposes usually require the application of the Slice pattern, for developers need to get an overview of the whole network of source code artifacts, including the different kinds of dependencies between them.

Part III

Implementation

8 Excursus: Technologies for Universal Traceability

This chapter introduces the main features of two technological spaces which are chosen as examples for analyzing the suitability for implementing a comprehensive, semantically rich traceability solution: the *TGraph approach* [Ebe08] and the *Web Ontology Language (OWL)* [Mot09b] together with related languages that are needed for querying.

The TGraph approach is covered in Section 8.1. Section 8.2.1 describes the Web Ontology Language together with the related languages *RDF* [Kly04] and *SPARQL* [Pru08].

8.1 The TGraph Approach

TGraphs, developed by Ebert et al. [Ebe95], are a very general and expressive kind of graphs. Together with a set of associated languages – the metamodeling language *grUML*, the query language *GReQL* [Kul99, Ebe10], and the transformation language *GReTL* [Hor11] – they form what is called the *TGraph approach*. Although there are some differences, the TGraph approach belongs to the family of well-known model-based technological spaces such as *MOF* [Obj06] or *EMF* [Ste08].

The TGraph approach has been used for various applications, including the development of meta-case tools [Ebe97], software reengineering [Ebe02], modeling geographic information [Fal09], or migration to service-oriented architecture [Zil11].

The different constituents of the TGraph approach are described in more detail in the following sections. Section 8.1.1 explains the basics of TGraphs themselves. In Section 8.1.2, grUML is introduced. The languages GReQL and GReTL are covered in Sections 8.1.3 and 8.1.4, respectively. Finally, Section 8.1.5 addresses the creation and usage of *event-condition-action* rules for TGraphs with *JGraLab*[1], a Java-based library that allows for the practical usage of TGraphs and its accompanying languages.

---

[1]http://jgralab.uni-koblenz.de

8.1.1 TGraph Basics

As already stated in the introduction of this section, TGraphs are very general kind of graph. In detail, TGraphs are

- *typed*, i.e., vertices, edges, and the graph itself have a type,

- *attributed*, i.e., vertices, edges, and the graph can carry attribute name-value pairs,

- *directed*, i.e., edges have a start and an end vertex, and

- *ordered*, i.e., vertices and edges are globally ordered within the graph. Furthermore, the edges incident to a vertex are ordered, too.

To visualize TGraphs, *UML object diagrams* [Obj10c] are employed. For an example, consider Figure 8.1 which depicts a TGraph modeling a small social network. The type of the graph itself is SocialNetwork, represented by the instance with the «graphclass» stereotype. Vertices are either instances of Place, Person, or Organization. Similarly, the types of the edges are IsParentOf, IsSiblingOf, Knows, and ResidesIn. There are various attributes used in the example, such as the name attribute of vertices of type Place which

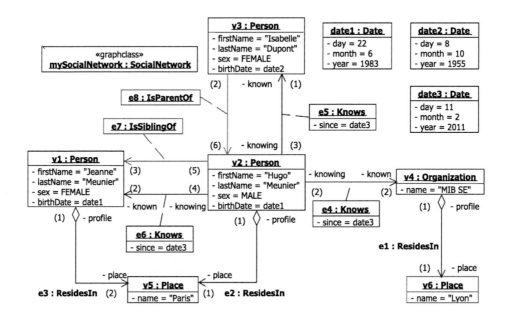

Figure 8.1: Example TGraph.

takes a string value or the sex attribute of Person vertices. The latter attributes are of an enumeration type, i.e., they can take one of the values FEMALE or MALE (see Figure 8.2). The birthDate and since attributes of Person vertices and Knows edges, respectively, are of the user-defined composite type Date, which is a so-called *record*. With day, month, and year, each Date record comprises three integer components. Edge directions are displayed as arrowheads. For illustrative purposes, the global orders of vertices and edges are indicated by an adequate choice of identifiers: v1 and v6 are the first and the last vertex in the global vertex order, respectively. Analogously, the identifiers e1 to e8 imply the global edge order. The order of the incident edges at a specific vertex is denoted by the numbers in parentheses.

A central idea of modeling with TGraphs is the representation of an object of the modeled world by a single vertex, while the object's *occurrences* are represented as edges. In the example TGraph, this is illustrated by vertex v5 and its incoming edges: instead of representing the residence of "Jeanne" and "Hugo" by two instances of Place with the name "Paris", two ResidesIn edges to a single vertex are used.

Note, that with respect to the IsSiblingOf and Knows edges, their directionality may imply that only the real-world persons represented by their sources "are siblings of" or "know" the target persons, but not vice versa. In reality, however, the "is sibling of" relationship is mutual. Furthermore, the "knows" relationship in well-known social networks is symmetric, too. In this example, it has been chosen to treat this issue as implicit knowledge of the modeler which has to be considered by the application logic. Alternatively, a counterpart for each of these edges, with source and target vertices switched, could be added.

The properties of TGraphs which are illustrated above are formally underpinned by Definition 8.

A feature that distinguishes TGraphs from related technological spaces such as Essential MOF, a subset of MOF, or EMF is its treatment of edges as first-class citizens. This means that edges are not merely anonymous references, but are seen as being coordinate with vertices. For instance, they can be explicitly referred to store them in variables.

JGraLab offers a Java API for the creation, manipulation, and traversal of TGraphs. The graph itself and its vertices and edges are implemented by plain Java objects that are instances of classes representing the types of the graph and its elements. Attributes are accordingly represented as Java member fields. The global order of vertices and edges as well as the order of incidences at each vertex are reflected by the referencing scheme between the various objects. TGraphs can be made persistent using the JGraLab-specific *TG* file format.

DEFINITION 8 (TGRAPH)

Let

- *Vertex* be the *universe of vertices,*
- *Edge* be the *universe of edges,*
- *TypeID* be the *universe of type identifiers,*
- *AttrID* be the *universe of attribute identifiers,* and
- *Value* be the *universe of attribute values.*

A *TGraph* G over the sets $V \subseteq Vertex$ and $E \subseteq Edge$ is a quintuple $G = (V_{seq}, E_{seq}, \Lambda_{seq}, type, value)$ with the following properties:

- $V_{seq} \in \text{iseq } V$ is the graph's *sequence of vertices,* reflecting the global vertex order.

- $E_{seq} \in \text{iseq } E$ is the graph's *sequence of edges,* reflecting the global edge order.

- $\Lambda_{seq} : V \rightarrow \text{iseq }(E \times \{in, out\})$ is the vertices' *incidence mapping,* where
  $\forall e \in E : \exists !v, w \in V : ((e, out) \in \text{ran } \Lambda_{seq}(v) \wedge (e, in) \in \text{ran } \Lambda_{seq}(w))$,
  i.e., to each vertex, the sequence of incident edges with their respective direction is assigned, reflecting the order of incident edges.

- $type : (G \cup V \cup E) \rightarrow TypeID$ is a *typing* of the graph and its elements.

- $value : (G \cup V \cup E) \rightarrow (AttrID \nrightarrow value)$ is an *attribution* of the graph and its elements.

Explanations:

- iseq S: the set of duplicate-free sequences over the set S

- ran R: the range of the binary relation R

- $X \nrightarrow Y$: a partial function from X to Y

8.1.2 Metamodeling TGraphs with grUML

Comparable to OMG's MOF, the TGraph approach adheres to a four-layered meta-hierarchy. TGraphs themselves are situated on the M1 level, with their run-time in-

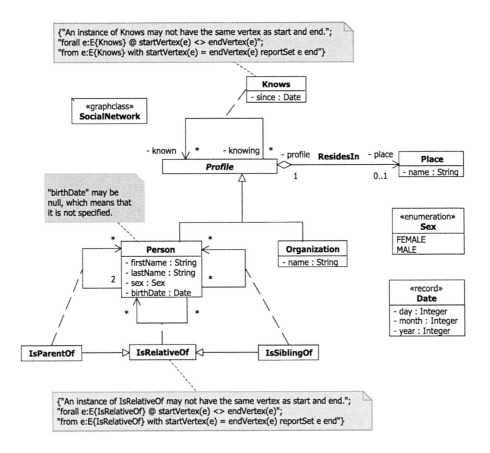

Figure 8.2: Example TGraph schema in grUML.

stances on M0. TGraph meta models on the M2 level, called *schemas*, are modeled using *graph UML* (*grUML*) and specify the possible structures of TGraphs. Schemas again conform to the predefined *grUML meta schema* on the M3 level.

grUML Schemas

Figure 8.2 shows an example schema for the graph in Figure 8.1. Essentially, grUML constitutes a subset of *UML class diagrams* [Obj10c], incorporating only those concepts which exhibit a graph-like semantics. In detail, the class of the graph itself is defined by a dedicated UML class adorned with a «graphclass» stereotype. Vertex classes, e.g., Person, and their attributes are visualized by UML classes with attributes.

Edge classes such as ResidesIn are represented by associations, which can also exhibit aggregation or composition semantics. If an edge type possesses attributes or participates in a generalization relationship, as in the case of Knows, IsParentOf, and IsSiblingOf, UML association classes are employed. The latter two edge types are defined to be subclasses of IsRelativeOf, which is not used in the example graph. Since edges cannot be connected by edges themselves, association classes may not be interrelated by associations. The direction of edges is usually specified by the reading direction of the associations representing the respective edge classes. Multiplicities denote degree restrictions, i.e., the multiplicity on the far end of an edge class incident to a given vertex class specifies the minimum and maximum number of vertices which may be connected to an instance of the given vertex class by respective edges. For instance, a Profile vertex may be connected to at most one Place vertex via a ResidesIn edge. Note, that in the example schema in Figure 8.2, the reading direction is omitted due to restrictions of the employed modeling tool. However, an agreed-upon convention is that the reading direction may be omitted if the edge class name clearly implies the edges' direction.

The semantics of generalization relationships between vertex classes and between edge classes is similar to standard UML: all subclasses inherit the attributes of their superclasses and instances of an edge class may connect vertices of the same classes as its super edge classes. Thus Person vertices may be incident to IsRelativeOf as well as to IsParentOf and IsSiblingOf edges. Furthermore, vertices of a given class may be incident to edges of all classes specified by its super vertex classes. Consequently, Person vertices may also be incident to Knows and ResidesIn edges. Generally speaking, instances of subclasses can be used anywhere an instance of a superclass is required [Lis87][2]. grUML supports multiple inheritance, i.e., any class can have more than one superclass. Furthermore, vertex and edge classes may be declared as being *abstract*. An abstract class, e.g., Profile, may not have direct instances which are not instances of some subclass.

Furthermore, it is possible to attach comments and constraints to schema elements. In the example schema, a comment is linked to Person and two constraints are imposed on Knows and IsRelativeOf, respectively. Constraints are identifiable by their tripartite *message-predicate query-offending elements query* structure. The message is intended to describe the nature of a possible violation of the constraint at hand to the users. The predicate query is the actual constraint: a boolean *GReQL* expression (see Section 8.1.3) whose evaluation indicates whether the constraint holds. The offending elements query is another GReQL query that returns the graph elements responsible for a constraint

---

[2]An exception to this rule exists with respect to *redefinition* [Bil11a], which is not covered in this introduction.

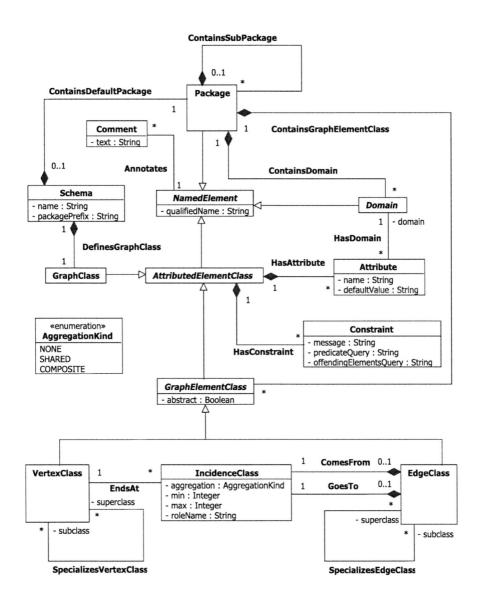

Figure 8.3: grUML meta schema, structure part.

violation. The generalization semantics imply that the constraint related to IsRelativeOf also applies to its subclasses.

The grUML Meta Schema

Figure 8.3 shows a slightly simplified version of the structure part of the grUML meta schema. Besides GraphClass, VertexClass, and EdgeClass, which serve to define graph and graph element classes and which are generalized by the abstract classes GraphElementClass, AttributedElementClass, and NamedElement, the meta schema specifies further concepts. The Schema itself is identifiable by its schemaPrefix and name. Apart from containing the GraphClass, it also indirectly comprises the GraphElementClasses via a default Package and possibly other, user-defined Packages. An edge class visualized as association in grUML is actually the concrete syntax for an instance of EdgeClass together with two IncidenceClasses connecting it to the VertexClasses. IncidenceClasses feature the attributes required for specifying aggregation kinds, multiplicities, and role names. While Comments may annotate any NamedElement, Constraints can be attached to AttributedElementClasses only.

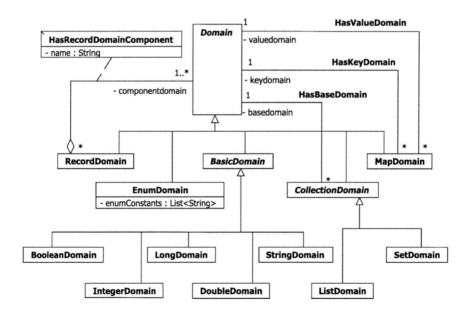

Figure 8.4: grUML meta schema, domain part.

The possible Domains of Attributes belonging to AttributedElementClasses are given in the domain part of the grUML meta schema, depicted in Figure 8.4. They are explained and further commented on in Table 8.1.

grUML domain	Comment
Boolean	represents a boolean value
Integer	represents a signed 32-bit integer number
Long	represents a signed 64-bit integer number
Double	represents a signed 64-bit floating point number
String	represents a string of any length
List	represents an ordered sequence of values of the domain basedomain (with the possibility of multiple occurrences)
Set	represents an (unordered) set of values of the domain basedomain (without multiple occurrences)
Map	represents a mapping of values of the keydomain to values of the valuedomain
Enum	represents a user-defined domain enumerating possible attribute values
Record	represents a user-defined domain composed of at least one name–componentdomain pairs

Table 8.1: Explanation of grUML domains. Taken and adapted from [Sch10a].

The JGraLab library fully supports the creation and manipulation of TGraph schemas. Schemas may also be modeled using an external UML tool, such as the *Rational Software Architect*[3] or *Enterprise Architect*[4], and then be imported by JGraLab. Using a code generation mechanism, Java code for the classes representing the graph, vertex, and edge classes is automatically created, including various methods to access and make use of the properties of TGraphs and their elements.

While keeping all the characteristics of TGraphs, the generated APIs allow for handling schemas and graphs by object-oriented concepts. Thus, they allow for the domain-specific and statically type-safe implementation of TGraph-based software. As an alternative to these schema-specific APIs, JGraLab also provides a generic API that is not dependent on a specific schema. It trades the benefits of schema-specific APIs for the possibility to handle all TGraphs in a uniform way.

---

[3]http://www-01.ibm.com/software/rational/products/swarchitect
[4]http://www.sparxsystems.com/products/ea/8/index.html

Furthermore, JGraLab provides a graph validator component to check the constraints specified in schemas.

8.1.3 Querying TGraphs with GReQL

GReQL, short for *Graph Repository Query Language*, is specifically tailored for querying TGraphs. In addition, the language also provides access to the TGraph schema. GReQL is designed as an *expression language*, i.e., every language construct is an expression which, obeying particular rules, can be combined to more complex expressions. A user-extensible function library offers about 100 functions that can be used in queries. The functions cover various aspects, e.g., arithmetics, logics, and path or graph analysis.

A GReQL parser and an evaluator are integral parts of the JGraLab library. Using the JGraLab API, queries can be evaluated on a given graph and the result be further processed.

Due to the multitude of different GReQL expressions and functions, the following description of the language only includes features with special significance to the retrieval of traceability information. These features are *regular path expressions, quantified expressions,* from-with-report *expressions, path systems,* and *slices.*

Regular Path Expressions

Regular path expressions (*RPEs*) describe the structure of paths in a graph. They are not usable as stand-alone expressions, but are nested in other expressions, most importantly in *path existence expressions,* which check if two vertices are connected by a path with a specific structure, in *forward vertex set expressions,* which compute the set of vertices reachable from a given vertex by such a path, or in *backward vertex set expressions,* which determine the set of vertices from which a given vertex can be reached.

Based on the graph in Figure 8.1, the GReQL expressions in Listing 8.1 exemplify the usage of RPEs in the three kinds of expressions mentioned above. For reasons of brevity, graph element identifiers in the example graph, e.g., v1 or e7, are directly employed as variables referring to the respective graph elements. In complete, proper queries, the binding of variables to elements has to be taken care of by the user by using appropriate GReQL constructs.

Listing 8.1: GReQL simple path expression examples.

```
1  v1 <−− v2
2  v4 −−>{ResidesIn}
3  v4 <>−−
```

```
4   <−>{Knows @ thisEdge.since.year > 2009} v2
```

The path existence expression in line 1 makes use of a *simple path expression* to test if vertex v2 can be reached from v1 by any single edge in backward direction. Due to the existence of e6 and e7, this expression would be evaluated to the boolean value *true*. Simple path expressions constitute the basic element of RPEs and describe single edges, optionally with a specific direction. Line 2 shows a forward vertex set expression which makes use of a simple path expression complemented by an *edge restriction*. The expression determines the set of vertices which are reachable from v4 by a single edge of the class ResidesIn (or its specializations, if they existed) in forward direction. The result is {v6}. The same result is yielded by the forward vertex set expression in line 3, where an edge with aggregation semantics is traversed in whole-to-part direction, starting from v4. The backward vertex set expression in line 4 returns the set of vertices from which v2 can be reached by following any Knows edge regardless of its direction, but where the value of the year component of the since attribute is greater than 2009 ({v1, v3, v4}).

Using regular expression operations, i.e., grouping, concatenation, option, alternation, and iteration, simple path expressions build more complex expressions.

Listing 8.2: GReQL complex path expression examples.

```
5   v1 <−−{IsRelativeOf} [<>−−]
6   <−−{ResidesIn} (<−>{IsRelativeOf} | <−>{Knows}) v3
7   v1 <−>{Knows}+ v6
```

In Listing 8.2, the expression in line 5 gives back the set of vertices which are reachable from v1 by traversing an edge of the class IsRelativeOf, which includes instances of its subclasses, in backward direction. Then, an aggregation may be optionally followed from whole to part ({v2, v5}). Line 6 determines the vertices from which v3 is reachable by a ResidesIn edge in backward direction followed by any IsRelativeOf or Knows edge ({v5}). Line 7 checks whether there is path of one or more Knows edges connecting v1 and v6 (*false*).

Other important features of RPEs are *start* and *goal vertex restrictions* for constraining the eligible start and end vertices of path descriptions, respectively.

Listing 8.3: GReQL start and goal vertex restriction examples.

```
8   {Person @ firstName = "Jeanne" or firstName = "Hugo"}&−−> v5
9   v2 −−>{Knows}&{Person}*
```

The backward vertex set expression in line 8 of Listing 8.3 employs a start vertex restriction for retrieving the Person vertices whose value for the firstName attribute is either "Jeanne" or "Hugo" and from which v5 can be reached by following any single edge in forward direction ({v1, v2}). Line 9 makes use of a goal vertex restriction to determine the vertices which are reachable from v2 by any number of Knows edges ending at a Person vertex ({v1, v2, v3}). Note, that the usage of the Kleene star, in contrast to the Kleene plus in line 7, also allows for not traversing any edge, resulting in v2 itself to be included in the forward vertex set.

Finally, using *intermediate vertex descriptions*, specific vertices on a path can be referred to. *Edge path descriptions* allow for referring to specific edges (see Listing 8.4).

Listing 8.4: GReQL intermediate vertex and edge path description examples.

```
10   v1 <−e6−− v3 <−e4−> v4
```

The intermediate vertex path description and two edge path descriptions in the expression in line 11 serve to check whether there is a path from v1 via e6 to v3 and further via e4 to v4, with e6 being traversed in backward direction and the direction of e4 being insignificant (*false*).

Quantified Expressions

Concerning quantified expressions, it can be distinguished between universal, existential, and unique quantification. They allow for testing whether all, some, or exactly one element(s) of a given collection fulfill a specific boolean expression, respectively. The examples in Listing 8.5 show the basic structure of quantified expressions: one of the keywords forall, exists, or exists! is followed by one or more variable declarations and, optionally, by further expressions which constrain the collection of elements. The boolean expression which has to be checked is appended after an *at* sign (@):

Listing 8.5: GReQL quantified expression examples.

```
1   forall p:V{Place} @ inDegree{ResidesIn}(p) > 0
2   forall p,q:V{Person}, p <−>{IsSiblingOf} q @ not p <−>{IsParentOf} q
3   not exists r:E{IsRelativeOf} @ startVertex(r) = endVertex(r)
4   exists! o:V{Organization} @ o.name = "MyNetwork"
```

The universally quantified expression in line 1 uses the inDegree() function to check that all Place vertices p have at least one incoming ResidesIn edge (*true*). In line 2, an additional expression constrains the variables p and q to only refer to pairs of Persons that are connected by an IsSiblingOf edge. The vertices forming such a pair must not be connected by an IsParentOf edge (*true*). Line 3 shows a negated existentially quantified expression which makes sure that there is no IsRelativeOf edge with its start and end vertices being identical (*true*). The uniquely quantified expression in line 4 enforces the – admittedly rather artificial – constraint that there must one single Organization vertex whose name is "MyNetwork", as a representative of the social network itself (*false*).

Note, that if the collection of elements for which the boolean expressions after the at sign is to be tested is empty, a universally quantified expression yields *true*, while an existentially or uniquely quantified expression returns *false*.

from-with-report Expressions

from-with-report (FWR) expressions are used to return tuples of values. The from part binds variables to domains, e.g., to a specific set of graph elements. The with part involves a boolean expression which imposes further constraints on the possible values of the declared variables. The report part specifies the structure of the FWR expression's result. Usually, the result is a bag of tuples. Consider the example in Listing 8.6, based on the graph in Figure 8.1.

Listing 8.6: GReQL from-with-report expression example (1).

```
from pr:V{Person}, pl:V{Place}
with pr −−>{ResidesIn} pl
report pr.firstName, pr.lastName, pl.name
end
```

This FWR expression assigns the variable pr to the set of Persons and the variable pl to the set of Places. For each combination of vertices where pr is connected to pl by a ResidesIn edge, a triple consisting of pr's firstName and lastName as well as pl's name is added to the result:

"Jeanne"	"Meunier"	"Paris"
"Hugo"	"Meunier"	"Paris"

Since edges are treated as first-class citizens of TGraphs, the same result can be achieved by the query in Listing reflst:GReQLFWR2. It only uses a single variable bound to the set of ResidesIn edges and accesses the start and end vertices of these edges with the startVertex() and endVertex() functions, respectively. As ResidesIn edges could also be incident to Organization vertices, the correct type is ensured in the with part.

Listing 8.7: GReQL from-with-report expression example (2).

```
from r:E{ResidesIn}
with hasType(startVertex(r), "Person")
```

```
report startVertex(r).firstName, startVertex(r).lastName, endVertex(r).name
end
```

Path Systems and Slices

Essentially, *path systems* and *slices* can be considered as subgraphs of a queried TGraph. A path system is computed with respect to a given vertex and a regular path expression. For each vertex that is reachable from the given vertex by a path conforming to the RPE, the path system contains exactly one of these paths. In contrast, slices take a set of vertices and an RPE as input and encompass all paths that start at some vertex in the set and conform to the RPE, except for paths where a loop is contained more than once. The slice concept and its implementation as a GReQL function have been introduced to cope with the requirements of traceability retrieval (see also Section 9.4).

The example GReQL expressions in Listing 8.8 for the computation of path systems and slices refer to the graph in Figure 8.1.

Listing 8.8: GReQL path system and slice examples.

```
1  pathSystem(v3, --> (-->{Knows} -->{ResidesIn} | -->{ResidesIn}))
2  slice({v3}, --> (-->{Knows} -->{ResidesIn} | -->{ResidesIn}))
```

The path system determined by the function call in line 1 includes two paths, e.g., (v3, e8, v2, e4, v4, e1, v6) and (v3, e8, v2, e2, v5). Note, that the path system only includes one path between v3 and v5 although there is a second one conforming to the given RPE: (v3, e8, v2, e6, v1, e3, v5). The slice computed in line 2 contains all three possible paths.

8.1.4 Transforming TGraphs with GReTL

GReTL stands for *Graph Repository Transformation Language* and is used for transforming one or more source TGraphs, conforming to possibly different source schemas, to a target graph conforming to a target schema. An important feature of GReTL is that target schemas do not need to be predefined, but can be created in the course of the transformations.

GReTL is based on the Java programming language and comes with a framework supporting the programmatic development of transformations, making use of the JGraLab library. In addition, a concrete syntax that is independent of any programming language is provided.

Subsequently, the basic principles of GReTL and its Java framework are explained, followed by a more detailed description of the elementary transformation operations.

The GReTL Framework

Transformations based on the GReTL framework are implemented according to the *Strategy* design pattern [Gam94]. The framework provides an abstract class Transformation and a set of predefined concrete subclasses that represent elementary transformation operations, such as the creation of vertices and edges in the target graph based on existing graph elements in the source graph(s). To write more complex transformations, developers are supposed to define their own subclasses of Transformation that override its abstract transform() method. In the body of overriding methods, calls to the elementary operations realize the transformation's behavior. Note, that Transformation is parameterized with with the type of the transform() method's return value. Usually, this type is Graph, the superclass of all user-defined graphclasses.

To specify the source graph(s) of the transformation, an instance of the helper class Context is to be passed to the constructor of Transformation. After the transformation has been executed, the Context instance will also contain a reference to the resulting target graph.

The implementation of GReTL transformations as Java classes enables their reuse. Two different schemes for reuse are thinkable. First, calls to transformations could be nested, thus allowing for transformations which are more complex than the elementary transformation operations but which are nevertheless frequently used to be factored out. Second, concrete transformations could be further specialized in order to inherit and extend their behavior.

The Context object also retains bijective mappings between the source and target elements of a transformation, called *archetypes* and *images*, respectively. In detail, the bijection img_T maps archetypes to their images and $arch_T$ maps images to archetypes, with T being the type the target elements conform to. Both bijections may be accessed by transformation operations other than those which initially created the mappings. They can even be used by other transformation objects which rely on the same Context object, e.g., if calls to transformations are nested as explained above. Furthermore, the mappings, which essentially represent the traceability relationships between the source and target graphs, may be recorded in an *XML*-based [Bra08] format.

115

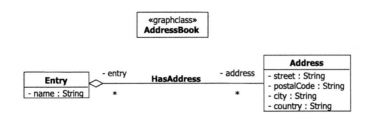

Figure 8.5: Target schema of GReTL example transformation.

Transformation Operations

As mentioned above, a set of predefined concrete subclasses of Transformation provide elementary transformation operations which are to be employed in user-defined transformations. These classes are based on the grUML meta schema (see Section 8.1.2) and serve to create the elements of the target schema together with their instances. Examples are the classes CreateVertexClass, CreateEdgeClass, and CreateAttribute. Their constructors take the static properties of the schema element to be created as parameters, e.g., the elements' names, or, for edge classes, the start and end vertex classes. In addition, a so-called *semantic expression* is passed to the constructors. A semantic expression is a GReQL expression that specifies which instances are to be created for the given schema element. Usually, the expression returns a set of source graph elements so that for each of them, a new element in the target graph is created. Thus, the elements of a semantic expression's result set constitute the archetypes. Essentially, GReTL's concrete syntax uses the same constructs, but does without syntactical details of the Java programming language, such as parentheses, commas, and semicolons.

Instead of creating graph elements along with entirely new schema elements, it is also possible to instantiate already existing schema elements. To this end, the classes Create-Vertices, CreateEdges, and SetAttributes are provided. Once a Transformation instance has been established, the actual transformation can be started by calling the execute() method.

The following example transformation illustrates the described concepts. It aims at the derivation of an initial data structure for an address book from data contained in a social network that is based on the TGraph schema in Figure 8.2. The final target schema that is to be created in the course of the transformation is shown in Figure 8.5. It features the vertex class Entry with the attribute name, for representing address book entries, and the vertex class Address with the attributes street, postalCode, city, and country.

Listing 8.9 shows the implementation of a Java class for the intended transformation.

Listing 8.9: Example GReTL transformation.

```java
public class SocialNetwork2AddressBook extends Transformation<Graph> {

    public SocialNetwork2AddressBook(Context context) {
            super(context);
    }

    @Override
    protected void transform() {
        VertexClass entry = new CreateVertexClass(context, "Entry",
            "V{Profile}").execute();

        Attribute name = new CreateAttribute(context, new AttributeSpec(
            entry, "name", getStringDomain()), "mergeMaps(
            "mergeMaps( "
            + "   from person: V{Person} "
            + "   reportMap person, person.firstName "
            + "        ++ \" \" ++ person.lastName "
            + "   end, "
            + "   from organization: V{Organization} "
            + "   reportMap organization, organization.name "
            + "   end "
            + ") ").execute();

        VertexClass address = new CreateVertexClass(context, "Address",
            "V{Place}").execute();

        new CreateAttribute(context, new AttributeSpec(entry, "street",
            getStringDomain()), "map()").execute();
        new CreateAttribute(context, new AttributeSpec(entry, "postalCode",
            getStringDomain()), "map()").execute();
        new CreateAttribute(context, new AttributeSpec(entry, "city",
            getStringDomain()),
            "from place: keySet(img_Address) "
            + "reportMap place, place.name "
            + "end ").execute();
        new CreateAttribute(context, new AttributeSpec(entry, "country",
            getStringDomain()), "map()").execute();

        new CreateEdgeClass(context, "HasAddress",
            new IncidenceClassSpec(entry, 0, Integer.MAX_VALUE,
                "entry"),
            new IncidenceClassSpec(address, 0, Integer.MAX_VALUE,
                "address"),
            "from residesIn: E{ResidesIn} "
            + "reportSet residesIn, startVertex(residesIn), "
            + "        endVertex(residesIn) "
            + "end ").execute();

        return context.getTargetGraph();
```

```
50      }
51   }
```

While the constructor of the class SocialNetwork2AddressBook in line 3 merely passes the Context instance, which holds information on the source and target graph, to the constructor of the superclass Transformation, the actual transformation is specified by the overridden transform() method. Line 9 creates the Entry vertex class. The GReQL query "V{Profile}" that is passed as semantic expression returns the set of all Profile vertices in the source graph. Thus, for each archetype vertex in this set, a corresponding image, i.e., an instance of Entry is created. Lines 12–22 create the name attribute of the Entry vertex class and set the attribute values of the Entry instances. A suitable semantic expression has to return a value of the GReQL data structure Map that maps the archetypes of the graph elements whose attribute values shall be set to the respective specific values. Here, the Entry instances are based on Person and Organization vertices in the source graph, which possess attributes with different identifiers. Consequently, the semantic expression uses the GReQL function mergeMaps() to merge a Map that maps Person vertices to the concatenations of firstName and lastName with another Map that maps Organization vertices to their names.

In lines 24–37, the Address vertex class, its instances, and the respective attributes are created analogously. Note, that for illustrative purposes, line 33 accesses the mapping of archetypes to images of the vertex class Address instead of using an expression such as V{Place}. More precisely, keySet(img_Address) returns the set of archetypes of all instances of Address in the target graph, which is exactly the set of Place vertices in the source graph.

Lines 39–47 finally create the HasAddress edge class and its instances. The instantiations of IncidenceClassSpec serve to specify the source and end vertex classes of the edge classes together with the respective multiplicities and role names. The semantic expression returns a set of triples. Such a triple consists of the archetypes of the created edge itself, of its start vertex, and of its end vertex.

Assuming the graph in Figure 8.1 as source graph, the target graph resulting from the transformation is depicted in Figure 8.6.

8.1.5 Event-Condition-Action Rules for TGraphs

To make the TGraph approach suitable for implementing semantically rich traceability relationship types, the JGraLab library has been extended by a framework for the specification of event-condition-action (ECA) rules for TGraphs (see also Section 9.1). Changes to a graph are constantly monitored, so that if a change corresponds to an

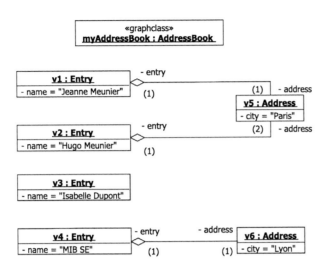

Figure 8.6: Target graph of GReTL example transformation.

event defined in a rule and the condition is evaluated to true, the action will be executed. The rules can either be specified with JGraLab's API or be loaded from an external file where the rules are stored using a special concrete syntax. On the basis of this syntax, three example rules are given in Listing 8.10.

Listing 8.10: JGraLab event-condition-action rule examples.

```
1  before deletedVertex(Profile) do print "Warning: A Profile will be deleted."
2
3  after createdEdge(IsParentOf)
4      with endVertex(context) --->{IsParentOf} startVertex(context)
5      do print "Warning: IsParentOf edge already exists in opposite direction."
6
7  E{Knows}: before deletedEdge() do DeleteConnectingEdges
```

Events

Possible kinds of events are the creation, deletion, or modification of a graph or graph element, where modification involves the update of an attribute value or the change of the start or end vertices of edges. Furthermore, it can be declared whether the rule should be triggered just before or after the actual execution of the change operation that triggers the event. To specify the elements for which the occurrence of an event

119

is to be monitored, a *context expression*, i.e., a GReQL expression that evaluates to a set of AttributedElements, can be passed to the event. If some element in the set, i.e, a graph, vertex, or edge, has just been created, is modified, or is going be deleted, the rule is triggered. Alternatively, an AttributedElementClass can be specified, so that all its instances are monitored for changes. In that case, the rule can also be triggered just before the creation or after the deletion of such an instance.

The event of the rule in line 1 of Listing 8.10 addresses the deletion of a Profile vertex. The rule is triggered before the actual deletion. The second rule, in lines 3 to 5, is triggered after a new IsParentOf edge has been created. The third rule, in line 7, fires before an edge out of the set of Knows instances, determined by the context expression E{Knows}, is deleted.

Conditions

Conditions correspond to GReQL expressions that are evaluated to boolean values. The element that is affected by the event can be referenced by the dedicated context variable. The specification of conditions is optional.

In Listing 8.10, only the second rule comprises a condition. It tests whether there already exists an IsParentOf edge from the end vertex of the newly created IsParentOf edge to the start vertex of that new edge.

Actions

Actions implement a special Action interface of the ECA framework. By implementing this interface, users are able to define their own actions in the form of Java methods. Two predefined kinds of actions are the output of a textual message and the execution of a GReQL transformation. To prevent infinite cascades of actions that trigger other rules, the number of rules in such a cascade can be limited. If the limit is reached, no further rule is triggered.

The actions of the first two rules in Listing 8.10 display messages to the users. The third rule invokes the user-defined action shown in Listing 8.11. It deletes all other edges between the start and the end vertex of the edge that is referred in the event, i.e., the Knows edge which is going to be deleted.

Listing 8.11: Example user-defined action for ECA rules in JGraLab.

```
1  public class DeleteConnectingEdges implements Action {
2
3      @Override
```

```
4    public void doAction(Event event) {
5        // get the start vertex of the edge referred in the event
6        Vertex startVertex = event.getEdge().getAlpha();
7
8        // get the end vertex of the edge referred in the event
9        Vertex endVertex = event.getEdge().getOmega();
10
11           // iterate over all edges incident to startVertex
12       for (Edge indicentEdge : startVertex.incidences()) {
13
14               // if the vertex at the opposite end of incidentEdge corresponds to endVertex
15           if (incidentEdge.getThat() == endVertex) {
16
17               // delete incidentEdge
18               incidentEdge.delete();
19           }
20       }
21   }
22 }
```

8.2 The Web Ontology Language and Related Technologies

In general, ontologies are a formal means for representing knowledge, describing concepts together with their instances and relationships. They are used in biomedical informatics [Ros08], linguistics [Far03], or geospatial semantics [Fon02], for instance. One of the most popular languages for describing ontologies is the *Web Ontology Language* (*OWL*). It is standardized by the *World Wide Web Consortium* (*W3C*) and actually constitutes a family of ontology languages with different degrees of expressiveness and complexity. The various sublanguages are formally based on *description logics* [Baa03]. The current second version of OWL, called OWL 2, reached W3C recommendation status in 2009 [Mot09b]. Although the contents of this section are based on OWL 2, for the sake of simplicity only the term *OWL* will be used in the following.

OWL ontologies can be mapped to *RDF* [Kly04], a W3C standard whose purpose is to describe resources on the World Wide Web. This makes it possible to query OWL ontologies with *SPARQL* [Pru08], which is yet another language standardized by the W3C and designed for querying RDF. Together, the three languages are referred to as the *OWL technological space* in the following.

In Section 8.2.1, the Web Ontology Language itself is described. This is followed by an explanation of the mapping of OWL to RDF in Section 8.2.2, which lays the foundations for an introduction to SPARQL in Section 8.2.3.

8.2.1 OWL Basics

The main part of this introduction to OWL is concerned with the various language constructs that can be used to represent knowledge. At the end of the section, a discussion of the *open world assumption* which is adopted by OWL and of entailment and reasoning in OWL ontologies is conducted.

Language Constructs

In general, syntactic constructs in OWL ontologies belong to one of three different categories: *entities, axioms,* and *expressions.* Entities correspond to the above-mentioned basic elements of ontologies: concepts, instances, and relationships. In OWL terminology, these three kinds of entities are called *classes, individuals,* and *properties,* respectively. Classes describe sets of individuals. Concerning properties, it can again be distinguished between *object properties,* interrelating two individuals, and *data properties,* connecting an individual to a *literal,* i.e., a data value. Axioms assert additional statements on an ontology's entities, such as subclass relationships between classes, instance-of relationships between individuals and classes, or characteristics of object properties. Finally, expressions are used to describe sets of individuals with specific characteristics. Normally, they are not used as stand-alone constructs, but are nested in axioms.

The constructs of an ontology can be coarsely grouped into two parts: the *terminological box (TBox)* and the *assertional box (ABox).* While the TBox contains entities and axioms over classes and properties, the ABox is concerned with knowledge on individuals. TBox and ABox are not OWL-specific terms, but stem from the field of description logics. Nevertheless, they are useful to further categorize an OWL ontology's constituents.

A fourth category of OWL ontology constructs – *annotations* – typically does not serve to directly represent information on the domain of discourse, but is used to attach additional information, e.g., comments, to entities or axioms. Annotations do not exhibit any formal semantics in OWL [Mot09a].

To illustrate the usage and purpose of the various OWL constructs, the social network example from Section 8.1 is taken up to stepwise develop an OWL ontology that models a similar scenario as the TGraph and its schema in Figures 8.1 and 8.2. To accommodate for the greater expressiveness of OWL ontologies compared to plain TGraphs [Wal10], i.e., without additional *GReQL* [Ebe10] constraints, further information is added to the scenario where required. Note, that due to the multitude of different OWL axioms and expressions, only the most important ones can be introduced here.

The initial example ontology depicted in Listing 8.12 merely defines a custom data type and declares a set of entities, without specifying further axioms. For representing the ontology, the OWL *functional syntax* is employed, which is one of various possible syntaxes, e.g., the Manchester Syntax [Hor09] or RDF/XML [Bec04].

Listing 8.12: OWL entity declaration examples.

```
Prefix( sn:=<http://www.socialnetworks.com/myNetwork#> )
Prefix( xsd:=<http://www.w3.org/2001/XMLSchema#> )
Ontology( <http://www.socialnetworks.com/myNetwork>

Declaration( Datatype( sn:sex ))
DatatypeDefinition( sn:sex DataOneOf( "Female" "Male" ))

Declaration( Class( sn:Profile ))
Declaration( Class( sn:Person ))
Declaration( Class( sn:Organization ))
Declaration( Class( sn:Place ))

Declaration( ObjectProperty( sn:knows ))
Declaration( ObjectProperty( sn:isRelativeOf ))
Declaration( ObjectProperty( sn:isParentOf ))
Declaration( ObjectProperty( sn:isSiblingOf ))
Declaration( ObjectProperty( sn:residesIn ))

Declaration( DataProperty( sn:hasFirstName ))
Declaration( DataProperty( sn:hasLastName ))
Declaration( DataProperty( sn:hasSex ))
Declaration( DataProperty( sn:hasBirthDate ))
Declaration( DataProperty( sn:hasName ))

Declaration( NamedIndividual ( sn:Jeanne ))
Declaration( NamedIndividual ( sn:Hugo ))
Declaration( NamedIndividual ( sn:Isabelle ))
Declaration( NamedIndividual ( sn:MIB ))
Declaration( NamedIndividual ( sn:Paris ))
Declaration( NamedIndividual ( sn:Lyon ))

Declaration( AnnotationProperty ( sn:since ))

)
```

The ontology itself as well as user-defined data types and entities are identified by *Internationalized Resource Identifiers* (*IRIs*) [Due05], an extended form of the more familiar URIs [Ber05]. Prior to the specification of the ontology, *prefixes* are declared that allow to abbreviate the potentially long IRIs. In addition to the prefix sn:, representing the social network ontology itself, the prefix xsd: is introduced to refer to *XML Schema*, whose data types [Bir01] are commonly used in OWL.

Inside the parentheses following the Ontology keyword, the ontology's IRI and then its contents are given. A data type sn:sex for specifying the sex of persons in the social network is declared first. Using DataOneOf, it is defined that the range of sn:sex consists of the two literals Female and Male. Following the data type definition, the ontology's entities are declared: the classes sn:Profile, sn:Person, sn:Organization, and sn:Place, the object properties sn:knows, sn:isRelativeOf, sn:isParentOf, sn:isSiblingOf and sn:residesIn; the data properties sn:hasFirstName, sn:hasLastName, sn:hasSex, sn:hasBirthDate, and sn:hasName; and the individuals sn:Jeanne, sn:Hugo, sn:Isabelle, sn:MIB SE, sn:Paris, and sn:Lyon. In addition, the *annotation property* sn:since is declared.

In Listing 8.13, *class expression axioms* are added to describe relations between classes or expressions describing classes. Two SubClassOf *class expression axioms* specify that sn:Person and sn:Organization are subclasses of sn:Profile. Subclassing implies that each instance of a subclass is also an instance of the superclass.

Listing 8.13: OWL class expression axiom examples.

```
SubClassOf( sn:Person sn:Profile )
SubClassOf( sn:Organization sn:Profile )
DisjointUnion( sn:Profile sn:Person sn:Organization )

SubClassOf( sn:Profile ObjectMaxCardinality( 1 sn:residesIn ))
SubClassOf( sn:Place ObjectExactCardinality( 1 ObjectInverseOf( sn:residesIn )))
SubClassOf( sn:Person ObjectExactCardinality( 2 ObjectInverseOf( sn:isParentOf )))

SubClassOf( sn:Person DataExactCardinality( 1 sn:hasSex ))
SubClassOf( sn:Person DataExactCardinality( 1 sn:hasFirstName ))
SubClassOf( sn:Person DataExactCardinality( 1 sn:hasLastName ))
SubClassOf( sn:Person DataExactCardinality( 1 sn:hasBirthDate ))
SubClassOf( sn:Organization DataExactCardinality( 1 sn:hasName ))
SubClassOf( sn:Place DataExactCardinality( 1 sn:hasName ))
```

To specify that each individuals that is an instance of sn:Profile either is an sn:Person individual or an sn:Organization individual, i.e., there are no individuals which are only sn:Profiles, the DisjointUnion axiom is used.

Another SubClassOf axiom makes use of an ObjectMaxCardinality *class expression* to state that the (named) class sn:Profile is a subclass of the (anonymous) class of individuals that possess at most one sn:residesIn object property. This implies that any individual which has more than one sn:residesIn property is not an sn:Profile. Furthermore, the existence of an object property, which can be interpreted as directed connection between a source individual i_1 and a target individual i_2, implies the existence of an inverse property from i_2 to i_1. This inverse property can be referred to with the ObjectInverseOf expression. Thus, according to Listing 8.13, any sn:Place individual must have exactly one property that is the inverse of sn:residesIn and any sn:Person individual must have exactly two properties which are the inverse of sn:isParentOf.

By adding SubClassOf axioms with DataExactCardinality class expressions, sn:Persons are restricted to possess exactly one sn:hasSex, sn:hasFirstName, sn:hasLastName, and sn:hasBirthDay data property, respectively. Finally, sn:Organizations and sn:Places must have exactly one name.

The *object property axioms* in Listing 8.14 define characteristics of object properties. ObjectPropertyDomain and ObjectPropertyRange axioms state the domains and ranges of object properties, respectively, i.e., the sets of instances to which the properties are connected. For example, each individual having an sn:residesIn property is an sn:Profile, and each individual to which an sn:Profile is linked via the sn:residesIn property is an sn:Place.

Listing 8.14: OWL object property axiom examples.

```
ObjectPropertyDomain( sn:knows sn:Profile )
ObjectPropertyRange( sn:knows sn:Profile )
SymmetricObjectProperty( sn:knows )

ObjectPropertyDomain( sn:isRelativeOf sn:Person )
ObjectPropertyRange( sn:isRelativeOf sn:Person )
SymmetricObjectProperty( sn:isRelativeOf )
TransitiveObjectProperty( sn:isRelativeOf )

SubObjectPropertyOf( sn:isParentOf sn:isRelativeOf )
SubObjectPropertyOf( ObjectPropertyChain( sn:isParentOf sn:isSiblingOf ) sn:isParentOf )
ObjectPropertyDomain( sn:isParentOf sn:Person )
ObjectPropertyRange( sn:isParentOf sn:Person )

SubObjectPropertyOf( sn:isSiblingOf sn:isRelativeOf )
ObjectPropertyDomain( sn:isSiblingOf sn:Person )
ObjectPropertyRange( sn:isSiblingOf sn:Person )
SymmetricObjectProperty( sn:isSiblingOf )
TransitiveObjectProperty( sn:isSiblingOf )

ObjectPropertyDomain( sn:residesIn sn:Profile )
ObjectPropertyRange( sn:residesIn sn:Place )
```

The object properties sn:isParentOf and sn:isSiblingOf are specified to be subproperties of sn:isRelativeOf. Thus, if an individual i_1 is connected by one of the two subproperties to another individual i_2, i_1 is also connected to i_2 via the superproperty. Furthermore, the chain consisting of an sn:isSiblingOf property followed by an sn:isParentOf property is considered to be a subproperty of isParentOf. This means that if an individual i_1 is connected to an individual i_2 via sn:isParentOf, and i_2 is linked to an individual i_3 via sn:isSiblingOf, then i_1 is connected to i_3 via the sn:isParentOf property.

OWL also allows to assign relational properties such as *reflexivity, symmetry,* or *transitivity* to object properties. In the example, sn:knows, sn:isRelativeOf, and sn:isSiblingOf are symmetric. Consequently, for any individual i_1 that has one of these properties connecting it to another individual i_2, i_2 possesses the same property relating it to i_1. The sn:isRelativeOf object property is transitive, meaning that for any chain of these properties where an individual i_1 is connected to an individual i_2 which is again related to a third individual i_3, i_1 is directly connected to i_3 via that property.

Listing 8.15 shows some examples for *data property axioms*. In detail, the domains and ranges of the various data properties in the social network ontology are specified by the DataPropertyDomain and DataPropertyRange axioms. While the domain of sn:hasFirstName, sn:hasLastName, sn:hasSex, and sn:hasBirthDate is sn:Person, individuals possessing the sn:hasName property can be sn:Organizations or sn:Places. This is specified by using the ObjectUnionOf class expression to build the class containing the instances of both. With the exception of sn:hasSex, whose range is the user-defined data type sn:sex, the ranges of the data properties are taken from the set of XML Schema data types.

Listing 8.15: OWL object property axiom examples.

```
DataPropertyDomain( sn:hasFirstName sn:Person )
DataPropertyRange( sn:hasFirstName xsd:string )

DataPropertyDomain( sn:hasLastName sn:Person )
DataPropertyRange( sn:hasLastName xsd:string )

DataPropertyDomain( sn:hasSex sn:Person )
DataPropertyRange( sn:hasSex sn:Sex )

DataPropertyDomain( sn:hasBirthDate sn:Person )
DataPropertyRange( sn:hasBirthDate xsd:dateTime )

DataPropertyDomain( sn:hasName ObjectUnionOf( sn:Organization sn:Place ))
DataPropertyRange( sn:hasName xsd:string )
```

All axioms that have been added so far belong to the ontology's TBox. Finally, the set of *assertions* in Listing 8.16, which are basically axioms about individuals, make up the ABox. They specify the membership of the declared individuals to their classes and define that individuals are connected to other individuals or to literals via object and data properties, respectively. Annotations on the basis of the sn:since annotation property specify the recording date of the sn:knows object property assertions.

Listing 8.16: OWL assertion examples.

```
ClassAssertion( sn:Person sn:Jeanne )
ClassAssertion( sn:Person sn:Hugo )
ClassAssertion( sn:Person sn:Isabelle )

ClassAssertion( sn:Organization sn:MIB )

ClassAssertion( sn:Place sn:Paris )
ClassAssertion( sn:Place sn:Lyon )


ObjectPropertyAssertion( Annotation( sn:since "2011−02−11T00:00:00Z"^^xsd:dateTime )
            sn:knows sn:Hugo sn:Jeanne )
ObjectPropertyAssertion( Annotation( sn:since "2011−02−11T00:00:00Z"^^xsd:dateTime )
            sn:knows sn:Hugo sn:Isabelle )
ObjectPropertyAssertion( Annotation( sn:since "2011−02−11T00:00:00Z"^^xsd:dateTime )
            sn:knows sn:Hugo sn:MIB )

ObjectPropertyAssertion( sn:isSiblingOf sn:Hugo sn:Jeanne )
ObjectPropertyAssertion( sn:isParentOf sn:Isabelle sn:Hugo )

ObjectPropertyAssertion( sn:residesIn sn:Jeanne sn:Paris )
ObjectPropertyAssertion( sn:residesIn sn:Hugo sn:Paris )
ObjectPropertyAssertion( sn:residesIn sn:MIB sn:Lyon )


DataPropertyAssertion( sn:hasFirstName sn:Jeanne "Jeanne"^^xsd:string )
DataPropertyAssertion( sn:hasLastName sn:Jeanne "Meunier"^^xsd:string )
DataPropertyAssertion( sn:hasSex sn:Jeanne "Female"^^sn:sex )
DataPropertyAssertion( sn:hasBirthDate sn:Jeanne "1983−06−22T00:00:00Z"^^xsd:dateTime )

DataPropertyAssertion( sn:hasFirstName sn:Hugo "Hugo"^^xsd:string )
DataPropertyAssertion( sn:hasLastName sn:Hugo "Meunier"^^xsd:string )
DataPropertyAssertion( sn:hasSex sn:Hugo "Male"^^sn:sex )
DataPropertyAssertion( sn:hasBirthDate sn:Hugo "1983−06−22T00:00:00Z"^^xsd:dateTime )

DataPropertyAssertion( sn:hasFirstName sn:Isabelle "Isabelle"^^xsd:string )
DataPropertyAssertion( sn:hasLastName sn:Isabelle "Dupont"^^xsd:string )
DataPropertyAssertion( sn:hasSex sn:Isabelle "Female"^^sn:sex )
DataPropertyAssertion( sn:hasBirthDate sn:Isabelle "1978−10−08T00:00:00Z"^^xsd:dateTime )

DataPropertyAssertion( sn:hasName sn:MIB "MIB SE"^^xsd:string )

DataPropertyAssertion( sn:hasName sn:Paris "Paris"^^xsd:string )

DataPropertyAssertion( sn:hasName sn:Lyon "Lyon"^^xsd:string )
```

Open World Assumption

If traditional database concepts or modeling technological spaces such as the TGraph approach (see Section 8.1), *MOF* [Obj06], or *EMF* [Ste08] are used to represent entities and relationships of the real world, information that is not explicitly recorded in the database or model is generally considered to be nonexistent. This notion is called *closed world assumption*. Consequently, queries operating on a closed world-based source of information return *false* if a looked-for fact is not contained.

In contrast, OWL adopts the *open world assumption*, which assumes incomplete knowledge of the world. Thus, the absence of a fact in an ontology does not allow to conclude its nonexistence. Querying for facts which are not contained in an ontology yield *unknown* rather than *false*. Thus, the nonexistence of facts has to be stated in the ontology explicitly.

Entailment and Reasoning

Entailment denotes the inference of knowledge from entities and axioms that are explicitly specified in the ontology. A simple example is based on the SubClassOf and ClassAssertion axioms: although Listing 8.16 only asserts that sn:Jeanne is an instance of Person, the specification of the SubClassOf(sn:Person sn:Profile) axiom allows to infer that sn:Jeanne is also an instance of sn:Profile. Another example is the entailment of an sn:isRelativeOf property between sn:Isabelle and sn:Hugo from the assertion of its subproperty sn:isParentOf. Finally, it can be inferred that sn:Isabelle has a sn:isParentOf property connecting it to sn:Jeanne. This is due to the existence of an indirect connection of the two individuals by an object property chain consisting of the sn:isParentOf property followed by sn:isSiblingOf. OWL is a *monotonic* language, i.e., inference only involves the generation of knowledge, but not its retraction. A full coverage of OWL entailment can be found in [Mot09a] and [Sch09a].

Reasoning refers to the process of performing various services on the ontology. Important reasoning services are *consistency checking, satisfiability checking, classification*, and *subsumption checking* [Sta10]. Consistency checking can test whether an ontology's ABox "conforms" to the TBox. For example, since the two classes sn:Person and sn:Organization are disjoint, adding an individual to the social network ontology and asserting that it is an instance of both would lead to the ontology to become inconsistent. Satisfiability of a concept means that the concept is instantiable. Unsatisfiability may be caused by the specification of contradictory class definitions. If the axiom EquivalentClasses(sn:Person sn:Organization) was to be added to the ontology, for instance, the disjointness of the two classes would cause them to be rendered unsatisfiable. Classification, making use of entailment, is used for the computation of class membership for an individual. Assuming that a new individual which possesses the sn:hasFirstName data property is added to the social network ontology, it can be reasoned that this individual is an instance of sn:Person, for sn:Person is given as the domain of sn:hasFirstName. Finally, subsumption checking denotes the testing for subclass relationships. A class is a subclass of another one if its set of instances is a subset of the set of instances of the other class.

Note, that the usage of certain combinations of OWL axioms may result in reasoning problems to become undecidable. More information on the required restrictions on axiom combinations can be found in [Mot09b].

8.2.2 Mapping OWL Ontologies to RDF

OWL ontologies can be mapped to *RDF*. RDF, short for *Resource Description Framework*, is a W3C standard language for describing information about and relations between *resources*. Resources are considered to be entities on the World Wide Web, e.g., a Web page, an item in an online shop, or a profile in a social network [Man04]. Basically, an RDF document is of a set of so-called *triples*. A triple consists of a *subject*, a *predicate*, and an *object*. Viewing subjects and objects as nodes and predicates as arcs starting at the subject node and ending at the object node, a set of triples forms an *RDF graph*.

Subject nodes in an RDF graph can be either *resources* or they can be *blank* without further means of identification. Predicates can be considered as being occurrences of resources. In addition to resources and blank nodes, object nodes may also represent *literals*, i.e., data values. Resources are globally identifiable by *URI references* [Ber05], which may be abbreviated by prefixes. To refer to specific blank nodes in an RDF graph, *blank node identifiers* are employed. Similar to OWL, XML Schema data types [Bir01] are commonly used as data types for RDF literals.

RDF predefines some resources. Among them are rdf:type[5], and rdf:Property. If rdf:type is used as predicate in a triple, the subject resource is considered to be an instance of the resource acting a object. Properties, i.e., instances of rdf:Property are the resources the predicates are occurrences of. More information on RDF concepts and their semantics can be found in [Kly04] and [Hay04].

Further special-purpose resources are provided by *RDF Schema* [Bri04], an extension to the RDF vocabulary. Among them are rdfs:Resources, rdfs:Class, rdfs:subClassOf[6], rdfs:subPropertyOf, rdfs:domain, and rdfs:range. All resources are considered to be instances of rdfs:Resource. All user-defined classes, i.e., resources acting as objects in

---

[5]The prefix rdf abbreviates `<http://www.w3.org/1999/02/22-rdf-syntax-ns#>`.
[6]The prefix rdfs abbreviates `<http://www.w3.org/2000/01/rdf-schema#>`.

rdf:type triples, are instances of rdfs:Class. rdfs:subClassOf and rdfs:subPropertyOf denote specialization relationships between classes and instances of rdf:Property, respectively. rdfs:domain and rdfs:range are used for the domains and ranges of instances of rdf:Property: resources acting as subjects (objects) in triples where that rdf:Property instance occurs as predicate are considered to be an instance of the class used as object in the corresponding rdfs:domain (rdfs:range) triple.

The details of the mapping from OWL to RDF are explained in [Pat09]. In essence, OWL entities are transformed to RDF resources. Most OWL axioms and expressions are represented by various classes and properties in the OWL namespace <http://www.w3.org/2002/07/owl#>. For some OWL constructs such as SubClassOf or ObjectPropertyDomain, the corresponding RDFS counterparts, in this case rdfs:subClassOf and rdfs:domain, are used. For illustrative purposes, Listing 8.17 provides an example RDF graph resulting from a mapping of some of the OWL entities and axioms around the individual sn:Jeanne of the social network ontology introduced in Section 8.2.1. The RDF graph is formatted using the *Turtle* syntax [Bec11]. It makes triples easily readable by writing the subjects, predicates, and object in their natural sequence and without further syntactic decorations. The OWL constructs that were used as source for the mapping are given as comments above the resulting RDF triples.

Listing 8.17: OWL to RDF mapping example.

```
@prefix sn:   <http://www.socialnetworks.com/myNetwork#> .
@prefix rdf:  <http://www.w3.org/1999/02/22−rdf−syntax−ns#> .
@prefix rdfs: <http://www.w3.org/2000/01/rdf−schema#> .
@prefix owl:  <http://www.w3.org/2002/07/owl#> .
@prefix xsd:  <http://www.w3.org/2001/XMLSchema#> .

# Ontology( <http://www.socialnetworks.com/myNetwork>
<http://www.socialnetworks.com/myNetwork> rdf:type owl:Ontology .

# Declaration( Class( sn:Profile ))
# Declaration( Class( sn:Person ))
# Declaration( Class( sn:Organization ))
# Declaration( Class( sn:Place ))
sn:Profile rdf:type owl:Class .
sn:Person rdf:type owl:Class .
sn:Organization rdf:type owl:Class .
sn:Place rdf:type owl:Class .

# Declaration( ObjectProperty( sn:residesIn ))
sn:residesIn rdf:type owl:ObjectProperty .

# Declaration( DataProperty( sn:hasFirstName ))
sn:hasFirstName rdf:type owl:DatatypeProperty .

# Declaration( NamedIndividual ( sn:Jeanne ))
```

```
# Declaration( NamedIndividual ( sn:Paris ))
sn:Jeanne rdf:type owl:NamedIndividual .
sn:Paris rdf:type owl:NamedIndividual .

# SubClassOf( sn:Person sn:Profile )
# SubClassOf( sn:Organization sn:Profile )
sn:Person rdfs:subClassOf sn:Profile .
sn:Organization rdfs:subClassOf sn:Profile .

# SubClassOf( sn:Profile ObjectMaxCardinality( 1 sn:residesIn ))
sn:Profile rdfs:subClassOf _:a .
_:a rdf:type owl:Restriction .
_:a owl:onProperty sn:residesIn .
_:a owl:maxCardinality "1"^^xsd:nonNegativeInteger .

# SubClassOf( sn:Person DataExactCardinality( 1 sn:hasFirstName ))
sn:Person rdfs:subClassOf _:b .
_:b rdf:type owl:Restriction .
_:b owl:onProperty sn:hasFirstName .
_:b owl:cardinality "1"^^xsd:nonNegativeInteger .

# ObjectPropertyDomain( sn:residesIn sn:Profile )
# ObjectPropertyRange( sn:residesIn sn:Place )
sn:residesIn rdfs:domain sn:Profile .
sn:residesIn rdfs:range sn:Place .

# DataPropertyDomain( sn:hasFirstName sn:Person )
# DataPropertyRange( sn:hasFirstName xsd:string )
sn:hasFirstName rdfs:domain sn:Person .
sn:hasFirstName rdfs:range xsd:string .

# ClassAssertion( sn:Jeanne sn:Person )
# ClassAssertion( sn:Paris sn:Place )
# ObjectPropertyAssertion( sn:residesIn sn:Jeanne sn:Paris )
# DataPropertyAssertion( sn:hasFirstName sn:Jeanne "Jeanne"^^xsd:string )
sn:Jeanne rdf:type sn:Person .
sn:Paris rdf:type sn:Place .
sn:Jeanne sn:residesIn sn:Paris .
sn:Jeanne sn:hasFirstName "Jeanne"^^xsd:string .
```

8.2.3 Querying OWL Ontologies with SPARQL

SPARQL is a recursive acronym standing for *SPARQL Protocol and RDF Query Language* [Pru08]. As its name implies, SPARQL is actually designed for querying RDF. However, since OWL can be mapped to RDF, the query language is frequently used for extracting information from OWL ontologies. The information given in this section is based on version 1.0, which is currently recommended by the W3C [Pru08]. An important characteristic of SPARQL (1.0) is the adoption of closed world semantics, i.e., only information that is explicitly specified in the queried ontology can be retrieved.

SPARQL queries can consist of the following five query parts:

- *prologue,*

- *query form,*

- *dataset,*

- *where clause,* and

- *solution modifiers.*

Depending on the nature of the *query form*, some query parts may be optional. Details are given in the following subsections that introduce the individual query parts. The explanations of the SPARQL query parts are a shortened version of the SPARQL tutorial in [Sch10a], with the examples being adapted to the social network example ontology presented in Sections 8.2.1 and 8.2.2.

At the time of writing these lines, work on SPARQL version 1.1 is in progress [Har11]. The expected new features with respect to each query part are shortly summarized at the end of the respective subsection.

Prologue

The prologue may contain a *base IRI* specification and a set of *prefixes*. A base IRI allows for the usage of relative IRIs within a SPARQL query: when using only the fragment part of an IRI, i.e, the part after the # sign, the base IRI is prepended. Similar to OWL and RDF, prefixes allow for the abbreviation of IRIs. The specification of a prologue is always optional. An example is shown in Listing 8.18.

Listing 8.18: SPARQL prologue example.

```
BASE <http://www.socialnetworks.com/myNetwork#>
PREFIX rdf: <http://www.w3.org/1999/02/22−rdf−syntax−ns#>
```

With this prologue, `<http://www.socialnetworks.com/myNetwork#Jeanne>` can be referred to by simply writing `<Jeanne>`. Furthermore, rdf:type can be used for `<http://www.w3.org/1999/02/22-rdf-syntax-ns#type>`.

Query Form

SPARQL provides four kinds of query forms: SELECT, ASK, CONSTRUCT, and DE-SCRIBE. To understand their purpose, it is necessary to introduce the notion of *solution mapping*. A solution mapping binds variables to *RDF terms*, i.e., resources, blank nodes, or literals. More precisely, a solution mapping is a partial function $\mu : V \nrightarrow T$. For a given query, V represents the set of all variables used in the query and T corresponds to the set of all RDF terms in the queried RDF graphs.

Specifying the query form is mandatory. Examples are given in the subsection discussing the where clause.

ASK queries check whether there exists any solution mapping for the structures in the where clause. The respective boolean value is returned.

SELECT queries project V to a subset $V_p \subseteq V$. V_p is the set of variables that is considered in the query's result, a bag of *solution mappings* Ω. This bag can be illustrated as a table with the variables in V_p serving as column titles and the solution mappings constituting the table rows. Each table cell contains the value $\mu(v)$, with $\mu \in \Omega$ being the solution mapping represented by the row of the table cell and $v \in V_p$ being the variable corresponding to the respective column. If $\mu(v)$ is not defined for some variable v, the according cell is empty. The variables in V_p are listed after the SELECT keyword. The concrete RDF terms each variable is bound to depend on the structures in the where clause.

In SPARQL 1.1, it will be possible to use expressions in SELECT queries. They allow for the assignment of values of expressions, possibly including variables used in the where clause, to new variables which are then included in the bag returned by the query. The applicable operations include aggregate functions, e.g., COUNT or AVG, which calculate the number of variable bindings or the average of the values bound to a given variable, respectively.

CONSTRUCT queries build and return new RDF graphs, using a template in the form of *triple patterns* (see below). The values of the solution mappings which fulfill the structures in the where clause form the triples of the new graph.

DESCRIBE queries return RDF graphs that describe resources. In contrast to CON-STRUCT, the graph's structure is not prescribed by the SPARQL user, but is rather determined by the provider of the queried RDF graph or the SPARQL processor.

Dataset

A given SPARQL query can be evaluated on more than one RDF graph. The set of queried graphs is given in the dataset query part.

This query part is optional because the RDF graphs to be queried can also be specified by the SPARQL protocol that facilitates the communication between a query client and a query processor. In that case, datasets specified in the query are overridden.

Where Clause

Usage of the where clause is mandatory except for DESCRIBE queries. It contains a set of *triple patterns* which forms the basis for determining the RDF triples to be considered in a query's result. A triple pattern resembles an ordinary RDF triple, except that in the triple pattern any part, i.e., subject, predicate, or object, can be represented by a variable. In the following, several example queries are given, showing the various SPARQL features usable in the where clause. The query results are based on an evaluation of the queries on the excerpt of the social network RDF graph in Listing 8.17.

The query in Listing 8.19 makes use of a variable, identifiable by the preceding question mark, to ask whether the social network contains an instance of sn:Person that has an sn:residesIn object property connecting it to sn:Lyon. The result is *no*.

Listing 8.19: SPARQL ASK query example.

```
PREFIX sn: <http://www.socialnetworks.com/myNetwork#>
PREFIX rdf: <http://www.w3.org/1999/02/22-rdf-syntax-ns#>

ASK
FROM <http://www.socialnetworks.com/myNetwork>
WHERE {
    ?person rdf:type sn:Person .
    ?person sn:residesIn sn:Lyon .
}
```

More precisely, it is queried whether there is any solution mapping that fulfills all the triple patterns in the where clause. Regarding the two patterns individually, the only solution mapping μ_1 for the first pattern is $\mu_1(?person) = sn : Jeanne$, while there is no mapping for the second pattern. Thus, $\Omega_1 = \{\mu_1\}$ and $\Omega_2 = \emptyset$. The bag of solution mappings for the whole query is the *join* ($\bowtie$) of Ω_1 and Ω_2. The join is defined as follows:

$$\Omega_1 \bowtie \Omega_2 = \{\mu_1 \cup \mu_2 \mid \mu_1 \in \Omega_1, \mu_2 \in \Omega_2, \forall v \in dom(\mu_1) \cap dom(\mu_2) : \\ \mu_1(v) = \mu_2(v)\}$$

Here, the result of computing the join of Ω_1 and Ω_2 is the empty set.

As mentioned above, the result of a SELECT query can be illustrated in tabular form. If the queried RDF graphs match the triple patterns in the where clause, i.e., if the graphs contain triples that result from replacing triple pattern variables by RDF terms, the respective variable bindings form a table row. If no further constructs are used in the where clause, all specified patterns have to be matched. In the query in Listing 8.20, however, the UNION keyword denotes that the two groups of triple patterns enclosed by braces, so-called *group graph patterns*, are alternatives. Consequently, solution mappings for either of the group graph patterns are included in the result, displayed below the query. The query returns all pairs of properties and declared classes used together in some rdfs:domain or rdfs:range triple.

Listing 8.20: SPARQL SELECT query example with UNION.

```
PREFIX sn:    <http://www.socialnetworks.com/myNetwork#>
PREFIX owl:   <http://www.w3.org/2002/07/owl#>
PREFIX rdf:   <http://www.w3.org/1999/02/22−rdf−syntax−ns#>
PREFIX rdfs:  <http://www.w3.org/2000/01/rdf−schema#>

SELECT ?property ?class
FROM <http://www.socialnetworks.com/myNetwork>
WHERE {
    {
        ?class rdf:type owl:Class .
        ?property rdfs:domain ?class .
    } UNION {
        ?class rdf:type owl:Class .
        ?property rdfs:range ?class .
    }
}
```

property	class
sn:residesIn	sn:Profile
sn:residesIn	sn:Place
sn:hasFirstName	sn:Person

The union ($\uplus$) of two bags of solution mappings Ω_1 and Ω_2 is defined as follows, where the function $card_\Omega(\mu)$ returns the number of occurrences of a solution mapping μ in Ω:

$$\Omega_1 \uplus \Omega_2 = \{\mu \mid \mu \in \Omega_1 \vee \mu \in \Omega_2\}$$
$$\wedge\, card_{\Omega_1 \uplus \Omega_2}(\mu) = card_{\Omega_1}(\mu) + card_{\Omega_2}(\mu)$$

According to this definition, if both alternatives denoted by UNION match the same triples, the respective solutions are returned twice.

Variables in triple patterns are also employed in CONSTRUCT queries to describe the RDF terms that should be considered when creating a new set of RDF triples. Furthermore, the CONSTRUCT query in Listing 8.21 uses the OPTIONAL keyword for denoting triple patterns which are not mandatory to be matched. An additional FILTER restricts the eligible solution mappings to those that cause the expression associated to the FILTER to evaluate to true. SPARQL provides a variety of operators and functions, partially imported from *XQuery* [Boa07] and *XPath* [Mal07], to be included in FILTER expressions. Examples are arithmetic and logical operators or regular expression matching. It is also possible to refer to user-defined functions.

For each class in the queried graph, the RDF graph constructed by the query (shown below the query) contains an rdfs:subClassOf triple which states that the class is a subclass of owl:Thing, the predefined OWL superclass of all other classes. Furthermore, rdfs:subClassOf triples for each superclass whose fragment starts with the letter "P" are added. Since the triple pattern with rdfs:subClassOf as predicate and the FILTER are optional, classes that do not have a superclass whose fragment starts with "P" are also considered in the result, but only form a triple that declares them as subclass of owl:Thing.

Listing 8.21: SPARQL CONSTRUCT query example with OPTIONAL and FILTER.

```
PREFIX sn:  <http://www.socialnetworks.com/myNetwork#>
PREFIX owl: <http://www.w3.org/2002/07/owl#>
PREFIX rdf: <http://www.w3.org/1999/02/22−rdf−syntax−ns#>
PREFIX rdfs: <http://www.w3.org/2000/01/rdf−schema#>

CONSTRUCT {
        ?class rdfs:subClassOf ?superClass .
        ?class rdfs:subClassOf owl:Thing .
}
FROM <http://www.socialnetworks.com/myNetwork>
WHERE {
   ?class rdf:type owl:Class .
   OPTIONAL {
      ?class rdfs:subClassOf ?superClass .
      FILTER regex(str(?superClass), "^http://www.socialnetworks.com/myNetwork#P.*")
   }
}
```

```
@prefix sn:  <http://www.socialnetworks.com/myNetwork#>
@prefix owl: <http://www.w3.org/2002/07/owl#>
@prefix rdfs: <http://www.w3.org/2000/01/rdf−schema#>

sn:Person rdfs:subClassOf sn:Profile .
sn:Profile rdfs:subClassOf owl:Thing .
sn:Person rdfs:subClassOf owl:Thing .
```

```
sn:Organization rdfs:subClassOf Thing .
sn:Place rdfs:subClassOf owl:Thing .
```

Essentially, the bag of solution mappings that fulfills the patterns in the where clause is computed as follows. First, the join of the mappings fulfilling the non-optional patterns (Ω_1) and the mappings fulfilling the optional patterns (Ω_2) is taken. Second, the bag of all mappings μ_3 from Ω_1 is computed, so that for all mappings μ_4 in Ω_2 which have variables in common with μ_3, there must be at least one variable v with $\mu_3(v) \neq \mu_4(v)$. Finally, the (set-)union of the bags that result from the two previous steps is taken. The whole operation is called *left (outer) join*:

$$\Omega_1 \text{ LEFTJOIN } \Omega_2 \;=\; (\Omega_1 \bowtie \Omega_2) \cup$$
$$\{\mu_3 \in \Omega_1 \;\mid\; \forall \mu_4 \in \Omega_2 : (\exists v \in dom(\mu_3) \cap dom(\mu_4) :$$
$$\mu_3(v) \neq \mu_4(v))\}$$

The OPTIONAL keyword is left-associative, i.e., a sequence of optional group graph patterns is evaluated in the order of their occurrence. Other orders can be achieved by using nested group graph patterns.

SPARQL 1.1 will introduce three important features that can be used in the where clause: *assignments, subqueries, negation,* and *property paths*.

The BIND keyword allows for assigning the value of expressions to variables, which can then be referred to in FILTER expressions, for instance.

The subqueries feature refers to the possibility to include complete SELECT queries in the where clause. The result of such a subquery is treated like any other bag of solution mappings that is determined by matching triple patterns, i.e., it can be used in join, union, or left join operations.

Negation is interpreted in two ways by SPARQL 1.1. First, solution mappings can be filtered using the new FILTER expression NOT EXISTS. If the triple pattern specified in the expression does not match some triple in the RDF graph, the FILTER expression evaluates to *true*, so that solution mappings resulting from matching triples patterns in the same group graph pattern as the FILTER construct are considered. Second, the MINUS keyword allows for removing triples from a set of solution mappings.

Finally, property paths are used in the predicate position of triple patterns and employ regular expression operations to denote sequences, alternatives, or iterations of properties. In this way, the structure of connections between non-adjacent nodes of an RDF graph can be described in a single triple pattern. Since property paths allow for the specification of paths of arbitrary length, they do away with the incapability of SPARQL 1.0 to express transitive closure.

Solution Modifiers

Solution modifiers can be employed for sorting or restricting the number of computed solution mappings. Sorting in ascending or descending order is specified by the OR-DER BY keyword together with ASC or DESC, respectively, followed by one or more variables as sorting criteria. The number of generated solution mappings can be controlled with the OFFSET and LIMIT keywords, followed by a number. OFFSET x states that the first x solutions found are not returned. LIMIT y ensures that no more than y solutions are included in the result.

SPARQL 1.1 will add the GROUP BY and HAVING solution modifiers. With GROUP BY, it is possible to group solution mappings on the basis of a given expression. HAVING can only be used in conjunction with GROUP BY and serves to filter groups, i.e., only groups for which the expression following the HAVING keyword evaluates to *true* are produced.

Usually, the usage of solution modifiers is optional. In ASK queries, they must not be specified.

9 Traceability with the TGraph Approach

In this chapter, the suitability of the *TGraph approach* [Ebe08] (see Section 8.1) for implementing comprehensive, semantically rich traceability is shown.

By mapping the properties of the Traceability Relationship Type Template (TRTT) (see Section 6.2) to various concepts of grUML, GReQL [Ebe10], and TGraph event-condition-action rules, Section 9.1 describes how traceability relationship types can be defined. Recording of traceability information with the JGraLab library is covered in Section 9.2. Thus, Research Question 2, asking how the customized definition of semantically rich traceability relationship types and the subsequent recording of relationships can be implemented (see Chapter 5 on research questions), is answered in the context of the TGraph approach. By providing an implementation for impact designators that can be used for identification and maintenance purposes, a contribution to Research Question 4 is provided. Section 9.3 further contributes to Research Question 4, as it describes the transformation-based identification of traceability relationships with GReTL [Hor11]. By demonstrating the usage of GReQL for realizing retrieval conforming to the traceability retrieval patterns introduced in Section 7.2, Section 9.4 gives a solution to Research Question 6.

Altogether, since the individual solutions to Research Questions 2, 4, and 6 facilitate comprehensive traceability, it becomes possible to affirm Research Question 7.

Note, as utilization is more related to specific applications of a traceability implementation than to the employed technological space, this activity is not considered here. Examples for the utilization of TGraph-based traceability information can be found in Chapters 11 and 12. The examples used throughout this chapter to illustrate the usage of the TGraph approach are based on the social network scenario that is used in Section 8.1 for introducing the TGraph approach.

9.1 Mapping of the TRTT Properties

In this section, the mapping of the TRTT to concepts of the TGraph approach is described in detail for each TRTT property. As examples, the Knows and the IsParentOf

Property	Value
Name	Knows
Description	A Knows relationship between two Profiles denotes that they know each other i.e., the user of the Profile p_1 has asked the user of the Profile p_2 to add him to p_1's *friends list* and the user of p_2 has accepted. The since attribute holds the date the relationship was established.
Supertypes	*none*
Schema fragment	
Attributes	since :Date
Relational properties	irreflexive, symmetric
Constraints	*none*
Impact designators	*none*
Examples	*see the graph in Figure 8.1*

Table 9.1: TRTT instantiation for Knows.

edge classes of the social network TGraph schema in Figure 8.2 are treated as traceability relationship types. The resulting instantiations of the TRTT are shown in Tables 9.1 and 9.2, respectively.

Name

A traceability relationship type's name is reflected by the name of the edge class or vertex class that represents the type (see also the description of the mapping of the *schema fragment*).

Description

The description of a traceability relationship type is usually part of its documentation and is not represented in a TGraph schema. If needed, grUML comments can be used in schemas to annotate the edge class or vertex class representing the relationship type with the description.

Property	Value
Name	IsParentOf
Description	An IsParentOf relationship between two Persons denotes that the source entity is a parent of the target entity. The since attribute holds the date the relationship was established.
Supertypes	IsRelativeOf
Schema fragment	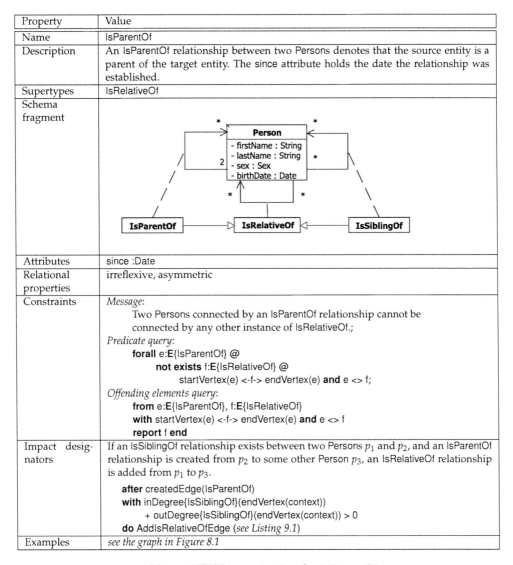
Attributes	since :Date
Relational properties	irreflexive, asymmetric

Constraints	*Message*:
	    Two Persons connected by an IsParentOf relationship cannot be connected by any other instance of IsRelativeOf.;
	Predicate query:
	    forall e:E{IsParentOf} @
	        not exists f:E{IsRelativeOf} @
	            startVertex(e) <-f-> endVertex(e) **and** e <> f;
	Offending elements query:
	    from e:E{IsParentOf}, f:E{IsRelativeOf}
	    with startVertex(e) <-f-> endVertex(e) **and** e <> f
	    report f **end**

Impact designators	If an IsSiblingOf relationship exists between two Persons p_1 and p_2, and an IsParentOf relationship is created from p_2 to some other Person p_3, an IsRelativeOf relationship is added from p_1 to p_3.
	
	    after createdEdge(IsParentOf)
	    with inDegree{IsSiblingOf}(endVertex(context))
	        + outDegree{IsSiblingOf}(endVertex(context)) > 0
	    do AddIsRelativeOfEdge (*see Listing 9.1*)

Examples	*see the graph in Figure 8.1*

Table 9.2: TRTT instantiation for IsParentOf.

Listing 9.1: Action for IsParentOf impact designator.

```
public class AddIsRelativeOfEdge implements Action {

    @Override
    public void doAction(Event event) {
```

```
// get the start vertex of the edge referred in the event
Vertex startVertex = event.getEdge().getAlpha();
// get the end vertex of the edge referred in the event
Vertex endVertex = event.getEdge().getOmega();

// get the IsSiblingOf EdgeClass
EdgeClass isSiblingOf = event.getEdge().getGraphClass().getEdgeClass("IsSiblingOf");
// get the IsRelativeOf EdgeClass
EdgeClass isRelativeOf = event.getEdge().getGraphClass().getEdgeClass("IsRelativeOf");

// iterate over all isSiblingOf edges incident to startVertex
for (Edge indicentEdge : startVertex.incidences(isSiblingOf)) {
    // create an IsRelativeOf edge from the vertex at the opposite end of incidentEdge to endVertex
    incidentEdge.getGraph().createEdge(isRelativeOf, incidentEdge.getThat(), endVertex);
  }
 }
}
```

Supertypes

The definition of a supertype is reflected by specifying the edge class or vertex class implementing the supertype to be a generalization of the edge class or vertex class representing the traceability relationship type at hand.

Schema Fragment

A binary traceability relationship type can be modeled as edge class. For an n-ary relationship type (with n > 2), a vertex class together with edge classes connecting to the vertex classes representing the traced entity types is to be used.

Attributes

Attributes are implemented as attributes of the edge class or vertex class that represents the relationship type.

Relational Properties

In general, it is thinkable to represent all relational properties by defining suitable constraints in a grUML schema. However, this approach is not recommended for properties that ensure the existence of possibly many edges, such as *transitivity* and *totality*. Such

Relationship type represented by edge class R is ...	Representation as GReQL constraint	Rewriting of GReQL RPEs
reflexive	**forall** v:**V** @ v -->{R} v	<--{R} ⇒ [<--{R}], -->{R} ⇒ [-->{R}], <->{R} ⇒ [<->{R}]
irreflexive	**not exists** v:**V** @ v -->{R} v	
coreflexive	**forall** e:**E**{R} @ startVertex(e) = endVertex(e)	
symmetric	**forall** e:**E**{R} @ endVertex(e) -->{R} startVertex(e)	<--{R} ⇒ <->{R}, -->{R} ⇒ <->{R}
asymmetric	**not exists** e:**E**{R} @ endVertex(e) -->{R} startVertex(e)	
antisymmetric	**not exists** e:**E**{R} @ endVertex(e) -->{R} startVertex(e) **and** startVertex(e) <> endVertex(e)	
transitive	**forall** e,f:**E**{R}, endVertex(e) = startVertex(f) @ startVertex(e) -->{R} endVertex(f)	<--{R} ⇒ <--{R}+, -->{R} ⇒ -->{R}+, <->{R} ⇒ <->{R}+
antitransitive	**not exists** e,f:**E**{R}, endVertex(e) = startVertex(f) @ startVertex(e) -->{R} endVertex(f)	
total	**forall** v,w:**V** @ v <->{R} w	
trichotomous	**forall** v,w:**V** @ v -->{R} w **xor** w -->{R} v **xor** v = w	
right-Euclidian	**forall** e,f:**E**{R}, endVertex(e) = endVertex(f) @ startVertex(e) -->{R} startVertex(f)	-->{R} <--{R} ⇒ -->{R}+ <--{R}+
left-Euclidian	**forall** e,f:**E**{R}, startVertex(e) = startVertex(f) @ endVertex(e) -->{R} endVertex(f)	<--{R} -->{R} ⇒ <--{R}+ -->{R}+

Table 9.3: Handling of relational properties with the TGraph approach (1). With properties taken from [Oli04, Leh04, Kom06, Iva10, Cam11].

constraints would require the population of the graph with a plethora of additional edges, probably causing an explosion of memory usage. Alternatively, those relational properties which specify the existence of additional edges with exactly defined start and end vertices, such as *reflexivity*, *symmetry*, and *transitivity*, could be dealt with at retrieval time. This means that GReQL regular path expressions in constraints and queries could be rewritten to reflect the relational property. For example, if some edge class R is transitive, any path expression -->{R} would be replaced by -->{R}+ if the Kleene plus is not already present. In short, this rule is written as -->{R} ⇒ -->{R}+.

Table 9.3 and 9.4 summarize the possibilities of handling relational properties with the TGraph approach. While the properties in Table 9.3 are only applicable for *endorelations*,

Relationship type represented by edge class R is ...	Representation as GReQL constraint	GReQL query rewriting rules
left-total	**forall** v:V @ outDegree{R}(v) > 0	
surjective	**forall** v:V @ inDegree{R}(v) > 0	

injective	**forall** e,f:E{R},
	    endVertex(e) = endVertex(f) @
	    startVertex(e) = startVertex(f)	

functional	**forall** e,f:E{R},
	    startVertex(e) = startVertex(f) @
	    endVertex(e) = endVertex(f)	

Table 9.4: Handling of relational properties with the TGraph approach (2). With properties taken from [Leh04].

i.e., for edge classes starting and ending at the same vertex class, the relational properties in Table 9.4 can be used for any edge class. For each relational property in the first column of the tables, the second column shows an appropriate GReQL constraint. Note, that the constraints assume that instances of R can be incident to vertices of any type. If the edge class R would be connected to some vertex class A instead, the appropriate irreflexivity constraint would be not exists v:V{A} @ v -->{R} v, for instance. The third column describes how GReQL regular path expressions must be rewritten to properly reflect the relational property. Here, in the case of reflexivity combined with transitivity, the rule -->{R} ⇒ -->{R}* could be applied instead of the individual rules for the two properties.

Considering generalization, if some subclass possesses a property not possessed by its superclass, then this subclass must be explicitly considered in path expressions. For example, if some intransitive edge class R has a transitive subclass S, a path expression -->{R} must be rewritten as (-->{R} | -->{S}+).

Constraints

Constraints can be specified using grUML's constraint concept. With the possibility to formulate messages for users if constraints are violated and to specify queries for determining the graph elements that cause a violation, important features for minimizing maintenance effort are provided.

In the example in Table 9.2, the syntax used for constraints conforms to the *message-predicate query-offending elements query* structure described in Section 8.1.2.

Impact Designators

To accommodate for the realization of impact designators, the TGraph approach was extended by the event-condition-action rule concept which has been implemented for the JGraLab library.

In Table 9.2, an ECA rule example is represented using the concrete syntax introduced in Section 8.1.5.

Examples

Example applications of a traceability relationship type are part of its documentation and are not represented in a TGraph schema.

9.2 Recording of TGraph-Based Traceability Information

With JGraLab, there exists an implementation of the TGraph approach that allows for creating, manipulating, traversing, and persisting TGraphs and their schemas. Thus, it constitutes a suitable technological basis for realizing a fact repository-based traceability solution.

To achieve a seamless representation of all traceable entities, suitable fact extractors have to be implemented for relevant entities which are not natively represented as TGraphs. To facilitate efficient retrieval of traceability information with GReQL, the various graphs resulting from fact extraction should be integrated into a single graph.

9.3 Transformation-Based Identification

As described in the introduction to GReTL in Section 8.1.4, traceability relationships between source and target elements of transformations are automatically maintained by the bijective mappings img_T and $arch_T$. While img_T maps archetypes, i.e., source elements, to images, i.e., target elements, $arch_T$ contains the inverse mappings, with T being the type of the concerned target elements. By storing the mappings to an XML file, they can be made persistent. A limitation of this approach is that the traceability information cannot be accessed by GReQL queries, for it is not represented as TGraph. To analyze this information, a program language must be used.

To create relationships that can be retrieved with GReQL, GReTL transformations can be modified to produce a target graph that contains the source graph and the original target graph as subgraphs. Then, traceability relationships between corresponding elements of these subgraphs can be generated. However, only vertices, but not edges, can be interconnected in this way. This approach can be automated by GReTL's predefined generic copy transformation, which copies the source schema and graphs to the target. Thus, user-defined transformations should first call the copy transformation and can then further extend the schema, create the target subgraph, and connect it to the source subgraphs.

9.4 Querying Conforming to the Retrieval Patterns

The three traceability retrieval patterns presented in Section 7.2 – *Existence, Reachable Entities*, and *Slice* – can all be implemented with GReQL. The requirement of the patterns stating that it must be possible to specify complex path structures, with various restrictions on the types and properties of involved relationships and entities, is satisfied by the availability of regular path expressions in GReQL.

In the following, the choice of GReQL constructs for implementing each pattern is described in detail.

9.4.1 Existence Pattern

The Existence pattern can be realized by GReQL existentially quantified expressions or stand-alone path existence expressions. The latter option is possible if variables have been bound to specific vertices externally, i.e., outside the GReQL query, by using the API of the GReQL evaluator.

In the example GReQL expression in Listing 9.2, it is checked whether there is a Knows relationship between any two Persons with the lastNames "Meunier" and "Dupont", respectively. While lines 2 and 3 narrow down the eligible vertices, the actual existence check is done in line 4.

Listing 9.2: Usage of an existentially quantified expression for implementing the Existence pattern.

```
1   exists p,q:V{Person} @
2       p.lastName = "Meunier" and
3       q.lastName = "Dupont" and
4       p <->{Knows}* q
```

Assuming that two variables, meuniers and duponts, have externally been bound to sets of Persons with the lastNames "Meunier" and "Dupont", the query in Listing 9.3 performs the same check as the one in Listing 9.2.

Listing 9.3: Usage of an existentially quantified expression with externally bound variables for implementing the Existence pattern.

```
exists p:meuniers, q:duponts @ p <->{Knows}* q
```

If the existence of a connection between two specific Person instances which have been bound externally is to be tested, the needed GReQL expression boils down to the path existence expression in Listing 9.4.

Listing 9.4: Usage of a path existence expression with externally bound variables for implementing the Existence pattern.

```
hugoMeunier <->{Knows}* isabelleDupont
```

9.4.2 Reachable Entities Pattern

Queries that conform to the Reachable Entities pattern make use of from-with-report expressions or, if the starting set of traced entities consists of a single vertex for which a variable has already been bound externally, stand-alone forward vertex set expressions.

The FWR expression in Listing 9.5 yields all Profiles that are directly connected to any Person with the firstName "Isabelle" via a Knows or an IsRelativeOf edge.

Listing 9.5: Usage of an FWR expression for implementing the Reachable Entities pattern.

```
1  from p:V{Person}, q:V{Profile}
2  with p.firstName = "Isabelle"
3       and p <->{Knows} | <->{IsRelativeOf} q
4  reportSet q
5  end
```

Provided that a single Person "Isabelle Meunier" has been bound to a variable externally, a single forward vertex set expression could be employed, as illustrated in Listing 9.6.

Listing 9.6: Usage of a forward vertex set expression with an externally bound variable for implementing the Reachable Entities pattern.

```
isabelleMeunier (<->{Knows} | <->{IsRelativeOf})
```

9.4.3 Slice Pattern

For realizing the Slice pattern, the slice function was added to the GReQL function library. As the function's first argument takes a set of vertices, a nested from-with-report expression that returns such a set could be used here. Alternatively, a set of vertices that has been externally bound by a variable can be used.

In Listing 9.7, the application of the slice function uses a FWR expression to determine the set of all Persons whose lastName is "Meunier". The result of the function call is a subgraph of the social network, consisting of the Persons in the determined set, all Places where a Person known by a relative of a "Meunier" resides, and all edges interconnecting the involved vertices.

Listing 9.7: Usage of the slice function for implementing the Slice pattern.

```
1  slice(from p:V{Person}
2      with p.lastName = "Meunier"
3      reportSet p end,
4      <->{IsRelativeOf} <->{Knows} -->{ResidesIn}
5  )
```

Assuming that the set of all Persons whose lastName is "Meunier" have been bound to externally, the GReQL expression in Listing 9.8 can be executed.

Listing 9.8: Usage of the slice function with an externally bound variable for implementing the Slice pattern.

```
slice(meuniers, <->{IsRelativeOf} <->{Knows} -->{ResidesIn})
```

10 Traceability with the Web Ontology Language

This chapter explains how to implement comprehensive, semantically rich traceability using the *OWL* technological space, including OWL itself [Mot09b], RDF as serialization format for OWL [Pat09,Kly04], and SPARQL [Pru08] as query language for RDF.

In detail, Section 10.1 shows the mapping of the Traceability Relationship Type Template's properties (see Section 6.2) to OWL and SPARQL concepts. In Section 10.2, the possibilities for storing traceability information represented in OWL are shortly discussed. By describing the definition and recording of custom, yet semantically rich traceability relationship types that support automatic identification and maintenance, Research Questions 2 and 4 (see Chapter 5) are answered in the context of the OWL technological space. Responding to Research Question 6, Section 10.3 illustrates the usage of SPARQL for retrieving traceability information according to the retrieval patterns described in Section 7.2.

By providing individual solutions to Research Questions 2, 4, and 6, the OWL technological space can be regarded as suitable for implementing comprehensive traceability as requested by Research Question 7. One shortcoming with respect to retrieval is the inability of SPARQL 1.0 to express object property paths of arbitrary length.

The activity of utilization is not considered as it is not within the scope of this work. An example for an OWL-based traceability solution is described in Chapter 13. The examples that illustrate the usage of OWL and SPARQL for realizing traceability are based on the ontology-based social network scenario used in Section 8.2.

10.1 Mapping of the TRTT Properties

In the following, the mapping of the TRTT's properties to concepts of the OWL technological space is described in detail. As examples, the sn:knows and sn:isParentOf object properties of the social network ontology in Listings 8.12 to 8.16 are taken. Tables 10.1 and 10.2 show the instantiated TRTT, respectively.

Property	Value
Name	sn:knows
Description	A sn:knows relationship between two sn:Profiles denotes that they know each other i.e., the user of the sn:Profile p_1 has asked the user of the sn:Profile p_2 to add him to p_1's *friends* list and the user of p_2 has accepted. Using the since annotation property, the date the relationship was established can be recorded.
Supertypes	*none*
Schema fragment	**Declaration(ObjectProperty(** sn:knows **))** **Declaration(AnnotationProperty (** sn:since **))** **ObjectPropertyDomain(** sn:knows sn:Profile **)** **ObjectPropertyRange(** sn:knows sn:Profile **)**
Attributes	sn:since *(modeled as annotation)*
Relational properties	irreflexive, symmetric
Constraints	*none*
Impact designators	*none*
Examples	*see Listing 8.16*

Table 10.1: Instantiated TRTT for sn:knows.

Name

A traceability relationship type's name is reflected by the name of the object property or class that represents the type (see also the description of the mapping of the *schema fragment*).

Description

The description of a traceability relationship type is usually part of its documentation and is not represented in an OWL ontology. If needed, OWL annotations can be used to attach the description to the object property or class representing the relationship type.

Supertypes

The definition of a supertype is reflected by specifying the object property or class implementing the supertype to be a superproperty or superclass, respectively, of the property or class representing the traceability relationship type at hand.

Property	Value
Name	sn:isParentOf
Description	An sn:isParentOf relationship between two Persons denotes that the source entity is a parent of the target entity. Using the since annotation property, the date the relationship was established can be recorded.
Supertypes	*none*
Schema fragment	**Declaration(ObjectProperty(** sn:isParentOf **))** **Declaration(AnnotationProperty(** sn:since **))** **SubObjectPropertyOf(** sn:isParentOf sn:isRelativeOf **)** **ObjectPropertyDomain(** sn:knows sn:Person **)** **ObjectPropertyRange(** sn:knows sn:Person **)**
Attributes	sn:since (*modeled as annotation*)
Relational properties	irreflexive, asymmetric

Constraints	An sn:Person must be the target entity of exactly two sn:isParentOf relationships.
	
	    SubClassOf(
	        sn:Person
	        ObjectExactCardinality(2 **ObjectInverseOf(** sn:isParentOf **))**
	    )
	
	Two sn:Persons connected by an sn:isParentOf relationship cannot be connected by an sn:isSiblingOf relationship.
	
	    DisjointObjectProperties(sn:isParentOf sn:isSiblingOf **)**

Impact designators	If an sn:isSiblingOf relationship exists between two sn:Persons p_1 and p_2, and an sn:isParentOf relationship exists between p_2 and some other sn:Person p_3, then an sn:isRelativeOf relationship is added from p_1 to p_3.
	
	    SubObjectPropertyOf(
	        ObjectPropertyChain(sn:isSiblingOf sn:isParentOf **)**
	        sn:isRelativeOf
	    )

Examples	*see Listing 8.16*

Table 10.2: Instantiated TRTT for sn:isParentOf.

Schema Fragment

A binary relationship type can be modeled as object property. For an n-ary relationship type (with n > 2), a class together with object properties connecting to the classes representing the traceable entity types is to be used.

Besides the arity of the relationship type, the choice between a single object property and a class together with object properties also depends on the intended usage of attributes. If a binary relationship type does not feature attributes or if the attributes shall not be referred to in constraints, impact designators, or anywhere else where reasoning services are involved, the relationship type can safely be modeled as object property and the attribute values be mapped to annotations to the respective object property assertions. In other cases, even binary relationship types have to be represented as classes together with object properties, so that attributes can be represented as data properties.

Using an object property chain, a binary relationship type modeled as class together with two object properties can be treated as a single object property.

Attributes

If the relationship type is modeled as object property, the object property assertions may involve annotations representing simple attributes that do not need to exhibit formal semantics, such as a comment or a rationale. If the relationship type is modeled as class, data properties can also be used to represent attributes (see also the description of the mapping of the *schema fragment*).

Relational Properties

The following relational properties can be directly represented using a corresponding OWL object property axiom: *reflexivity, irreflexivity, symmetry, asymmetry, transitivity, injectivity*, and *functionality*. Table 10.3 gives an overview of these axioms.

Other relational properties have to be specified by more complex axioms. For example, adding SubClassOf(owl:Thing ObjectSomeValuesFrom(OP owl:Thing)) to an ontology declares the object property OP to be left-total. However, since the implications of adding relational properties which are not natively supported by OWL on its decidability are unclear, a comprehensive list is not included here.

Object Property OP is ...	Representation as OWL axiom
reflexive	ReflexiveObjectProperty(OP)
irreflexive	IrreflexiveObjectProperty(OP)
symmetric	SymmetricObjectProperty(OP)
asymmetric	AsymmetricObjectProperty(OP)
transitive	TransitiveObjectProperty(OP)
injective	InverseFunctionalObjectProperty(OP)
functional	FunctionalObjectProperty(OP)

Table 10.3: Representation of relational properties as OWL axioms.

To be able to specify relational properties for a binary traceability relationship type modeled as class with two object properties, an object property chain over the two object properties has to be defined.

Constraints

Constraints in the OWL technological space can be specified by different axioms, most notably SubClassOf axioms, in conjunction with class expressions, or DisjointObject-Properties axioms. For some kinds of constraints, SPARQL ASK queries could be employed.

Using OWL SubClassOf axioms, constraints are represented as special classes. Classes of individuals which are supposed to fulfill a constraint are specified to be subclasses of such a special class. An example of this approach is the specification of cardinality restrictions, where a SubClassOf axiom states that a given class is a subclass of an (anonymous) class that is limited with respect to the minimum or maximum number of its properties (see Listing 8.13, for instance). Using the reasoning service of consistency checking, it can be tested whether all constraints are obeyed.

The DisjointObjectProperties axiom specifies that all object properties out of a set of given object properties are pairwise disjoint, i.e., no individual can possess two or more of the given properties.

SPARQL ASK queries implement existential quantification. They can be employed for ensuring that there is at least one individual, property, or combination of different entities, that adheres to a given restriction.

Impact Designators

One possibility to represent impact designators in the OWL technological space is to use SubObjectPropertyOf or SubClassOf axioms in conjunction with class expressions. SubObjectPropertyOf axioms allow for the entailment of object properties between individuals if there already exists some subproperty or some chain of properties between those individuals. With SubClassOf, it can be specified that an anonymous class whose individuals possess a specific number of properties is a subclass of some named class, for instance. Thus, any individual is classified as being an instance of the named class.

On the basis of OWL axioms only, complex impact designators can become rather convoluted. For the formulation of more concise and also more expressive impact designators, the OWL-compatible dialects of the *Rule Interchange Format (RIF)* [Bol10a, Bol10b, Bru10] or the *Semantic Web Rule Language (SWRL)* [Hor04] can be used.

However, the representation of impact designators using OWL or one of the mentioned rule languages does not allow for the retraction or modification of already existing knowledge in an ontology, but only for the inference of new facts. Another shortcoming is that such impact designators essentially constitute *condition-action* rules. They do not support the specification of events, such as the addition or removal of an entity to the ontology. Thus, the point in time at which the inference of facts is conducted is not an inherent characteristic of the rules, but depends on the usage of reasoning tools. In contrast, *event-condition-action* rules are executed immediately before or after the occurrence of the event.

To implement ECA rules in the OWL technological space, solutions based on ontology APIs such the *OWLAPI*[1] or as provided by the *Jena* framework[2] can be employed. They allow for the detection of events, i.e., changes to ontologies, for posing queries representing conditions, and for the modification of ontologies, including the deletion of entries or the update of data values, for instance.

Examples

Example applications of the traceability relationship type are part of its documentation and are not represented in an OWL ontology.

10.2 Recording of OWL-Based Traceability Information

Persistence of OWL ontologies is usually facilitated by storing them in text files. Mostly, the RDF/XML syntax [Bec04] is used for that purpose. For a more efficient storage and handling of large ontologies, frameworks such as *Sesame* [Bro02] or *Jena* [Car03] can be employed. They provide an abstraction layer for persistence, consequently allowing to rely on other means of storage, e.g., relational database systems. Sesame and Jena both include Java APIs which offer querying and reasoning services. Building on these frameworks, it is thinkable to realize an external, fact repository-baed recording concept in the OWL technological space.

Large ontologies may also be partitioned into several smaller ones that capture specific parts of the available traceability information, consequently improving comprehensibility. For example, such subontologies could contain the information for individual

---

[1]http://owlapi.sourceforge.net
[2]http://jena.sourceforge.net

subsystems. OWL provides an *import* concept, so that the subontologies can be integrated into a single ontology that establishes the traceability relationships between subsystems.

10.3 Querying Conforming to the Retrieval Patterns

In general, the three traceability retrieval patterns *Existence*, *Reachable Entities*, and *Slice* can be implemented by using SPARQL queries. However, the representation of complex structures such as alternative paths of traceability relationships between traceable entities results in rather verbose queries. Furthermore, SPARQL 1.0 does not support the computation of transitive closure, so that the connection of entities by paths of arbitrary length cannot be specified. In SPARQL 1.1, the property paths feature is expected to remedy these problems.

To make SPARQL 1.0 better suit the requirements of traceability retrieval, an approach for the transformation of GReQL existentially quantified expressions and from-with-report expressions to SPARQL ASK and SELECT queries, respectively, was developed. This way, long SPARQL queries could be replaced by more concise GReQL queries with regular path expressions. However, since SPARQL does not support the computation of transitive closure over properties, the Kleene star or plus must not be used in GReQL RPEs. More information on this transformation can be found in [Sch10a].

In the following, the choice of SPARQL constructs for implementing each pattern is described in detail.

10.3.1 Existence Pattern

The Existence pattern can be realized by SPARQL ASK queries. The where clause can be divided into three parts. While the first two parts specify the two sets of individuals representing the entities whose interconnection is to be tested, the third part describes the structure of the traceability relationship path between them.

The example in Listing 10.1 asks whether any two Persons with the lastNames "Meunier" and "Dupont", respectively, are interconnected by an sn:knows property.

Listing 10.1: Usage of an ASK query for implementing the Existence pattern.

```
1  PREFIX sn:   <http://www.socialnetworks.com/myNetwork#>
2  PREFIX rdf:  <http://www.w3.org/1999/02/22-rdf-syntax-ns#>
3
4  ASK
```

```
 5   WHERE {
 6      # Description of the first set of traced entities
 7      ?p rdf:type sn:Person .
 8      ?p sn:lastName "Meunier"^^xsd:string .
 9
10      # Description of the second set of traced entities
11      ?q rdf:type sn:Person .
12      ?q sn:lastName "Dupont"^^xsd:string .
13
14      # Description of the path structure
15      { ?p sn:knows ?q . } UNION { ?q sn:knows ?p . }
16   }
```

If the existence of a path of sn:knows properties of arbitrary length is to be checked, similar to the GReQL query in Listing 9.2, an OWL axiom stating the transitivity of sn:knows would temporarily have to be added to the ontology. Then, the transitive closure could be inferred and considered by SPARQL.

10.3.2 Reachable Entities Pattern

The Reachable Entities pattern is implemented by SPARQL SELECT queries. The where clause consists of two parts. The first one serves to specify the set of individuals that act as starting points for the reachability analysis. The second part describes the eligible structures of the paths between some individual i_1 in that set and an individual i_2 which is to be returned if it is reachable from i_1.

The SELECT query in Listing 10.2 yields all individuals that are connected to any sn:Person with the firstName "Isabelle" via an sn:knows or an sn:isRelativeOf object property.

Listing 10.2: Usage of a SELECT query for implementing the Reachable Entities pattern.

```
 1   PREFIX sn:   <http://www.socialnetworks.com/myNetwork#>
 2   PREFIX rdf:  <http://www.w3.org/1999/02/22−rdf−syntax−ns#>
 3
 4   SELECT ?q
 5   WHERE {
 6      # Description of the set of traced entities
 7      ?p rdf:type sn:Person .
 8      ?p sn:firstName "Isabelle"^^xsd:string .
 9
10      # Description of the path structure
11      { ?p sn:knows ?q . } UNION { ?q sn:knows ?p . } UNION
12      { ?p sn:isRelativeOf ?q . } UNION { ?q sn:isRelativeOf ?p . }
13   }
```

The SPARQL query in Listing 10.2 would be the result of applying the GReQL-to-SPARQL transformation presented in [Sch10a] to the GReQL query in Listing 9.5.

10.3.3 Slice Pattern

Compared to the Reachable Entities pattern, the Slice pattern intends to also return the traceability relationships forming the paths between entities, together with the intermediate entities lying on these paths. Slices can be computed using SELECT or CONSTRUCT queries, depending on whether the result should be represented in tabular form or as an RDF graph. Hence, CONSTRUCT queries allow for the generation of subgraphs of the queried RDF graph, as originally specified by the Slice pattern. The where clause features three parts. The first part specifies the set of individuals that act as starting points for the Slice computation. The second part assigns additional variables to the object properties representing the traceability relationships, so that they can be returned by the query. Similar to the SPARQL implementation of the other patterns, the final part describes the structures of the paths to be considered.

The example SELECT query in Listing 10.3 returns all tuples ?p ?op1 ?q ?op2 ?r ?op3 ?s. Here, ?p denotes an sn:Person individual with the lastName "Meunier". ?op1, ?op2, and ?op3 are bound to the object properties sn:isRelativeOf, sn:knows, and sn:residesIn, respectively. ?q represents individuals that are connected to some individual ?p via an object property ?op1. ?r is bound to individuals that are connected to some ?q via ?op2. Finally, ?r must have an object property ?op3 connecting it to some individual ?s.

Listing 10.3: Usage of a SELECT query for implementing the Slice pattern.

```
1   SELECT ?p ?op1 ?q ?op2 ?r ?op3 ?s
2   WHERE {
3       # Description of the set of traced entities
4       ?p rdf:type sn:Person .
5       ?p sn:lastName "Meunier"^^xsd:string .
6
7       # Binding of traceability relationship variables
8       ?op1 rdf:type sn:isRelativeOf .
9       ?op2 rdf:type sn:knows .
10      ?op3 rdf:type sn:residesIn .
11
12      # Description of path structure
13      { { ?p ?op1 ?q . } UNION { ?q ?op1 ?p . } }
14      { { ?q ?op2 ?r . } UNION { ?r ?op2 ?q . } }
15      ?r ?op3 ?s .
16  }
```

The CONSTRUCT query in Listing 10.4 features the same where clause as the query in Listing 10.3. However, instead of returning a table, a new RDF graph containing the sought-after information is created.

Listing 10.4: Usage of a CONSTRUCT query for implementing the Slice pattern.

```
1   CONSTRUCT {
2       ?p ?op1 ?q .
3       ?q ?op2 ?r .
4       ?r ?op3 ?s .
5   }
6   WHERE {
7       # Description of the set of traced entities
8       ?p rdf:type sn:Person .
9       ?p sn:lastName "Meunier"^^xsd:string .
10
11      # Binding of traceability relationship variables
12      ?op1 rdf:type sn:isRelativeOf .
13      ?op2 rdf:type sn:knows .
14      ?op3 rdf:type sn:residesIn .
15
16      # Description of path structure
17      { { ?p ?op1 ?q . } UNION { ?q ?op1 ?p . } }
18      { { ?q ?op2 ?r . } UNION { ?r ?op2 ?q . } }
19      ?r ?op3 ?s .
20  }
```

Part IV

Application

11 Requirements-Based Reuse of Software Artifacts

The *ReDSeeDS* project (*Requirements-Driven Software Development System*)[1] pursued the usage of traceability information for identifying software artifacts that fulfill a set of given requirements. These requirements belong to various already completed software development projects and are identified as being similar to the requirements of a system that is currently being developed [Amb08]. In this chapter, the application of the generic traceability concepts introduced in Chapters 6 and 7 for facilitating this idea of requirements-based reuse is presented. The concepts are implemented on the basis of the TGraph approach [Ebe08], as explained in Chapter 9.

Section 11.1 details the idea of the ReDSeeDS project, including a general overview of the role of traceability information. In Section 11.2, the *ReDSeeDS Engine*, a prototypical tool for finding reusable software artifacts is described. Section 11.3 explains the implementation of a traceability solution in the context of the ReDSeeDS Engine. The description is structured along the six traceability-related activities introduced in Chapter 3.

11.1 The ReDSeeDS Project

The main idea of the ReDSeeDS project was to conceive and implement an approach for the requirements-based reuse of software artifacts. Given a software system that is currently under development, its requirements specification is compared with the requirements specifications of already completed software development projects. This comparison aims at the identification of similar requirements of "old" software systems. Software artifacts that fulfill these similar requirements are candidates for reuse in the current project.

Furthermore, ReDSeeDS advocates a model-driven development process: the requirements specification is transformed to an architecture model, further on to a detailed design model, and finally to source code. The notion of "Software Case", illustrated in

---

[1]http://www.redseeds.eu

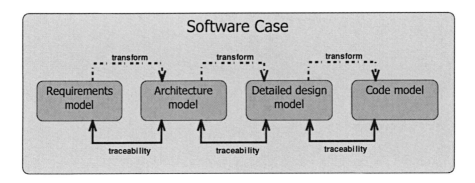

Figure 11.1: Structure of a Software Case.

Figure 11.1, has been introduced to refer to the entirety of artifacts on these four abstraction levels. Traceability relationships are automatically established between the source and target elements of these transformations. In addition to relying on model transformations, requirements can also be implemented manually. In that case, adequate traceability relationships have to be identified and recorded by the developers.

Figure 11.2 illustrates the reuse concept of ReDSeeDS: first, the requirements model of a current Software Case is compared with the requirements models of completed Software Cases recorded in a dedicated repository. Starting from requirements which have been identified to be similar, traceability relationships are traversed to find implementing elements in architecture, detailed design, and code models. These elements can then be adopted into the current Software Case and linked to its requirements model. Requirements which cannot be fulfilled by reusing some part of an "old" Software Case are realized by applying model transformations or by manual implementation. Once completed, the Software Case is recorded in the Software Case repository.

11.2 The ReDSeeDS Engine: a Platform for Finding Reusable Artifacts

The *ReDSeeDS Engine*, developed under the direction of the Warsaw University of Technology in collaboration with the other ReDSeeDS partners, implements the reuse approach detailed in Section 11.1. It is realized as an *Eclipse RCP (Rich Client Platform)* application [Rei08]. The Rich Client Platform consists of the Eclipse basic infrastructure and user interface components [McA10]. Building applications on top of the RCP, software with the well-established Eclipse look-and-feel can be developed efficiently.

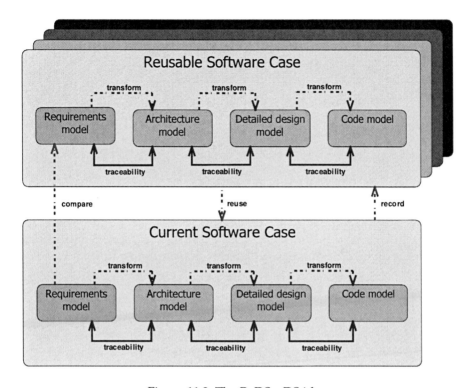

Figure 11.2: The ReDSeeDS idea.

For the representation of Software Cases, the *Software Case Language* (*SCL*) [Bil09a] has been developed in a joint effort of the ReDSeeDS project team. By using JGraLab, the ReDSeeDS Engine records Software Cases as *TGraphs* [Ebe95], based on an SCL TGraph schema.

Section 11.2.1 introduces the SCL and its sublanguages. In Section 11.2.2, an overview of the features of the ReDSeeDS Engine is given.

11.2.1 The Software Case Language

To represent the various Software Case parts, i.e., the requirements, architecture, detailed design, and source code models, the SCL includes appropriate sublanguages. In detail, these are the *Requirements Specification Language* (*RSL*) [Wol09], used for the requirements specification, the *UML* [Obj10c], for the architecture and design models, and an adaptation of the grammar of the Java programming language for the source

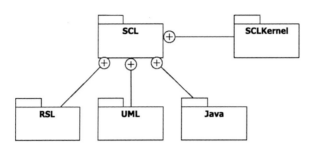

Figure 11.3: SCL package diagram.

code. The package diagram in Figure 11.3 illustrates the structure of the SCL TGraph schema. The SCL package includes subpackages for each of the sublanguages, and an SCLKernel package that contains basic concepts and inter-level traceability relationship types.

The RSL has been developed in the context of ReDSeeDS for facilitating the model-based representation of requirements. An important feature of the RSL is its distinction between a requirement itself and its representations, as expressed by the two vertex classes Requirement and RequirementRepresentation shown in the RSL schema excerpt in Figure 11.4. Requirements per se can be UseCases, FunctionalRequirements, or Constraints, i.e., non-functional requirements. Independent of the specific type, Requirements may be represented diagrammatically or textually. Possible diagram forms are InteractionScenarios, similar to UML sequence diagrams, or ActivityScenarios, which are comparable to UML activity diagrams. ConstrainedLanguageScenarios allow for the textual description of scenarios based on a constrained form of English. Sentences formulated in this constrained language may be broken down into their various parts of speech and are represented as a graph. SentenceLists contain individual statements on the system, phrased in constrained or natural language. Traceability relationships between Requirements can be recorded using the subclasses of RequirementRelationship. Requirement and RequirementRepresentation are subclasses of the SCLKernel vertex class SCLElement. Similarly, all kinds of RequirementRelationships are considered to be SCLRelationships.

Besides SCLElement and SCLRelationship, the SCLKernel package features the vertex classes SoftwareCase, SoftwareArtifact and its subclasses, and TraceabilityLink (see Figure 11.5). While SoftwareCases represent Software Cases themselves, SoftwareArtifacts model their four main parts. TraceabilityLink subsumes all types of inter-level traceability relationship types (see Figure 11.6). Note, that while the naming of the Dependency vertex class may seem unfortunate at first glance, this actually results from the adoption

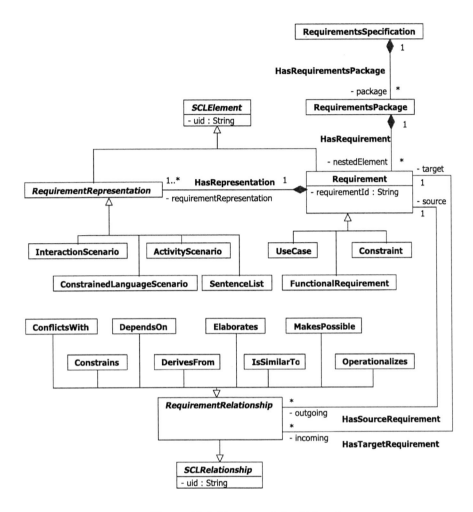

Figure 11.4: Excerpt of the RSL schema.

of the traceability concepts of the UML, discussed in Section 3.1. Refer to Section 11.3 and Appendix A.1 for more details on the traceability-related concepts of the SCL.

Note the modeling of all traceability relationship types as vertex classes together with two edge classes connecting them to the vertex classes that represent the traced entity types. This design decision was made to accommodate for the integration of JGraLab with the *MOLA* transformation framework (see Section 11.2.2). MOLA interprets the

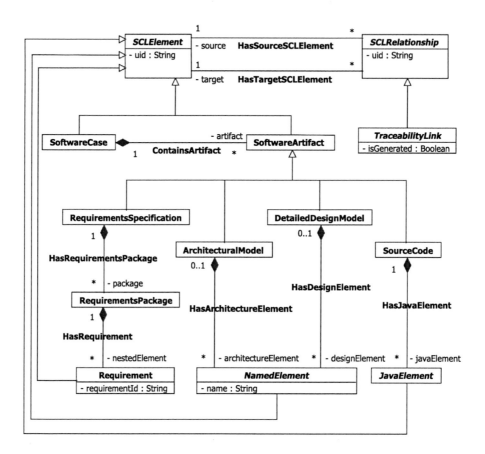

Figure 11.5: SCL kernel.

SCL schema as an *EMOF* meta model [Obj06]. EMOF does not feature an equivalent for grUML edge classes that possess attributes.[2]

The UML and Java parts of the SCL, which mainly conform to standard UML or are an adaptation of the Java grammar for representing Java abstract syntax graphs, respectively, are not detailed here. More information can be found in [Kal07b].

---

[2]Using GReTL [Hor11] as transformation language instead, the relationship types could have been modeled as mere edge classes.

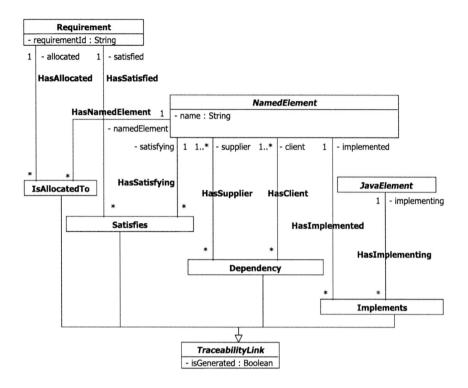

Figure 11.6: SCL inter-level traceability concepts.

11.2.2 Features

As an Eclipse RCP application, the ReDSeeDS Engine provides an integrated environment for accomplishing the various tasks presented by the ReDSeeDS approach. These tasks involve

- the modeling of requirements based on the RSL,

- the transformation of models along the model-driven development chain,

- the modeling of architecture and detailed design based on the UML,

- the comparison of requirements of a current Software Case with those of completed cases,

- the identification, recording, and retrieval of traceability information with the purpose to find potentially reusable software artifacts, and

- the import of reusable artifacts into a current Software Case

Note, that although supported by the underlying SCL schema, the transformation to Java source code and its reuse is not part of the developed ReDSeeDS Engine prototype.

The solutions offered by the ReDSeeDS Engine for performing the first four tasks are described in the following. The Engine's traceability support and the utilization of traceability information for the reuse of software artifacts is more extensively covered in Section 11.3.

11.2.2.1 Modeling of Requirements

The ReDSeeDS Engine offers various editors and views to allow for the modeling of requirements specifications conforming to the RSL. The choice of editor depends on the chosen type of requirement to be added, i.e., FunctionalRequirement, Constraint, or UseCase, and the desired form of representation.

Figure 11.7 shows a sample screenshot detail of the Engine's scenario editor. On the left, the *Software Case browser* illustrates the artifacts of a current Software Case in a tree-like structure. In the upper right part, the sentences in constrained English making up the "User registration" scenario of the "User registration" use case are listed. The choice of color and font makes it possible to distinguish between the constituents of such a sentence: subject, verb, and object. In the lower right part, one of the potentially many senses of a given term can be selected, which is essential for the correct similarity computation between requirements. The senses are read from the lexical database *WordNet* [Fel98] which is integrated with the ReDSeeDS Engine.

11.2.2.2 Transformation

At the time the ReDSeeDS Engine prototype was developed, the TGraph transformation language GReTL had not been conceived. For the transformation of RSL requirements specifications to UML architecture and further on to detailed design models, the *MOLA* transformation language [Kal04] has been employed instead.

MOLA *programs* are formulated using a graphical notation that combines both pattern matching and model element generation aspects. The execution of rules in a MOLA program may be controlled using sequences or loops. As illustrated in the following example, loops are the predominant type of control structure in MOLA.

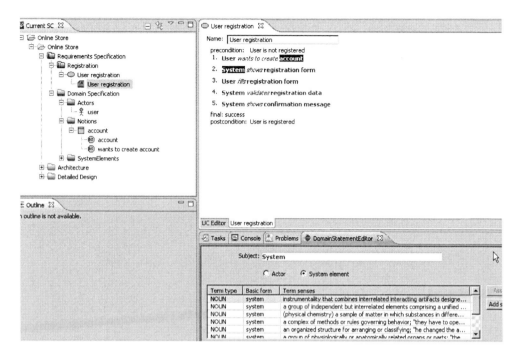

Figure 11.7: ReDSeeDS Engine screenshot detail of the scenario editor. Taken from the ReDSeeDS Engine presentations on http://www.redseeds.eu.

Taken from [Sch10c], Figure 11.8 depicts a MOLA program for the transformation of RSL RequirementsPackages to UML Components. The program consists of three loops, recognizable by the large bold rectangles. The loops are organized in a sequence. Each loop iterates a single rule, represented as a gray rectangle with rounded corners. The elements in a rule that are drawn with solid lines denote the pattern that has to be matched: the loop iterates over all instances in the model that match the element with a bold black border and its context, illustrated by the elements with thin borders. For each such instance, the dashed instances are added to the model.

The example MOLA program transforms RequirementsPackages and nested UseCases into architectural Components, Ports, and Interfaces. For illustrative purposes, the transformation has been simplified in that the Satisfies traceability relationships are modeled as edge classes instead of vertex classes with two incident edge classes. The transformation is performed in three steps:

- Step 1: For each RequirementsPackage rp1, a Component c1 is created. A Satisfies edge connects c1 to rp1.

169

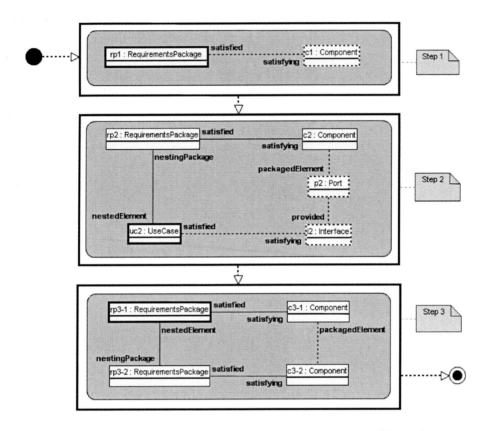

Figure 11.8: Example MOLA transformation. Taken from [Sch10c].

- Step 2: For each UseCase uc2 that is nested in a RequirementsPackage for which a corresponding Component c2 has been generated in Step 1, an Interface i2 and a Port p2 are generated. While an Owns edge connects c2 to p2, p2 is linked to i2 via a Provides edge. A Satisfies edge connects i2 to uc2.

- Step 3: For each RequirementsPackage rp3-1 that is nested in another Requirements-Package rp3-2, and where both RequirementsPackages are linked to satisfying Components c3-1 and c3-2, respectively, an Owns edge indicating the containment of c3-1 in c3-2 is generated.

The architecture resulting from the transformation of the requirements specification in Figure 11.7 is shown in the Software Case browser part of the screenshot detail in Figure 11.9. A full description of the MOLA transformation programs used in ReDSeeDS can be found in [Kal07a].

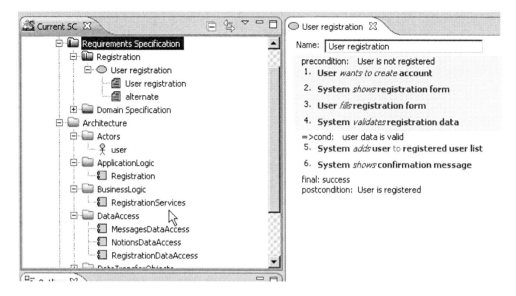

Figure 11.9: ReDSeeDS Engine screenshot detail showing the generated architecture in the Software Case browser. Taken from the ReDSeeDS Engine presentations on http://www.redseeds.eu.

11.2.2.3 Modeling of Architecture and Design

Besides showing the architecture and detailed design models in the Software Case browser, the ReDSeeDS Engine prototype does not allow for directly modifying these models. Instead, a third-party modeling tool is employed: *Enterprise Architect* by Sparx Systems (see also Section 4.2.4). Using an XMI import/export mechanism, UML models are exchanged between the ReDSeeDS Engine and Enterprise Architect.

11.2.2.4 Comparison of Requirements

The comparison of the requirements specification of a current Software Case with the requirements specification of completed Software Cases makes use of a hybrid technique. Their application depends on the specific type of the requirements to be compared [Wol08]. Graph differencing algorithms are used for comparing the structures of the requirements specifications [Bil09b]. They are especially effective with respect to requirements that are represented as instance networks internally, such as InteractionScenarios, ActivityScenarios, or representation forms that make use of constrained language. For pure natural language requirements, information retrieval techniques

171

are employed. To deal with linguistic aspects, e.g., synonyms or homonyms, Word-Net is used. Moreover, experiments with ontology-based similarity measures [Hot09] and case-based reasoning [Aam94] have been conducted. A detailed description of the similarity computation in ReDSeeDS can be taken from [Wol07].

Figure 11.10 shows a screenshot detail of the ReDSeeDS Engine's query manager, where the Software Case "WebStore" is compared with the Software Cases "Car registration" and "OnlineStore". The degree of similarity between Software Cases is expressed as a value between 0 (completely dissimilar) and 1 (equal). This overall value is calculated on the basis of similarity values between individual elements of the requirements specifications. To get a more detailed picture, these values may be browsed in a special view, displayed on the lower right of the screenshot.

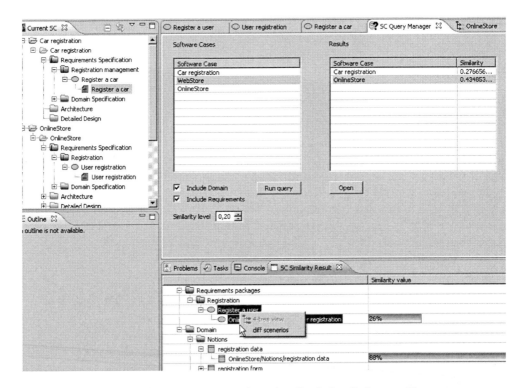

Figure 11.10: ReDSeeDS Engine screenshot detail of the Software Case query manager. Taken from the ReDSeeDS Engine presentations on http://www.redseeds.eu.

11.3 Using Traceability for Finding Reusable Artifacts

In the following, a description of the comprehensive traceability solution in the ReD-SeeDS project is given. Sections 11.3.1 to 11.3.6 structure it in accordance with the six traceability-related activities.

11.3.1 Definition

The SCL comprises a variety of intra-level and inter-level traceability relationship types. While the intra-level relationship types are specified by the schemas of the SCL's sub-languages, i.e., RSL, UML, and Java, the inter-level types are contained in the SCLKernel package.

With respect to intra-level traceability, the RSL provides eight relationship types for connecting Requirements: ConflictsWith, Constrains, DependsOn, DerivesFrom, Elaborates, IsSimilarTo, MakesPossible, and Operationalizes (see Figure 11.4). UML Dependencys, besides their function as inter-level relationship type connecting architecture and detailed design models (see below), can also be used for modeling intra-level traceability relationships within the architecture or detailed design. The Java schema does not include explicit traceability relationship types. However, generalization relationships between classes or call relationships between methods may serve as implicit traceability relationships if required by particular applications.

Concerning inter-level relationship types, IsAllocatedTo and Satisfies relationships connect UML NamedElements in a Software Case's architecture to Requirements. Dependencys, adopted from UML, interrelate architecture and design NamedElements. Finally, Implements relationship types link JavaElements to NamedElements in the design model. These relationship types are depicted in Figure 11.6.

Since the classes NamedElement and JavaElement rank high in the generalization hierarchy of the UML and Java schemas, i.e., they are generalizations of most concepts in the UML schema and all classes in the Java schema, Dependency and Implements inter-level traceability relationships can connect to virtually any architecture, design, or code element.

Three SCL traceability relationship types are presented in detail here: DependsOn, Satisfies, and Implements. Tables 11.1, 11.2, and 11.3 show the respective instantiation of the TRTT. As traceability relationships in ReDSeeDS Software Cases mainly serve the identification of reusable artifacts, they do not feature any constraints or impact designators. For reasons of simplicity and comprehensibility, the used examples present

Property	Value
Name	DependsOn
Description	A DependsOn relationship expresses that the implementation of the target Requirement is a prerequisite for the implementation of the source Requirement.
Schema fragment	*see Figure 11.4*
Attributes	uid :String – an ID which is unique within the scope of the current Software Cases and the completed Software Cases recorded in a Software Case repository
Examples	**FunctionalRequirement**: Customers must be able to make online reservations. *DependsOn* **FunctionalRequirement**: The reservation system must provide a web interface.

Table 11.1: TRTT instantiation for DependsOn.

Property	Value
Name	Satisfies
Description	A Satisfies relationship indicates that the source NamedElement, which is part of a Software Case's architecture, has been ensured to fulfill the target Requirement. If a generated architecture NamedElement which is connected to the originating Requirement via an IsAllocatedTo relationship has been modified manually, recording an additional Satisfies relationship marks that the NamedElement has been inspected to be suitable for fulfilling the Requirement.
Schema fragment	*see Figure 11.6*
Attributes	uid :String – an ID which is unique within the scope of the current Software Cases and the completed Software Cases recorded in a Software Case repository
	isGenerated :Boolean – indicates whether an instance of this relationship type was generated in the course of a model transformation or has been installed manually
Examples	**Component** (subclass of NamedElement): ReservationWebInterface *Satisfies* **FunctionalRequirement**: The reservation system must provide a web interface.

Table 11.2: TRTT instantiation for Satisfies.

the involved traced entities in a textual form. Refer to Appendix A.1 for a complete overview of the SCL's relationship types.

11.3.2 Identification

The identification of the inter-level traceability relationships IsAllocatedTo, Dependency, and Implements is conducted automatically along with the transformations from requirements to architecture, from architecture to detailed design, and from detailed design to source code, respectively. In [Kal07a], the involved MOLA transformation pro-

Property	Value
Name	Implements
Description	An Implements relationship indicates that the source JavaElement is responsible for the implementation of the target NamedElement in a Software Case's detailed design model.
Schema fragment	*see Figure 11.6*
Attributes	uid :String – an ID which is unique within the scope of the current Software Cases and the completed Software Cases recorded in a Software Case repository
	isGenerated :Boolean – indicates whether an instance of this relationship type was generated in the course of a model transformation or has been installed manually
Examples	**Class** (subclass of JavaElement): Reservation
	Satisfies
	Component (subclass of NamedElement): Reservation

Table 11.3: TRTT instantiation for Implements.

grams are explained in detail. Naturally, these relationship types, as well as the Satisfies type, may also be created manually.

The intra-level traceability relationships provided by the RSL and UML are intended to be identified purely manually in the course of specifying a Software Case's requirements or modeling its architecture and detailed design. With respect to Java source code, users are not supposed to directly modify the code's graph representation. Instead, it is envisioned that using a suitable parsing mechanism, changes to the (textual) source code are automatically adopted by the graph.

11.3.3 Recording

As explained in Section 11.2, the ReDSeeDS Engine represents Software Cases, including traceability information, as TGraphs conforming to the SCL schema. As such, they are recorded using the JGraLab API.

11.3.4 Retrieval

To find potentially reusable elements of a completed Software Case, based on a set of SCL Requirements that have been identified to be similar to those of a current Case, the *Slice* pattern on the basis of GReQL's slice function [Ebe10] is employed. Consequently, that set of Requirements serves as starting vertex set for the slice computation.

Concerning the regular path expression that is taken as parameter, three different configurations are distinguished: *minimal slice*, *maximal slice*, and *ideal slice* [Amb08]. The corresponding path expressions are referred to as rpe_{min}, rpe_{max}, and rpe_{ideal}, respectively.

For computing a minimal slice, only intra-level traceability relationships on the requirements specification level and inter-level traceability relationships are traversed. Listing 11.1 shows the regular path expression. Since the SCL represents relationship types as vertex classes, two GReQL simple path expressions have to be sequenced in order to traverse one traceability relationship.

Listing 11.1: rpe_{min} regular path expression.

```
1   rpe_min = (<---{HasTargetRequirement}
2                 &{Constrains,DerivesFrom,Elaborates,IsSimilarTo,MakesPossible,Operationalizes}
3                 --->{HasSourceRequirement}
4               | <---{HasSourceRequirement}&{DependsOn,IsSimilarTo}--->{HasTargetRequirement}
5             )*
6             [<---{HasAllocated}--->{HasNamedElement} | <---{HasSatisfied}--->{HasSatisfying}
7               [<---{HasClient}--->{HasSupplier}
8                 [<---{HasImplemented}--->{HasImplementing}]]
9             ]
10            ]
```

Starting from the set of similar requirements, intra-level traceability relationship types are traversed to reach interrelated requirements (lines 1–5). For most relationship types, except IsSimilarTo, it is reasonable to consider them in one specific direction only, dependent on their intended semantics. For example, the requirement that *constrains* or *operationalizes* some other requirement should be added to the slice, but not vice versa. In line 6, IsAllocatedTo and Satisfies relationships are traversed in order to include automatically or manually created architecture elements. With the traversal of UML Dependencys in line 7, elements of the detailed design model are incorporated. Finally, by traversing Implements relationships, line 8 is concerned with the inclusion of source code fragments. Note the usage of brackets denoting optional expression parts. Without them, only graph elements which lie on a path starting at some requirement and ending at a code element could be included in the slice. For instance, not yet implemented detailed design elements would not be considered.

A maximal slice considers any connection between traced entities, effectively resulting in the usage of <->* as path expression (see Listing 11.2).

Listing 11.2: rpe_{max} regular path expression.

```
1   rpe_max = <->*
```

In most cases, however, such a slice will correspond to the whole Software Case, for any software artifact is supposed to be somehow interrelated to another artifact.

Similar to minimal slices, ideal slices also consider intra-level traceability relationships between requirements and inter-level relationships. Furthermore, intra-level relationships on the architecture, design, and code levels are traversed. These include implicit relationships, such as nestings or generalizations, as well as explicit ones. Consequently, ideal slices ensure that the set of reused software artifacts constitutes a self-contained subsystem. See Listing 11.3 for the corresponding path expression.

Listing 11.3: rpe_{ideal} regular path expression.

```
1   rpeideal = (<−−{HasTargetRequirement}
2                 &{Constrains,DerivesFrom,Elaborates,IsSimilarTo,MakesPossible,Operationalizes}
3                 −−>{HasSourceRequirement}
4              | <−−{HasSourceRequirement}&{DependsOn,IsSimilarTo}−−>{HasTargetRequirement}
5            )*
6            [(<−−{HasAllocated}−−>{HasNamedElement} | <−−{HasSatisfied}−−>{HasSatisfying})
7             (<>−− | <−−{HasClient}−−>{HasSupplier}
8              | <>−−{Generalization,ElementImport,PackageImport}−−>)*
9             [<−−{HasClient}−−>{HasSupplier}
10              (<>−− | <−−{HasClient}−−>{HasSupplier}
11               | <>−−{Generalization,ElementImport,PackageImport}−−>)*
12             [<−−{HasImplemented}−−>{HasImplementing}]
13               <−−*
14            ]
15           ]
```

Compared to rpe_{min}, rpe_{ideal} adds lines 7–8, 10–11, and 13. In lines 7–8 and 10–11, intra-level traceability relationships on the architecture and design levels are taken into account, respectively. They comprise nesting relationships, represented by edges with aggregation semantics, Dependencys, Generalizations, ElementImport, and PackageImport relationships. As a generalized element inherits the properties of its generalization, the latter has to be included by a self-contained ideal slice. Thus, the given path expression traverses Generalizations from the specific to the general element. Importing some element in UML allows for referencing them without using their fully qualified name. Therefore, ElementImport and PackageImport relationships are strong indicators for possible dependencies. Line 13 includes nesting and dependency relationships on the source code level. Since in the Java subschema, nested or dependent elements are the sources for these relationships, the direction of traversal is from target to source.

11.3.5 Utilization

Users of the ReDSeeDS Engine may specify which type of slice is to be computed. The results are displayed in the *four-tree view*, illustrated in the upper right of Figure 11.11). The four-tree view juxtaposes the elements of the four abstraction levels as

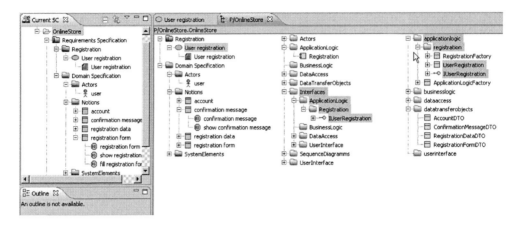

Figure 11.11: ReDSeeDS Engine screenshot detail of a slice in the 4-tree view. Taken from the ReDSeeDS Engine presentations on `http://www.redseeds.eu`.

trees. The trees' structure is based on nesting relationships and ignores all other intra-level crosslinks. The contents of a slice are highlighted. Recall that the ReDSeeDS Engine prototype does not include support for source code, so the screenshot shows three trees only.

The contents of the slice can be merged with a current Software Case. Potential conflicts, e.g., because of duplicate names, may be resolved using a special dialog (see Figure 11.12).

11.3.6 Maintenance

With the current ReDSeeDS Engine prototype, traceability relationships are maintained manually.

In future releases, automatic support for the maintenance of traceability information in the context of transformation reexecution is envisioned. Once a transformation is reexecuted, possibly due to a modification to the source model, manual changes to the previously generated transformation results have to be handled. Users should be able to decide if a manually changed element shall be overwritten by the reexecution. Traceability relationships between non-overwritten elements and the transformation source are candidates for maintenance, for it needs to be checked if they are still valid subsequent to the modification of the source.

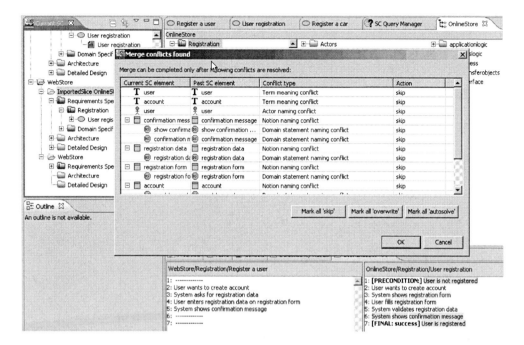

Figure 11.12: ReDSeeDS Engine screenshot detail of the merge conflicts dialog. Taken from the ReDSeeDS Engine presentations on `http://www.redseeds.eu`.

12 Validation of Business Process Model Refinements

In service-oriented software development, the functionality of software systems is implemented by the reuse and proper composition of software services [Cer05]. To develop software support for business processes, potentially high-level models of these processes have to be refined to fine-grained, more operational models whose individual tasks can be directly mapped to existing services.

In the $MOST^1$ project, one case study was concerned with the conception and implementation of tools that aid analysts and developers in the correct refinement of business processes. One possibility for achieving this was to use traceability information[2] [Sch10b].

Section 12.1 describes the problems the business process model refinement case study is confronted with. Section 12.2 introduces the *MOST Workbench*, a tool suite that includes a component for aiding developers in refining business processes. Section 12.3 elaborates on the implementation of a traceability solution for ensuring correct refinement and its integration in the process refinement component of the MOST Workbench.

12.1 Refining Business Process Models

The stepwise refinement of high-level business process models into more detailed models was pursued in a case study of the MOST project, with the goal to finally map tasks of a sufficiently fine-grained process model to existing software services. Such a refinement results in a chain of increasingly fine-grained process models, shortly referred to as *refinement chain* in the following. The mapping of tasks to services, which are represented in so-called *component models*, is called *grounding*.

Section 12.1.1 introduces the *Business Process Modeling Notation* (*BPMN*) [Obj11]. It is employed to specify process models in refinement chains as well as component models.

---

[1] http://www.most-project.eu
[2] Another investigated technique was based on ontology reasoning (see [Ren09]).

Building on the examples in that section, Section 12.1.2 defines the constraints that have to be obeyed for a refinement chain and a grounding to be consistent.

12.1.1 The Business Process Modeling Notation

As its name implies, BPMN was designed for the description of business processes. While BPMN offers a variety of language concepts, such as data objects, different process participants, or messages passed between them, the MOST case study made use of a limited selection of BPMN elements only. Table 12.1 shortly describes them.

Element name	Description	Symbol
Task	A task is an activity that is usually performed by an end-user and/or applications.	Name
Start event	A start event indicates the start of a process.	
End event	An end event ends the flow of a process.	
Exclusive gateway	An exclusive gateway creates or merges alternative flows. At an exclusive gateway, the control flow can only take one of the outgoing paths.	
Parallel gateway	A parallel gateway creates or synchronizes parallel flows. Tasks in parallel flows can be performed simultaneously.	
Sequence flow	A sequence flow defines the chronological order of execution of flow elements, e.g., tasks, events, and gateways. A sequence flow may define a condition expression on the state of the process, indicating that the path starting with that sequence flow can only be taken if the expression evaluates to true. The configuration of sequence flows connecting the various tasks, events, and gateways of a process or component model specifies the control flow of the model.	

Table 12.1: Overview of BPMN elements used in the context of the MOST business process refinement case study. Adapted from [Obj11].

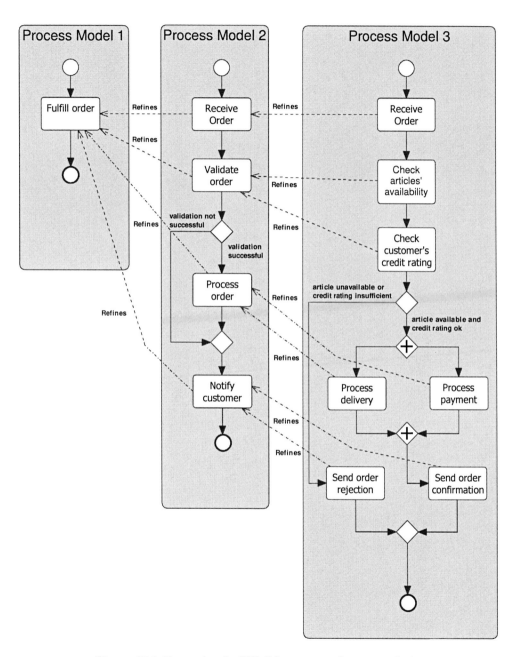

Figure 12.1: Example of a BPMN process refinement chain.

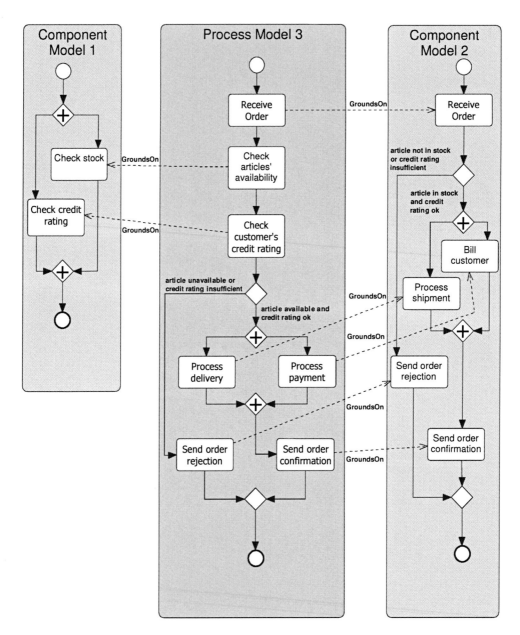

Figure 12.2: Example of a BPMN process grounding.

The behavior of BPMN process models is based on *token semantics*, comparable to *UML activity diagrams* [Obj10c], for instance. At the occurrence of the start event, a token is generated and passed to the target element of the outgoing sequence flow. If the token arrives at a task, that task is executed. Upon the completion of the task, the token traverses further via the task's outgoing sequence flow. Exclusive gateways accept exactly one token on one of their incoming sequence flows and pass the token to exactly one of their outgoing sequence flows. Parallel gateways expect one token on every incoming sequence flow before they put a token on every outgoing sequence flow. The order of execution in parallel flows is arbitrary. Finally, the end event consumes an incoming token and the flow through the process is ended. For the sake of simplicity, it is assumed here that only gateways may possess more than one incoming or outgoing sequence flow.

Figure 12.1 shows an example of a process model refinement chain. The single task Fulfill order in *Process Model 1* is first refined to the four tasks Receive order, Validate order, Process order, and Notify customer in *Process Model 2*. The execution of Process order may be skipped, depending on the outcome of the validation. In *Process Model 3*, Receive Order is adopted without further decomposition, i.e., there is a task of the same name refining Receive Order in *Process Model 3*. Validate order is decomposed to Check articles' availability and Check customer's credit rating, which are to be performed consecutively. In contrast, Process delivery and Process payment, as refinements of Process order, can be performed in parallel. Finally, Notify customer is refined to Send order rejection and Send order confirmation. Note, that the Refines and GroundsOn relationships are not inherent to the OMG's original BPMN specification, but have been introduced in the context of this case study.

According to the token semantics, one possible execution sequence of the tasks in *Process Model 3* is: Receive order → Check articles' availability → Check customer's credit rating → Process payment → Process delivery → Send order confirmation.

Component models specified in BPMN use tasks for representing software services. The structure of the BPMN model with its usage of sequence flows and gateways prescribes possible orders of service execution. In Figure 12.2, the tasks in *Process Model 3* are grounded on services in *Component Model 1* and *Component Model 2*. Note, that *Component Model 1* allows for a parallelization of the order validation tasks, whereas they are strictly sequenced in *Process Model 3*. *Component Model 2* facilitates order reception, shipment, payment, and customer notification, with a sequence flow configuration similar to *Process Model 3*.

12.1.2 Constraints on Process Refinement Chains and Groundings

Figures 12.1 and 12.2 show a *consistent* process refinement and grounding, respectively. For a process refinement chain to be valid, various constraints have to be obeyed, e.g.:

- Two different tasks of one process model may not refine tasks belonging to two different process models.

- Every task in a process model must either be refined by a task of the subsequent process model in the refinement chain or be grounded to a service in a component model.

- Every task in a process model may only refine at most one other task of the preceding process model.

- Every task in a process model may only be grounded on at most one service of a component model.

In addition, a given process model has to adhere to further, more complex constraints, adopting the notion of *maximum execution set semantics* [Wyn01]. They are imposed by the control flow of the process model's predecessor in the refinement chain, and, if the model's tasks are grounded, by the control flow of the respective component model. A formalization of these constraints, taken from [Ren09], is shown below. For the sake of clarity, the names of the tasks in the examples illustrating the formalization are abbreviated according to Table 12.2.

First, Definition 9 specifies the notion of *task execution sequence*.

DEFINITION 9 (TASK EXECUTION SEQUENCE)

A task execution sequence is one of possibly several orders in which the tasks of a given BPMN model can be executed according to the BPMN token semantics.

Examples for task execution sequences are $< ABD >$ for *Process Model 2* or $< SWVY >$ for *Component Model 2*.

Making use of the definition of task execution sequences, consistent refinement between two consecutive process models in a refinement chain is specified by Definition 10.

Task in Process Model 2	Symbol	Task in Process Model 3	Symbol	Task in Component Models 1 and 2	Symbol
Receive order	A	Receive order	a	Receive order	S
Validate order	B	Check articles' availability	b_1	Check stock	T
		Check customer's credit rating	b_2	Check credit rating	U
Process order	C	Process delivery	c_1	Process shipment	V
		Process payment	c_2	Bill customer	W
Notify customer	D	Send order rejection	d_1	Send order rejection	X
		Send order confirmation	d_2	Send order confirmation	Y

Table 12.2: Abbreviation of task names.

DEFINITION 10 (CONSISTENT REFINEMENT)

Let

- P be a BPMN process model in a refinement chain,

- Q be the BPMN process model succeeding P in the refinement chain, i.e., every task in Q refines some task in P,

- TES_P be the set of possible task execution sequences in P,

- TES_Q be the set of possible task execution sequences in Q.

Q consistently refines P iff, after performing the following transformations on TES_Q, $TES_Q \subseteq TES_P$.

- *Renaming*: Every task in a task execution sequence *tes* $\in TES_Q$ is renamed to the task it refines.

- *Compaction*: Every continuous sequence of tasks with the same name in some *tes* $\in TES_Q$ is replaced by a single task of that name.

As an example, consider the set of possible task execution sequences of *Process Model 3*:

$$TES_{Process\ Model\ 3} = \{< ab_1b_2c_1c_2d_2 >, < ab_1b_2c_2c_1d_2 >, < ab_1b_2d_1 >\}$$

Renaming and compaction lead to the following sets:

$$\begin{aligned} TES_{Process\ Model\ 3,\ renamed} &= \{< ABBCCD >, < ABBCCD >, < ABBD >\} \\ &= \{< ABBCCD >, < ABBD >\} \\ TES_{Process\ Model\ 3,\ renamed\ and\ compacted} &= \{< ABCD >, < ABD >\} \end{aligned}$$

Finally, it can be shown that the refinement of *Process Model 2* by *Process Model 3* is consistent:

$$TES_{Process\ Model\ 3,\ renamed\ and\ compacted} \subseteq TES_{Process\ Model\ 2} = \{< ABCD >, < ABD >\}$$

Concerning a process model in the refinement chain and a component model, consistent grounding is specified by Definition 11.

DEFINITION 11 (CONSISTENT GROUNDING)

Let

- C be a component model represented in BPMN,

- P be a BPMN process model in a refinement chain, where every task in P grounds on some task in C,

- TES_C be the set of possible task execution sequences in C,

- TES_P be the set of possible task execution sequences in P.

P consistently grounds on C iff, after performing the following transformations on TES_P and TES_C, $TES_P \subseteq TES_C$.

- *Renaming*: Every task in a task execution sequence $tes \in TES_P$ is renamed to the task it grounds on.

- *Reduction*: Every task in some $tes \in TES_P$ that does not ground on a task in C is removed from tes.

Renaming the tasks in $TES_{Process\ Model\ 3}$ to the tasks they ground on yields:

$$TES_{Process\ Model\ 3,\ renamed} = \{< STUVWY >, < STUWVY >, < STUX >\}$$

Reducing the tasks in $TES_{Process\ Model\ 3,\ renamed}$ to those that are contained in *Component Model 2* results in:

$$TES_{Process\ Model\ 3,\ renamed\ and\ reduced} \quad = \quad \{< SVWY >, < SWVY >, < SX >\}$$

Now it becomes evident that *Process Model 3* consistently grounds on *Component Model 2*:

$$TES_{Process\ Model\ 3,\ renamed\ and\ reduced} \quad \subseteq \quad TES_{Component\ Model\ 2}$$
$$= \{< SVWY >, < SWVY >, < SX >\}$$

12.2 The *MOST Workbench*: Tool Support for Process Model Refinement

In the MOST project, the *MOST Workbench* [Wen10] has been developed as an integrated tool environment for the project's various case studies. As such, it also includes a component dedicated to the business process refinement case study: the *BPM Tool*.

Section 12.2.1 gives some details on the technological background of the MOST Workbench and the BPM Tool. Subsequently, Section 12.2.2 describes special services offered by the BPM Tool.

12.2.1 The ADOxx Metamodeling Platform

The MOST Workbench is based on the *ADOxx metamodeling platform*[3] of the BOC Group. Employing product line engineering, various modeling tools have been developed using ADOxx, with the probably best-known being *ADONIS*, a business process management tool [Jun00]. The following overview of the ADOxx platform is taken and adapted from [Sch10b].

ADOxx provides a *platform kernel* and so-called *platform mechanisms*. The kernel provides key features required by any derived product, such as meta model libraries, model repositories, or security management. Mechanisms represent components such as model editors, model comparison modules, and import/export facilities, which can be reused by products if needed. The BPM Tool adopts ADOxx model editing and analysis mechanisms.

---

[3]ADOxx® is a registered trademark of the BOC Group, http://www.boc-group.com.

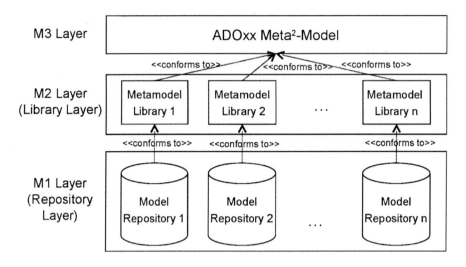

Figure 12.3: The ADOxx metamodeling hierarchy. Taken from [Sch10b].

With respect to metamodeling, the ADOxx platform implements a meta-hierarchy similar to *MOF* [Obj06], *EMF* [Ste08], or the *TGraph approach* [Ebe08] (see Section 8.1). The meta-meta model, referred to as *ADOxx Meta²-Model* here, resides on the M3 level. Apart from some ADOxx-specific concepts, it features the "expected" elements, such as Classes, Relation Classes, or Attributes. Thus, it is comparable to the grUML meta schema, for instance. On the M2 level, so-called *libraries* contain the meta models used by a specific product derived from the ADOxx platform. *Model repositories* on the M1 level are configured by the libraries, i.e., each model element in a model repository conforms to an element of the respective library. An overview of the meta-hierarchy of ADOxx is depicted in Figure 12.3.

The BPM Tool uses a product-specific BPMN meta model, of which an excerpt is shown in Figure 12.4. With Task, Event, and Gateway, the excerpt features the BPMN concepts employed by the business process refinement case study. Note, that the enumerations GatewayType and EventType also contain literals for gateway and event types not used in the case study. All process model elements belong to an instance of BPMNModel. The value of its attribute isComponentModel denotes whether the BPMNModel is a process model in a refinement chain or a component model. The meta model is complemented by the Refines and GroundsOn Relation Classes which have been introduced for representing the refinement and grounding relationships between BPMN tasks, respectively.

Due to the similarity of the ADOxx Meta^2-Model to the grUML meta schema, it was possible to implement an adapter for integrating the JGraLab library (see Section 8.1) with ADOxx. This way, the BPMN meta model can act as grUML schema, and BPMN refinement chains together with relevant component models may be treated as a single graph conforming to that schema. Consequently, for effective constraint checking as well as impact and origin analysis, the models can be queried using GReQL [Ebe10].

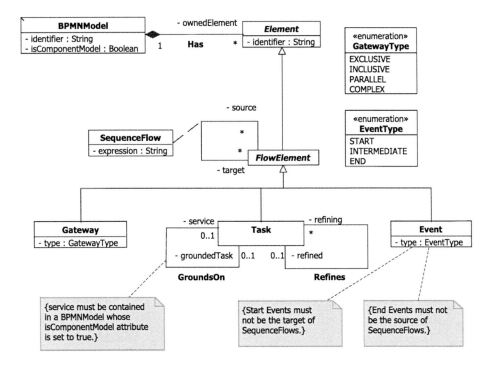

Figure 12.4: Excerpt of the BPMN meta model used by the MOST Workbench.

12.2.2 Services of the BPM Tool

The BPM Tool offers three services specially tailored to the business process refinement case study [Ziv10]:

- *Process guidance*: The BPM Tool infers possible next steps in the workflow of business process modeling, refinement, and grounding. Thus, the tool actively guides its users through the process of creating and changing process models.

191

- *Consistency guidance*: The constraints introduced in Section 12.1.2 are monitored by the BPM tool to ensure correct refinement and grounding of business process models. Constraint violations are reported so that users can resolve them.

- *Impact and origin analysis*: The BPM tool allows for retrieval conforming to the *Slice* pattern for facilitating impact and origin analysis (see Section 7.1). Given a specific task, its refining and refined tasks as well as the grounded-on services can be determined.

Process guidance is facilitated by reasoning on a special guidance ontology that integrates knowledge on the workflow with the status of the currently edited business process models [Bar11]. The inferred actions that can be performed as next steps in the workflow are proposed to the user.

For consistency guidance, an ontology reasoning-based [Ren09] as well as a graph querying-based solution [Sch10b] have been investigated. The latter ensures consistent refinement and grounding by formulating constraints on the structure of a process model when compared to its predecessor in the refinement chain or of a component model, respectively. Although both approaches to consistency guidance yield similar results [Sch09b], the final BPM Tool prototype implements the reasoning-based approach, for it turned out to be better maintainable and adaptable to changed definitions of consistency.

Navigation and visualization of traceability information for impact and origin analysis is supported by special extensions to the user interface (see also Section 12.3).

12.3 Using Traceability for Consistent Process Model Refinement

This section describes the implementation of a traceability solution for supporting business process model refinement. Each of the following Sections 12.3.1 to 12.3.6 is concerned with one of the six traceability-related activities. The instantiation does not only cope with impact and origin analysis, but, as an alternative to the reasoning-based solution to consistency guidance, also formulates constraints that ensure correct refinement and grounding.

12.3.1 Definition

To facilitate consistency guidance, impact analysis, and origin analysis, it is necessary to treat the Refines and GroundsOn Relation Classes as traceability relationship types.

Property	Value
Name	Refines
Description	A Refines relationship maps a refining Task to its refined Task in the preceding process model in the refinement chain.
Schema fragment	*see Figure 12.4*

Constraints	*Message*:
	    Every Task in a process model must either be refined by a Task of the subsequent process model in the refinement chain or be grounded to a Task in a component model.;
	Predicate query:
	    forall t:V{Task},
	        count(t <--{Has}&{ @ isComponentModel = false}) = 1 @
	        inDegree{Refines}(t) = 1 **xor** outDegree{GroundsOn}(t) = 1;
	Offending elements query:
	    from t:V{Task}
	    with count(t <--{Has}&{ @ isComponentModel = false}) = 1
	        and not (inDegree{Refines}(t) = 1 **xor** outDegree{GroundsOn}(t) = 1)
	    report t **end**

Examples	*see Figure 12.1*

Table 12.3: TRTT instantiation for Refines.

Tables 12.3 and 12.4 show the instantiated TRTT for the two types. For reasons of clarity, only an excerpt of the entire set of relationship type constraints required for preserving refinement and grounding correctness can be shown here. A complete overview can be found in Appendix A.2. The constraints have been validated against a test suite of refinement chains [Sch09b].

12.3.2 Identification

The identification of Refines and GroundsOn traceability relationships in the BPM Tool is done manually, as business process refinement is a cognitive design task that cannot be automated. As users create a new BPMN task, they can create relationships to other tasks in the *notebook*, a special view that allows to edit the properties of a selected model element. In the screenshot detail in Figure 12.5, a Refines relationship is being created from the Task Interview Applicant to the Task Select Applicant.

12.3.3 Recording

As explained in Section 12.2.1, Refines and GroundsOn are modeled as concepts of an ADOxx BPMN meta model whose instances are held in the BPM Tool's model repos-

Property	Value
Name	GroundsOn
Description	A GroundsOn relationship maps a Task in a process model in a refinement chain to the component model Task it is grounded on.
Schema fragment	(see Figure 12.4)

Constraints	*Message*:
	     Every Task in a process model of a refinement chain may only
	     be grounded on at most one Task in a component model.;
	 Predicate query:
	     forall t:V{Task},
	         count(t <--{Has}&{ @ isComponentModel = false}) = 1 @
	         outDegree{GroundsOn}(t) < 2;
	 Offending elements query:
	     from t:V{Task}
	     with count(t <--{Has}&{ @ isComponentModel = false}) = 1
	     and not outDegree{GroundsOn}(t) < 2
	     report t **end**

Examples	*see Figure 12.2*

Table 12.4: TRTT instantiation for GroundsOn.

itory. For the purpose of retrieval, the traceability relationships and the traced entities are treated as edges and vertices of a TGraph that can be queried using GReQL.

12.3.4 Retrieval

To perform impact and origin analysis, GReQL's slice function is used for querying conforming to the Slice pattern. In this case, the function takes a specific BPMN task in the refinement chain and the regular path expressions <--{Refines}*, -->{Refines}*, or -->{GroundsOn} as parameters.

12.3.5 Utilization

For consistency guidance, the predicate queries of the constraints associated with the Refines and GroundsOn traceability relationship types have to be evaluated in specific time intervals or in conjunction with suitable actions, e.g, when the refinement chain is saved. Then, the model elements determined by the concerned offending elements queries are presented to the user.

The results of slice function applications for impact and origin analysis are visualized in a tree-like view.

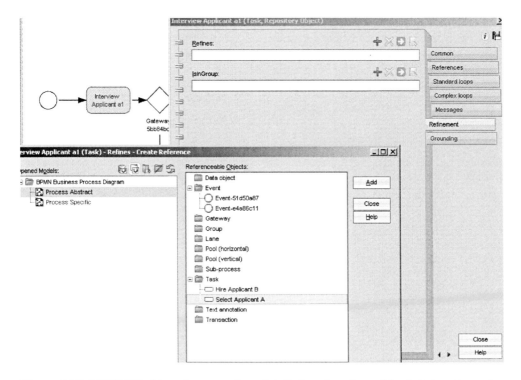

Figure 12.5: MOST Workbench screenshot detail showing the *notebook*. Taken from the "BPMN Tool" screencast on http://www.redseeds.eu.

12.3.6 Maintenance

Similar to their identification, maintenance of Refines and GroundsOn traceability relationships has to be performed manually by editing a BPMN task's properties in its notebook. However, users are hinted at invalid refinements and groundings in the context of consistency guidance, i.e., there is a certain degree of automatic assistance.

13 Support of Requirements Management

In the context of the MOST project, an ontology for supporting requirements management, including requirements traceability had been developed (henceforth referred to as the *Requirements Ontology*) [Sie11]. To allow for its usage in practice, the *OntoRT* Eclipse plug-in has been prototypically developed around the Requirements Ontology, thus complementing the well-established software development environment with requirements management and traceability features. OntoRT implements the generic traceability concepts presented in Chapters 6 and 7 on the basis of the *OWL* [Mot09b] technological space, as specified in Chapter 10.

Section 13.1 introduces the challenges and tasks associated with requirements management, especially concerning requirements traceability, which have led to the development of the Requirements Ontology. Section 13.2 describes the Requirements Ontology and gives an overview of OntoRT. In Section 13.3, OntoRT's traceability features are explained in more detail.

13.1 Requirements Management Challenges and Tasks

The requirements specification of a software system is subject to constant change in the course of its development process. The reasons for this change are manifold: they range from shifted stakeholder interests to a late perception of limitations of the employed implementation technologies. The arising need for controlled handling of changes, together with other requirements-related challenges, e.g., the analysis of requirements, the handling of impending risks, or the traceability to other software artifacts, leads to *requirements management*.

Requirements management forms the basis for activities such as change management, risk management, and requirements traceability [Hoo08]. The successful accomplishment of these activities relies on the possibility to perform the following tasks, adapted and extended from [Sie11]:

- the structured recording of requirements themselves together with important attributes, including their cost, priority, and state of implementation,

- the recording of traceability relationships between requirements, e.g., to denote dependencies,

- the recording of traceability relationships to non-requirement entities, especially risks, stakeholders, and artifacts that implement of requirements,

- the checking of the requirements specification's consistency,

- the checking of the requirements specification's completeness, and

- the effective retrieval of traceability information in order to perform elementary analyses (see Section 7.1).

13.2 Ontology-Based Requirements Management in Eclipse

To provide a data structure that is capable of supporting the requirements management-related challenges and tasks presented in Section 13.1, the Requirements Ontology has been developed at the Dresden University of Technology. Besides the reasoning-based checking of the completeness and consistency of requirements specifications, the ontology is also employed for implementing requirements traceability in the context of the well-established software development environment Eclipse[1]. To this end, it has been extended with concepts that represent Eclipse-specific artifacts of the later stages of software development.

The extended Requirements Ontology is used by *OntoRT*, an Eclipse plug-in that allows for the recording and maintenance of requirements, for relating them to other software development artifacts via traceability relationships, and for analyzing the recorded traceability information.

In the following, Section 13.2.1 details the structure of the Requirements Ontology. Section 13.2.2 describes the OntoRT plug-in, including a general overview of its features and an explanation of how the Requirements Ontology has been integrated.

13.2.1 The Requirements Ontology

The OWL-based Requirements Ontology offers various concepts for representing entities on the requirements abstraction level and Eclipse-specific software artifacts. Figure 13.1 shows an excerpt of the ontology's class hierarchy. At the top level, the Requirements Ontology distinguishes, among others, between ro:Stakeholders[2], ro:Artifacts, and

---

[1] http://www.eclipse.org
[2] ro is used as prefix for the Requirement Ontology.

198

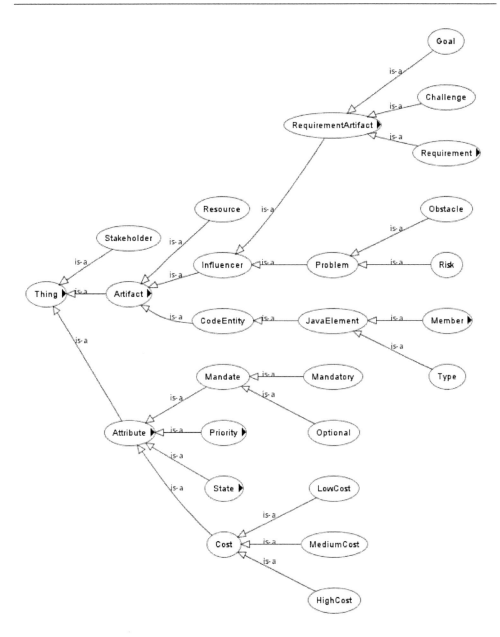

Figure 13.1: Excerpt of the Requirements Ontology's class hierarchy.

ro:Attributes. Note, that the arrows inside the ovals denote the existence of further sub-classes that are not displayed. Subclasses of ro:Artifact are ro:Influencer, ro:Resource, and ro:CodeEntity. ro:Influencers are entities on the requirements specification level, in-cluding ro:Requirements themselves, as well as ro:Goals, ro:Challenges, ro:Obstacles, and ro:Risks. ro:Resource is a concept originating from Eclipse, comprising projects, folders, and files. Finally, ro:CodeEntity encompasses more fine-grained source code elements. Examples are Java ro:Types, including classes, and ro:Members of Java classes, such as ro:Fields and ro:Methods (not displayed).

Specializations of ro:Attribute are ro:Mandate, ro:Priority, ro:State, or ro:Cost, for instance. To assign attributes to an individual, that individual is declared as an instance of the desired subclass of ro:Attribute.

Furthermore, the Requirements Ontology defines a set of intra-level and inter-level traceability relationship types, described in Section 13.3.1.

The Requirements Ontology is complemented by a set of rules for checking the com-pleteness and consistency of recorded requirements. These rules are implemented as SPARQL queries and OWL axioms. The results of the checks have to be interpreted so that suitable follow-up actions can be recommended to the users.

13.2.2 OntoRT

OntoRT, short for *Ontology-based Requirements Traceability*, is the prototype of an Eclipse plug-in that extends the software development environment with the possibility to manage requirements and inter-relate them to Eclipse projects, files, or even more fine-grained source code entities such as Java methods and fields.

The plug-in allows to enable (and subsequently disable) requirements management and traceability for specific projects. Effectively, enabling assigns a blank copy of the Requirements Ontology, i.e., without any asserted knowledge, to the selected project. However, such an assignment does not imply that the respective Requirements On-tology copy may only be used to record information on a single project. Rather, it is possible to create traceability relationships to any entity in the workspace. Thus, on the one hand, it is thinkable to maintain the requirements and traceability information for a set of inter-related projects in a single "master" project. On the other hand, if the projects in a workspace are independent of each other, requirements traceability could be enabled for every single one.

Figure 13.2 depicts a screenshot detail of the Eclipse workbench. The *Package Explorer* shows two projects: "HiringSystem" and "SocialNetwork". The bullet adorning "Hir-

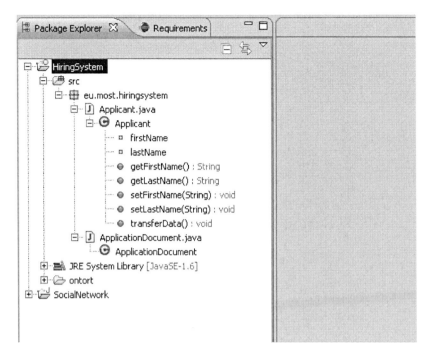

Figure 13.2: Eclipse project with the requirements traceability nature.

ingSystem" indicates that requirements management and traceability has been enabled for that project.

For adding, modifying, and deleting requirements, OntoRT adds the dedicated *Requirements* view to the Eclipse workbench (see the screenshot in Figure 13.3). The *Requirements* view represents the classes of the Requirements Ontology as folders, with the subclass hierarchy reflected by the folder's nesting structure. Instances of a specific class are contained in the respective folder and are represented by icons depicting stylized documents. Besides the *Requirements* view, Figure 13.3 also depicts the *Properties* dialog that allows for changing a requirement's ID, its description, and its various attributes.

Further, traceability-related features of OntoRT are described in detail in Section 13.3.

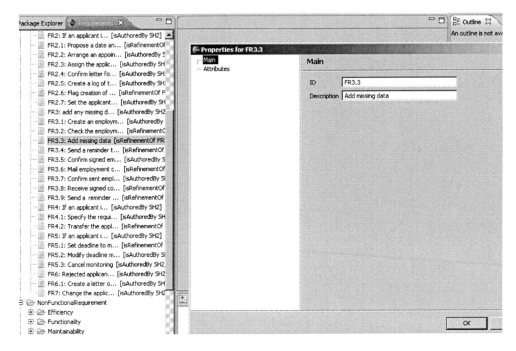

Figure 13.3: Editing requirements with OntoRT.

13.3 Establishing Traceability in Eclipse

In the following, OntoRT's implementation of a comprehensive traceability solution is described. The concept facilitates traceability of the requirements managed by OntoRT as well as traceability of other Eclipse artifacts. Sections 13.3.1 to 13.3.6 structure the description in accordance with the six traceability-related activities.

13.3.1 Definition

The Requirements Ontology predefines a variety of intra-level and inter-level traceability relationship types.

Some of the intra-level traceability relationship types on the requirements level are shown in Table 13.1. For interrelating traceable entities on the code level, i.e., Eclipse ro:Resources and ro:CodeEntitys, the intra-level relationship types ro:calls, ro:creates,

Traceability relationship type	Domain	Range
ro:isAlternativeTo, ro:isDependentOn, ro:isInConflictWith, ro:isRefinementOf, ro:isRevisionOf	ro:Requirement	ro:Requirement
ro:hasChallenge	ro:Requirement	ro:Challenge
ro:hasGoal	ro:UseCase	ro:Goal
ro:hasObstacle	ro:RequirementArtifact	ro:Obstacle
ro:hasRisk	ro:RequirementArtifact	ro:Risk
ro:isAuthoredBy	ro:Artifact	ro:Stakeholder

Table 13.1: The requirements-level traceability relationship types provided by the Requirements Ontology.

ro:derivesFrom, and ro:uses are provided. With ro:fulfills, only one single inter-level relationship type is included. Its instances are supposed to link non-requirement Eclipse entities to the requirement they fulfill.

Tables 13.2, 13.3, and 13.4 present the instantiated TRTT for three traceability relationship types: ro:isInConflictWith, ro:uses, and ro:fulfills. Refer to Appendix A.3 for the TRTT instantiations of all relationship types mentioned here. Listing A.1, showing an example instantiation of the Requirements Ontology, can also be found in the appendix.

By complementing the Eclipse *Preferences* dialog with a *Traceability* page, the OntoRT plug-in supports the modification of the traceability relationship types provided by a project-specific instance of the Requirements Ontology. It is possible to modify the predefined relationship types as well as to add new types. Figure 13.4 shows a screenshot detail of the preference page. At the top of the page, a requirements traceability-enabled project and one of its relationship types can be selected. Below, the user interface elements reflect the structure of the TRTT in order to allow for the editing of the selected relationship type's properties.

13.3.2 Identification

Traceability relationships in OntoRT can be identified either manually or automatically based on impact designators.

In Figure 13.5, the *Create Traceability Relationship from/to"* dialog used for manual identification (and maintenance, see Section 13.3.6) is depicted. It can be called by selecting the corresponding menu item in the context menu of some entity in the *Package Explorer* or *Requirements* view. The dialog allows for the creation of new traceability relationships between that entity and some other entity which is selected in the tree view on the right. Alternatively, if two entities are selected in the *Package Explorer* or *Requirements* view,

Property	Value
Name	ro:isInConflictWith
Description	An ro:isInConflictWith relationship between two ro:Requirements specifies that only one of them can be fulfilled, but not both.
Supertypes	ro:hasRequirementRelationship
Schema fragment	**Declaration(ObjectProperty(** ro:isInConflictWith **))** **ObjectPropertyDomain(** ro:isInConflictWith ro:Requirement **)** **ObjectPropertyRange(** ro:isInConflictWith ro:Requirement **)**
Attributes	ro:creationDate, ro:rationale (*modeled as annotations*)
Relational properties	symmetric
Constraints	Any two ro:Requirements that are connected by an ro:isInConflictWith relationship may not be connected by an ro:isAlternativeTo, ro:isDependentOn, ro:isRefinementOf, or ro:isRevisionOf relationship. **DisjointObjectProperties(** ro:isInConflictWith ro:isDependentOn **)** **DisjointObjectProperties(** ro:isInConflictWith ro:isRefinementOf **)** **DisjointObjectProperties(** ro:isInConflictWith ro:isRevisionOf **)**

Impact designators	If an ro:isRefinementOf relationship exists from ro:Requirement r_1 to ro:Requirement r_2, and r_2 is connected to another ro:Requirement r_3 via an ro:isInConflictWith relationship, then an ro:isInConflictWith relationship is added between r_1 and r_3.
	
	SubObjectPropertyOf(
	    ObjectPropertyChain(ro:isRefinementOf ro:isInConflictWith **)**
	    ro:isInConflictWith
	)

Examples	*see Listing A.1 in Appendix A.3*

Table 13.2: TRTT instantiation for ro:isInConflictWith.

Property	Value
Name	ro:uses
Description	An ro:uses relationship specifies that the semantics of the source ro:Resource or ro:CodeEntity depend on the semantics of the target ro:Resource or ro:CodeEntity.
Supertypes	ro:hasDesignOrCodeRelationship
Schema fragment	**Declaration(ObjectProperty(** ro:uses **))** **ObjectPropertyDomain(** ro:uses **ObjectUnionOf(** ro:Resource ro:CodeEntity **))** **ObjectPropertyRange(** ro:uses **ObjectUnionOf(** ro:Resource ro:CodeEntity **))**
Attributes	ro:creationDate, ro:rationale (*modeled as annotations*)
Examples	*see Listing A.1 in Appendix A.3*

Table 13.3: TRTT instantiation for ro:uses.

the *Create Traceability Relationship between* dialog facilitates the creation of traceability relationships between these two entities only.

Using the impact designators of traceability relationship types, which correspond to OWL axioms [Mot09b] here, additional traceability relationships can be inferred auto-

Property	Value
Name	ro:fulfills
Description	An ro:fulfills relationship indicates that the source ro:Resource or ro:CodeEntity realizes the functionality or constraint specified by the target ro:Requirement.
Supertypes	ro:hasInterLevelRelationship
Schema fragment	**Declaration(ObjectProperty(** ro:fulfills **))**
	ObjectPropertyDomain(ro:fulfills **ObjectUnionOf(** ro:ResourceCodeEntity **))**
	ObjectPropertyRange(ro:fulfills Requirement **)**
Attributes	ro:creationDate, ro:rationale (*modeled as annotations*)
Examples	*see Listing A.1* in Appendix A.3

Table 13.4: TRTT instantiation for ro:fulfills.

matically. For an example, refer to the impact designator of the ro:isInConflictWith relationship type. Note, that the user interface of the current OntoRT prototype currently does not support the invocation of this inference. Instead, external tools such as the Protégé ontology editor[3] must be used.

13.3.3 Recording

Identified traceability relationships are recorded as object property assertions within a project-specific Requirements Ontology instance. The ontology is physically recorded as an RDF/XML file.

13.3.4 Retrieval

Retrieval of traceability information in OntoRT is facilitated by the *Query Traceability Information* dialog, illustrated in Figure 13.6. Starting from a set of entities that has previously been selected in the *Package Explorer* or the *Requirements* view, queries conforming to the three traceability retrieval patterns *Existence*, *Reachable Entities*, and *Slice* can be executed. For the Existence pattern, a set of end entities has to be selected in the tree view on the dialog's right side. In the text field labeled by *Enter Path Description*, a GReQL regular path expression [Ebe10] is to be entered. It specifies the possible structures of paths by which the start and end entities have to be connected. The query results are returned in a special *Query Result* view.

The computation of query results is based on the *GReQL-SPARQL* query transformation approach presented in [Sch10a]. In a first step, the regular path expressions are used to construct GReQL queries suitable for retrieving the desired traceability information.

---

[3]http://protege.stanford.edu

205

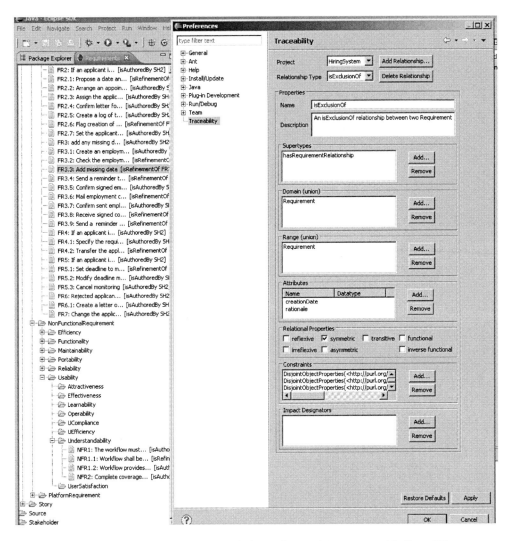

Figure 13.4: Definition of traceability relationship types with OntoRT.

Second, these GReQL queries are transformed to SPARQL queries [Pru08] which are executed on a project-specific instantiation of the Requirements Ontology. Relying on this solution, users are relieved from formulating of rather cumbersome and verbose SPARQL queries. However, due to limitations of SPARQL 1.0 (see Section 10.3, the choice of GReQL concepts is limited. For example, the usage of the Kleene star or plus is not permitted.

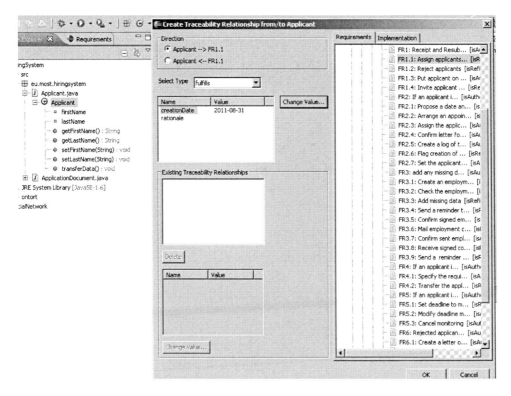

Figure 13.5: Manual identification of traceability relationships with OntoRT.

Note, that the computation of slices has not been implemented in the current OntoRT prototype.

13.3.5 Utilization

In the current OntoRT prototype, there is no utilization going beyond the visualization of traceability information to the users. As explained in the following, OntoRT presents this information in three different places.

First, the *Requirements* view displays traceability relationships incident to a specific requirement directly after that requirement's description (see the information enclosed in brackets on the left of the screenshot detail in Figure 13.4). Second, existing relationships between two entities are listed by the *Create Traceability Relationship from/to* and

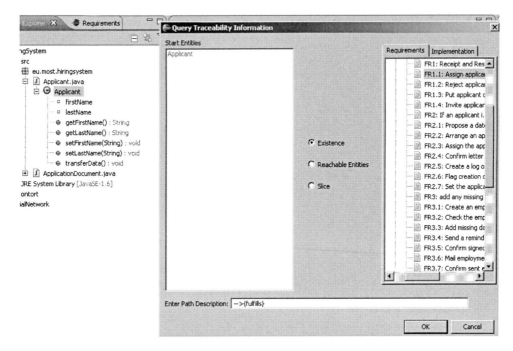

Figure 13.6: Retrieval of traceability information with OntoRT.

Create Traceability Relationship between dialogs. Finally, the results of traceability queries are listed in a *Query Result* view.

In future, the rules mentioned in Section 13.2.1 for automatically checking the completeness and consistency of the recorded requirements could be integrated. The results of these checks should then be adequately visualized.

13.3.6 Maintenance

The *Create Traceability Relationship from/to* and *Create Traceability Relationship between* dialogs introduced in Section 13.3.2 also support the maintenance of already existing traceability relationships between two entities. This includes their deletion and the change of their attribute values.

Since reasoning on the basis of OWL axioms does not allow for the retraction of knowledge from the ontology, maintenance of traceability relationships cannot be fully automated by impact designators.

14 Conclusion

In this final chapter, the results of the research work presented by this book are recapitulated and appraised, followed by an outlook on possible future research activities.

First, Section 14.1 summarizes the contents of this work. In Section 14.2, the results and gained insights are discussed and appraised against the initially defined research questions, including an overview of further contributions that are not directly attributable to a research question. Finally, Section 14.3 gives an outlook on possible actions following up this work.

14.1 Summary

Sections 14.1.1 to 14.1.4, each one dedicated to one part of this book, briefly summarize the contents of each chapter.

14.1.1 Part I: Foundation

Part I builds the foundations for being able to understand the concept of traceability and its relevance in research and practice.

Chapter 2 analyzes common definitions for *traceability* that exist in literature and derives a new definition that suits the purposes of this work. Important *related terms* such as *traceable entity* and *traceability relationship* are also defined. Furthermore, various *dimensions* of traceability are discussed, classifying different notions, views, and kinds of traceability relationships.

In Chapter 3, the state of the art of traceability research is presented, structured with respect to six traceability-related activities. The activity of *definition* addresses the determination of traceable entity and traceability relationship types that are relevant for a traceability application. The *identification* activity is concerned with the manual or automatic discovery of traceability relationships. *Recording* of traceability information refers to the physical representation of traceability information in a data structure. *Retrieval* involves the localization and gathering of recorded traceability information answering a specific purpose. The activity of *utilization* treats the processing of retrieved traceability information for different applications. Finally, *maintenance* describes the manual or automatic updating of recorded traceability relationships in response to modifications of traced entities or other relationships.

The application of traceability in practice is the subject of Chapter 4. Following an overview of potential fields of application, such as change management, maintenance, or quality assurance, the traceability features of four commercial requirements management and modeling tools are investigated. The chapter concludes with a discussion of the role of traceability in industry, highlighting existing obstacles for the widespread adoption of traceability concepts.

14.1.2 Part II: Conception

Part II elaborates generic, technology-independent, and semantically rich concepts for the description of traceability solutions.

First, Chapter 5 analyzes existing deficiencies of the state of the art and formulates research questions that aim at the elimination of these deficiencies. The research questions are structured along the traceability-related activities, except for utilization, which is out of the more technical scope of this work.

Chapter 6 introduces the *Traceability Relationship Type Template (TRTT)*. Based on requirements gathered in the *MOST* project[1], the TRTT generically specifies a set of desired properties of semantically rich traceability relationship types. With the TRTT being technology-independent, its properties are supposed to be mapped to concepts of suitable technological spaces. Subsequent to establishing such a mapping, application-specific traceability relationship types can be defined in the context of a concrete technological space.

In Chapter 7, the identification of elementary traceability tasks leads to the specification of the three *traceability retrieval patterns Existence, Reachable Entities*, and *Slice*, which reflect typical retrieval problems in a generic and technology-independent way. Since these problems are common to many traceability applications, retrieval conforming to the patterns should be supported by technological spaces used for implementing traceability.

---

[1]http://www.most-project.eu

14.1.3 Part III: Implementation

Part III investigates the suitability of two technological spaces – the *TGraph approach* and the *OWL* technological space – for facilitating comprehensive traceability. This includes the mapping of the TRTT's properties to specific concepts of the spaces and the realization of retrieval according to the traceability retrieval patterns.

The "excursus" in Chapter 8 introduces the two technological spaces. Regarding the TGraph approach, *TGraphs* themselves, the metamodeling language *grUML*, the query language *GReQL*, the transformation language *GReTL*, and the specification of *event-condition-action rules* for TGraphs are described in detail. The introduction of the latter was motivated by the research conducted in the context of this work. The OWL technological space consists of the ontology language *OWL*, its serialization syntax *RDF*, and the query language *SPARQL*.

Chapter 9 addresses the implementation of comprehensive traceability on the basis of the TGraph approach. The properties of the TRTT are mapped to grUML and GReQL concepts, complemented by event-condition-action rules that permit automatic identification and maintenance. GReTL transformations constitute a further means of relationship identification. The JGraLab library for handling and persisting TGraphs can be used as basis for implementing a fact repository for the recording of traceability information. Retrieval is facilitated by suitable GReQL queries.

The implementation of comprehensive traceability in the OWL technological space is explained in Chapter 10. In detail, the TRTT properties are mapped to OWL and SPARQL concepts. Traceability information can be recorded using text files or, with the help of frameworks such as *Sesame* or *Jena*, using better scaling repository technologies, e.g., relational databases. The SPARQL query language allows for the retrieval of traceability information. Since SPARQL queries are generally less concise than GReQL queries, an approach to the transformation of GReQL to SPARQL was developed, thus reducing the users' effort for writing traceability queries.

14.1.4 Part IV: Application

Part IV illustrates the application of the traceability concepts and implementations on the basis of three case studies.

In Chapter 11, the implementation of a TGraph-based comprehensive traceability solution in the *ReDSeeDS*[2] project is described. Partly relying on model transformations,

---

[2]http://www.redseeds.eu

ReDSeeDS envisions to identify traceability relationships from the requirements specification to the architecture, detailed design, and source code of a software system and to record the traced entities together with the relationships in a fact repository. If the requirements of a new system to be developed are similar to the requirements of an already completed system, the latter ones serve as starting point for finding potentially reusable artifacts. The retrieval of such artifacts is facilitated by adequate GReQL queries on the recorded traceability information. The ReDSeeDS approach is supported by an Eclipse-based tool that integrates the JGraLab library as fact repository.

The MOST case study presented in Chapter 12 pursues the application of traceability for ensuring the correct refinement of process models. To develop software support for business processes, these processes are stepwise refined to operational process models that can finally be mapped to existing software services. Such a refinement and mapping has to obey certain integrity constraints. Instantiating the TRTT, these constraints are specified as properties of suitable traceability relationship types whose instances connect the different refinement steps. Tool support is offered on the basis of the ADOxx metamodeling platform, whose modeling concepts are similar to those of the TGraph approach. Thus, it was possible to develop an adapter to the JGraLab library, so that the constraints could be specified with GReQL.

Finally, Chapter 13 introduces *OntoRT*, an Eclipse plug-in that extends the integrated development environment by requirements management and comprehensive traceability features. Based on an OWL ontology for recording traceability information, OntoRT allows for the definition of custom traceability relationship types conforming to the TRTT. Identification and maintenance are supported by the respective TRTT properties. For the retrieval of traceability information, the plug-in integrates a GReQL-to-SPARQL transformation component that allows for the usage of more concise GReQL expressions instead of SPARQL queries.

14.2 Discussion

The main goal of this work is the elaboration of a *universal* approach that describes required features of traceability solutions, including an investigation of the suitability of existing technological spaces to implement respective solutions. This involves possibly needed extensions to those spaces. The term "universal" refers to the approach being

- *comprehensive*, i.e., offering support for all traceability-related activities,
- *generic*, i.e., applicable to different projects and applications,
- *technology-independent*, i.e., describing the features free of technological bias so that they are implementable by different technological spaces, and

- *semantically rich*, i.e., providing precise, formalized traceability relationship semantics that support the automation of traceability-related activities.

Research Questions 1 to 6, formulated in Chapter 5, concretize this overall goal by stating specific challenges that can be attributed to individual traceability-related activities. The achievements that provide solutions to these questions are discussed in Sections 14.2.1, 14.2.2, and 14.2.3, dealing with definition and recording, identification and maintenance, and retrieval, respectively.

Research Question 7 asks if existing technological spaces are suitable for implementing comprehensive traceability. The results with respect to this question are addressed in Section 14.2.4.

Finally, Section 14.2.5 gives an overview of additional contributions that are not related to some research question.

14.2.1 Solutions for Definition and Recording

Concerning the activity of definition, Research Question 1 calls for an approach that combines a generic, technology-independent means for the definition of traceability relationships types with the possibility of defining rich, formalized relationship semantics.

To this end, the Traceability Relationship Type Template was conceived to act as generic, technology-independent guideline for the definition of traceability relationship types. By specifying desired properties of relationship types, the TRTT allows for the definition of custom, domain- or project-specific, yet semantically rich traceability relationship types. With attributes, relational properties, constraints, and impact designators, the TRTT integrates different state-of-the-art techniques for the specification of relationship semantics.

For the application of the TRTT in practice, its properties have to be mapped to the concepts of suitable, concrete technological spaces. The investigation and, possibly, the extension of existing technological spaces' capabilities to support the implementation of the properties is the subject of Research Question 2. Besides the activity of definition, this also includes the recording of the respective traceability information.

The analyzed technological spaces, i.e, the TGraph approach and the OWL technological space, both proved to be suitable for defining and recording traceability relationship types conforming to the TRTT. With respect to relational properties, it has been investigated how to handle these properties using GReQL constraints. To support the mapping of impact designators, the TGraph approach was extended by a concept for the specification of event-condition-action rules. Here, it also has to be noted that the OWL technological space lacks inherent concepts for reacting to events that indicate changes to an ontology and for specifying the retraction of information from an ontology.

In general, both technological spaces are suitable for realizing a fact repository-based recording concept, provided that needed fact extractors are implemented.

14.2.2 Solutions for Identification and Maintenance

Research Question 3 asks if the rich semantics of the combined definition approach, i.e., the TRTT, can support the (semi)automatic identification and maintenance of traceability relationships.

With the inclusion of constraints and impact designators as traceability relationship type properties, the TRTT supports the usage of effective techniques for the automation of identification and maintenance. By reporting relationships which are responsible for the violation of some constraint to the user, the possibility of specifying constraints mainly contributes to semiautomatic maintenance. Impact designators, which are usually represented by some sort of rules, can help to achieve a full automation of identification and maintenance.

The support of (semi)automatic identification and maintenance by existing technological spaces is addressed by Research Question 4. It considers the implementation of constraints and impact designators as well as other techniques that are not assignable to single traceability relationship types and therefore, are not covered by the TRTT.

Both the TGraph approach and the OWL technological space support the specification of constraints and impact designators. However, as already mentioned in Section 14.2.1, in the OWL space it is not possible to react on events and to retract information from ontologies using OWL or SPARQL alone.

With the transformation language GReTL, the TGraph approach also facilitates the transformation-based identification of traceability relationships. Here, one shortcoming is the non-native, i.e., not in the form of some TGraph concept, recording of traceability relationships between source and target elements. If the source and target elements are not within the same graph, it is not possible to generate edges for representing traceability relationships, either. Thus, this information cannot be accessed using GReQL, but must be retrieved with the help of some external tool or programming language.

14.2.3 Solutions for Retrieval

With respect to retrieval, Research Question 5 demands the generic, technology-independent, yet formalized categorization of typical retrieval problems.

Based on an analysis of the retrieval-related aspects of elementary traceability tasks that abstract from concrete fields of application, the three identified traceability retrieval patterns Existence, Reachable Entities, and Slice provide such a categorization. The patterns come with a precise description of their purpose and of the queries that are required to obtain the sought-after traceability information.

The possibilities of implementing these categories by existing technological spaces is the subject of Research Question 6.

Prior to the work done in the context of this book, the GReQL query language of the TGraph approach has already supported queries according to the Existence and Reachable Entities patterns. To allow for queries that conform to the Slice pattern, a slice function was added. Retrieving traceability information from OWL ontologies using SPARQL (1.0) has two disadvantages: the length of queries that express complex path structures and the incapability to express transitive closure over arbitrary path descriptions. The first disadvantage was remedied by an approach for transforming GReQL queries to SPARQL queries, so that GReQL's more concise regular path expressions could be employed for denoting the structure of object property paths in OWL ontologies. With the adoption of the SPARQL 1.1 standard and its property paths feature, both deficiencies are expected to be eliminated.

14.2.4 Solutions for Comprehensive Traceability

Research Question 7 asks if existing technological spaces are suitable for implementing comprehensive traceability.

It has been shown that the TGraph approach as well as the OWL technological space offer satisfactory solutions in response to the activity-specific challenges that are captured by Research Questions 2, 4, and 6. The ability to combine these individual solutions into comprehensive ones as explained by this work, one for each technological space, allows for an affirmation of Research Question 7.

To demonstrate the practicality of the comprehensive traceability solutions, they were applied in the in the context of three case studies, dealing with the reuse of software artifacts, process model refinement, and requirements management, respectively. While each of the three developed traceability concepts essentially covered all traceability-related activities, each one had its focal points, too. Concerning the ReDSeeDS approach, these were the identification of relationships in the course of model transformations and the dependency on retrieval according to the Slice pattern, which led to the addition of the slice function to the GReQL function library. The process refinement case study of the MOST project made heavy use of traceability relationship type constraints that were used for consistency checking and maintenance purposes. The integration of traceability functionality to the Eclipse integrated development framework, facilitated by the OntoRT plug-in, allowed the users to directly configure their preferred traceability environment. OntoRT makes use of the full breadth of relationship type properties specified by the TRTT. Furthermore, queries conforming to all three patterns are possible.

14.2.5 Further Contributions

Apart from the solutions discussed above, this work contributes to the establishment of a consistent terminology for the traceability field of research. First, the definition of the term *traceability* given in Section 2.1 tries to mitigate the deficiencies of various definitions that can be found in literature. Second, the existing, in many cases inconsistent and ambiguous terminology used to describe the different dimensions of traceability is amended. Third, the introduced six traceability-related activities help to structure the different technical aspects of traceability research.

Furthermore, the survey of related work conducted in this book achieves a structuring of the examined publications with respect to the techniques they employ to support traceability.

Finally, the extensions to the TGraph approach, i.e., the investigation of how to treat relational properties, the addition of the slice function to GReQL, and the specification and implementation of the event-condition-action rule concept are to be regarded as fundamental additions to the technological space whose range of applications are not limited to traceability.

14.3 Outlook

A first category of extensions to the traceability solutions described by this work addresses the closing of existing gaps of the two investigated technological spaces. Concerning the TGraph approach, the probably most prominent gap that is relevant to traceability is GReTL's recording of automatically identified traceability relationships in a non-TGraph format. Here, an approach that allows for the querying of these relationships using GReQL should be conceived. To facilitate the definition of more expressive impact designators in the OWL technological space, the possibility of reacting to events and the retraction of knowledge from ontologies should be integrated. However, due to OWL's design as a monotonic language, it is unlikely that some sort of retraction can be integrated into the OWL language itself.

Distributed Hierarchical Hyper-TGraphs (*DHHTGraphs*), which are currently in development [Bil11b], promise to offer new, valuable features for implementing traceability. First, distribution, referring to the ability to retain different parts of a graph in different nodes of a network, allows for the convenient tracing of entities situated in different locations within a single graph. Second, hierarchy, denoting the refinement of graph elements by nested graphs, enables the seamless representation of traceability relationships on different levels of granularity. For example, a coarse-grained relationship interrelating two architectural components could be refined by a set of more fine-grained relationships which connect individual classes within these components. Thus, users could "zoom in" and "out" of the traceability model as required. Third, hyperedges, which are edges that connect to more than two vertices, facilitate a more natural representation of n-ary traceability relationships than the currently pursued approach which employs vertices as auxiliary constructs.

Going beyond (DHH)TGraphs and OWL, future work also should comprise the evaluation of other technological spaces for their suitability to implement comprehensive traceability, including their extension to fill potential gaps. Spaces with considerable relevance in practice are, for example, relational databases, MOF, and the XML world.

Finally, the lessons learned from developing the GReQL-to-SPARQL transformation approach mentioned in this work could be employed for the conception of a generic query language that can be applied in the context of different technological spaces. Using such a query language, traceability implementations which integrate different spaces with their individual strengths are still able to guarantee a uniform retrieval of traceability information.

Appendix A

Traceability Relationship Types

This appendix lists the TRTT instantiations of the traceability relationship types defined by the applications in Chapters 11, 12, and 13.

Section A.1 describes the traceability relationship types defined by the *Software Case Language* used in the *ReDSeeDS* project. In Section A.2, the relationship types used in the BPMN process model refinement case study of the *MOST* project are listed. Section A.3 gives the instantiated TRTT for the relationship types provided by the *OntoRT* Eclipse plug-in for requirements management and traceability.

A.1 Traceability Relationship Types used in ReDSeeDS

In the following, the traceability relationship types included by the Software Case Language (*SCL*), developed in the ReDSeeDS project (see Chapter 11), are described in detail by accordingly instantiating the TRTT. The definition is based on the TGraph approach.

For reasons of brevity, instead of including schema fragments in every such instantiation, an excerpt of the schema of the *Requirements Specification Language* (*RSL*), one of the SCL's sublanguages, and an excerpt of the SCL schema showing the inter-level traceability relationship types are depicted in Figures A.1 and A.2, respectively.

TRTT instantiation for ConflictsWith.

Property	Value
Name	ConflictsWith
Description	A ConflictsWith relationship expresses that the two connected Requirements cannot be both satisfied simultaneously.
Schema fragment	*see Figure A.1*

Attributes	uid :String – an ID which is unique within the scope of the current Software Cases and the completed Software Cases recorded in a Software Case repository
Examples	**FunctionalRequirement**: Users must log in to access the reservation system. *ConflictsWith* **FunctionalRequirement**: The reservation system shall provide guest access without requiring to enter user credentials.

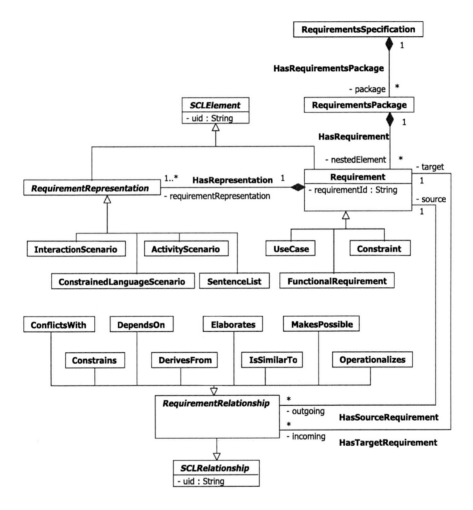

Figure A.1: Excerpt of the RSL schema.

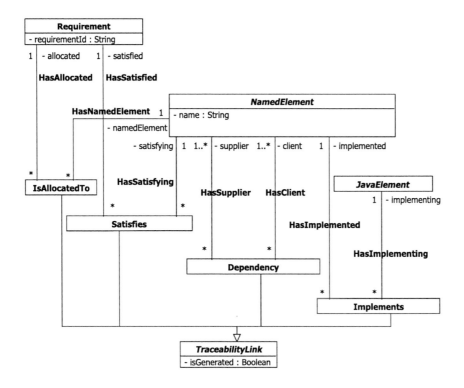

Figure A.2: SCL inter-level traceability concepts.

TRTT instantiation for Constrains.

Property	Value
Name	Constrains
Description	A Constrains relationship describes that the source Requirement imposes some restriction on the target Requirement. Usually, relationships of this type link Constraints to FunctionalRequirements.
Schema fragment	*see Figure A.1*
Attributes	uid :String – an ID which is unique within the scope of the current Software Cases and the completed Software Cases recorded in a Software Case repository
Examples	**Constraint**: Reservations should be encrypted when transmitted over the Internet. *Constrains* **FunctionalRequirement**: The reservation system must provide a web interface.

TRTT instantiation for Dependency.

Property	Value
Name	Dependency
Description	"A Dependency is a relationship that signifies that a single or a set of model elements requires other model elements for their specification or implementation. This means that the complete semantics of the depending elements is either semantically or structurally dependent on the definition of the supplier element(s)." [Obj10c]. Dependencys denote intra-level relationships on the architecture and detailed design abstraction levels as well as inter-level relationships between the two levels.
Schema fragment	*see Figure A.2*
Attributes	uid :String – an ID which is unique within the scope of the current Software Cases and the completed Software Cases recorded in a Software Case repository isGenerated :Boolean – indicates whether an instance of this relationship type was generated in the course of a model transformation or has been installed manually
Examples	**Component** (subclass of NamedElement): ReservationWebInterface *Dependency* **Component** (subclass of NamedElement): Billing

TRTT instantiation for DependsOn.

Property	Value
Name	DependsOn
Description	A DependsOn relationship expresses that the satisfaction of the target Requirement is a prerequisite for the satisfaction of the source Requirement.
Schema fragment	*see Figure A.1*
Attributes	uid :String – an ID which is unique within the scope of the current Software Cases and the completed Software Cases recorded in a Software Case repository
Examples	**FunctionalRequirement**: Customers must be able to make online reservations. *DependsOn* **FunctionalRequirement**: The reservation system must provide a web interface.

TRTT instantiation for DerivesFrom.

Property	Value
Name	DerivesFrom
Description	A DerivesFrom relationship indicates that the source Requirement has its origins in the target Requirement.
Schema fragment	*see Figure A.1*
Attributes	uid :String – an ID which is unique within the scope of the current Software Cases and the completed Software Cases recorded in a Software Case repository

Examples	**FunctionalRequirement**: The reservation system shall register payments.
	DerivesFrom
	FunctionalRequirement: The reservation system shall automatically bill customers.

TRTT instantiation for Elaborates.

Property	Value
Name	Elaborates
Description	An Elaborates relationship describes that the source Requirement extends the target Requirement by adding more details.
Schema fragment	*see Figure A.1*
Attributes	uid :String – an ID which is unique within the scope of the current Software Cases and the completed Software Cases recorded in a Software Case repository
Examples	**FunctionalRequirement**: The reservation system shall automatically print bills on the basis of customer activities.
	Elaborates
	FunctionalRequirement: The reservation system shall automatically bill customers.

TRTT instantiation for Implements.

Property	Value
Name	Implements
Description	An Implements relationship indicates that the source JavaElement is responsible for the implementation of the target NamedElement in a Software Case's detailed design model.
Schema fragment	*see Figure A.2*
Attributes	uid :String – an ID which is unique within the scope of the current Software Cases and the completed Software Cases recorded in a Software Case repository
	isGenerated :Boolean – indicates whether an instance of this relationship type was generated in the course of a model transformation or has been installed manually
Examples	**Class** (subclass of JavaElement): Reservation
	Satisfies
	Component (subclass of NamedElement): Reservation

223

TRTT instantiation for IsAllocatedTo.

Property	Value
Name	IsAllocatedTo
Description	An IsAllocatedTo relationship expresses that the target NamedElement, which is part of a Software Case's architecture, has been created in response to the source Requirement. After reviewing the NamedElement, it is linked to the originating Requirement via a Satisfies relationship. IsAllocatedTo relationships are automatically generated when transforming requirements to architecture, but may also be created manually.
Schema fragment	*see Figure A.2*
Attributes	uid :String – an ID which is unique within the scope of the current Software Cases and the completed Software Cases recorded in a Software Case repository isGenerated :Boolean – indicates whether an instance of this relationship type was generated in the course of a model transformation or has been installed manually
Examples	**FunctionalRequirement**: The reservation system must provide a web interface. *IsAllocatedTo* **Component** (subclass of NamedElement): ReservationWebInterface

TRTT instantiation for IsSimilarTo.

Property	Value
Name	IsSimilarTo
Description	An IsSimilarTo relationship describes that the connected Requirements refer to the same issue and differ only slightly, possibly with respect to their wording.
Schema fragment	*see Figure A.1*
Attributes	uid :String – an ID which is unique within the scope of the current Software Cases and the completed Software Cases recorded in a Software Case repository
Examples	**FunctionalRequirement**: The reservation system shall automatically print bills on the basis of customer activities. *IsSimilarTo* **FunctionalRequirement**: The reservation system shall automatically print invoices depending on customers' activities.

TRTT instantiation for MakesPossible.

Property	Value
Name	MakesPossible
Description	A MakesPossible relationship links a source FunctionalRequirement to a target UseCase. If the FunctionalRequirement is satisfied, the behavior described by the UseCase is enabled.
Schema fragment	*see Figure A.1*
Attributes	uid :String – an ID which is unique within the scope of the current Software Cases and the completed Software Cases recorded in a Software Case repository

| Examples | **FunctionalRequirement**: The reservation system shall automatically print bills on the basis of customer activities.
 MakesPossible
 UseCase: Print bill |

TRTT instantiation for Operationalizes.

Property	Value
Name	Operationalizes
Description	An Operationalizes relationship describes that the source Requirement adds some specific information to the rather target Requirement.
Schema fragment	*see Figure A.1*
Attributes	uid :String – an ID which is unique within the scope of the current Software Cases and the completed Software Cases recorded in a Software Case repository
Examples	**FunctionalRequirement**: The data storage server shall be protected by a ICSAcertified firewall. *Operationalizes* **FunctionalRequirement**: Customer data shall be stored securely.

TRTT instantiation for Satisfies.

Property	Value
Name	Satisfies
Description	A Satisfies relationship indicates that the source NamedElement, which is part of a Software Case's architecture, has been ensured to fulfill the target Requirement. If a generated architecture NamedElement which is connected to the originating Requirement via an IsAllocatedTo relationship has been modified manually, recording an additional Satisfies relationship marks that the NamedElement has been inspected to be suitable for fulfilling the Requirement.
Schema fragment	*see Figure A.2*
Attributes	uid :String – an ID which is unique within the scope of the current Software Cases and the completed Software Cases recorded in a Software Case repository isGenerated :Boolean – indicates whether an instance of this relationship type was generated in the course of a model transformation or has been installed manually
Examples	**Component** (subclass of NamedElement): ReservationWebInterface *Satisfies* **FunctionalRequirement**: The reservation system must provide a web interface.

A.2 Traceability Relationship Types used for Business Process Refinement

Here, the two traceability relationship types Refines and GroundsOn which are featured by the BPMN meta model of the MOST Workbench are described.

As explained in Section 12.2.1, although the MOST Workbench relies on the ADOxx metamodeling platform, the meta model can be treated as grUML schema due to the similarity of the platform's metamodeling concepts to the TGraph approach. Therefore, the TRTT instantiations for Refines and GroundsOn employs GReQL to describe the relationship type's constraints.

Instead of including schema fragments in every TRTT instantiation, Figure A.3 shows an excerpt of the BPMN meta model that includes the relationship types. For an example on their usage, refer to Chapter 12.1.1. There, Figure 12.1 illustrates the usage of Refines relationships, while Figure 12.2 employs GroundsOn relationships.

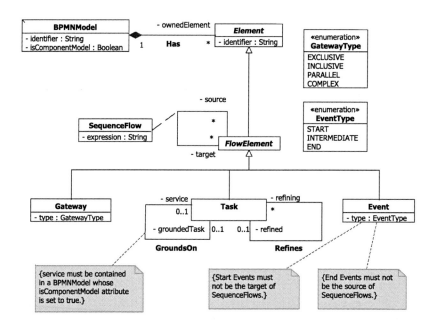

Figure A.3: Excerpt of the BPMN meta model used by the MOST Workbench.

TRTT instantiation for Refines.

Property	Value
Name	Refines
Description	A Refines relationship maps a refining Task to its refined Task in the preceding process model in the refinement chain.
Schema frag-ment	*see Figure A.3*

Constraints	*Message*:
	    Two different Tasks of one process model must refine Tasks that belong to the same process model.;
	Predicate query:
	    forall s,t:**V**{Task},
	        s <->{SequenceFlow}+ t @
	        s -->{Refines}<--{Has}-->{Has}<--{Refines} t;
	Offending elements query:
	    from t:**V**{Task}
	    with s <->{SequenceFlow}+ t
	        and not s -->{Refines}<--{Has}-->{Has}<--{Refines} t
	    report s, t **end**
	
	Message:
	    Every Task in a process model must either be refined by a Task of the subsequent process model in the refinement chain or be grounded to a Task in a component model.;
	Predicate query:
	    forall t:**V**{Task},
	        count(t <--{Has}&{ @ isComponentModel = false}) = 1 @
	        inDegree{Refines}(t) = 1 **xor** outDegree{GroundsOn}(t) = 1;
	Offending elements query:
	    from t:**V**{Task}
	    with count(t <--{Has}&{ @ isComponentModel = false}) = 1
	        and not (inDegree{Refines}(t) = 1 **xor** outDegree{GroundsOn}(t) = 1)
	    report t **end**
	
	Message:
	    Every Task in a process model may refine at most one task of the preceding process model.;
	Predicate query:
	    forall t:**V**{Task} @ outDegree{Refines}(t) < 2;
	Offending elements query:
	    from t:**V**{Task}
	    with not outDegree{Refines}(t) < 2
	    report t **end**
	
	Message:
	    Every Refines relationship must connect two Tasks belonging to different process models.;

Predicate query:
> **forall** r:E{Refines} @
>> count(startVertex(r) <--{Has}&{ @ isComponentModel = false}) = 1
>> **and** count(endVertex(r) <--{Has}&{ @ isComponentModel = false}) = 1
>> **and not** startVertex(r) <--{Has}-->{Has} endVertex(r);

Offending elements query:
> **from** t:E{Refines}
> **with not** (count(startVertex(r) <--{Has}&{ @ isComponentModel = false}) = 1
>> **and** count(endVertex(r) <--{Has}&{ @ isComponentModel = false}) = 1
>> **and not** startVertex(r) <--{Has}-->{Has} endVertex(r));
> **report** r **end**

Message:
> Two successive Tasks in a refining process model cause an inconsistent
> refinement, i.e., they may not be directly sequenced according to the refined
> process model.;

Predicate query:
> **forall** s,t:V{Task},
>> s -->{SequenceFlow}&{^Task}* -->{SequenceFlow} t @
>> s -->{Refines}<--{Refines} t
>> **or** s -->{Refines} -->{SequenceFlow}&{^Task}*
>>> -->{SequenceFlow} <--{Refines} t
>> **or** ((**exists** f:V{FlowElement}, f -->{SequenceFlow}* <--{Refines} s @
>>> f <--{SequenceFlow}&{Gateway @ thisVertex.type = "PARALLEL"}
>>>> -->{SequenceFlow}&{ @ thisVertex <> f} -->{SequenceFlow}*
>>>> <--{Refines} t)
>>> **and not** s -->{Refines} -->{SequenceFlow}+ <--{Refines} t
>>> **and not** s -->{Refines} <--{SequenceFlow}+ <--{Refines} t);

Offending elements query:
> **from** s,t:V{Task}
> **with** s -->{SequenceFlow}&{^Task}* -->{SequenceFlow} t
>> **and not** (s -->{Refines}<--{Refines} t
>>> **or** s -->{Refines} -->{SequenceFlow}&{^Task}*
>>>> -->{SequenceFlow} <--{Refines} t
>>> **or** ((**exists** f:V{FlowElement}, f -->{SequenceFlow}* <--{Refines} s @
>>>> f <--{SequenceFlow}&{Gateway @ thisVertex.type = "PARALLEL"}
>>>>> -->{SequenceFlow}&{ @ thisVertex <> f}
>>>>> -->{SequenceFlow}* <--{Refines} t)
>>>> **and not** s -->{Refines} -->{SequenceFlow}+ <--{Refines} t
>>>> **and not** s -->{Refines} <--{SequenceFlow}+ <--{Refines} t)
>>)
> **report** s,t **end**

Message:
> Two parallel Tasks in a refining process model cause an inconsistent
> refinement, i.e., they may not be parallelized according to the refined process
> model.;

Predicate query:
    forall s,t:**V**{Task},
        (**exists** g:**V**{FlowElement}, g -->{SequenceFlow}* s @
            g <--{SequenceFlow}&{Gateway @ thisVertex.type = "PARALLEL"}
                -->{SequenceFlow}&{ @ thisVertex <> g} -->{SequenceFlow}* t) @
        s -->{Refines}<--{Refines} t
        or ((**exists** f:**V**{FlowElement}, f -->{SequenceFlow}* <--{Refines} s @
            f <--{SequenceFlow}&{Gateway @ thisVertex.type = "PARALLEL"}
                -->{SequenceFlow}&{ @ thisVertex <> f} -->{SequenceFlow}*
                <--{Refines} t)
            and not s -->{Refines} -->{SequenceFlow}+ <--{Refines} t
            and not s -->{Refines} <--{SequenceFlow}+ <--{Refines} t);
Offending elements query:
    from s,t:**V**{Task}
    with (**exists** g:**V**{FlowElement}, g -->{SequenceFlow}* s @
        g <--{SequenceFlow}&{Gateway @ thisVertex.type = "PARALLEL"}
            -->{SequenceFlow}&{ @ thisVertex <> g} -->{SequenceFlow}* t)
        and not (s -->{Refines}<--{Refines} t
            or s -->{Refines} -->{SequenceFlow}&{^Task}*
                -->{SequenceFlow} <--{Refines} t
            or ((**exists** f:**V**{FlowElement}, f -->{SequenceFlow}* s @
                f <--{SequenceFlow}&{Gateway @ thisVertex.type = "PARALLEL"}
                    -->{SequenceFlow}&{ @ thisVertex <> f}
                    -->{SequenceFlow}* t)
                and not s -->{Refines} -->{SequenceFlow}+ <--{Refines} t
                and not s -->{Refines} <--{SequenceFlow}+ <--{Refines} t)
)
    report s,t **end**

Message:
    The entry Event and some directly sequenced Task in a refining
     process model cause an inconsistent refinement, i.e., they may not be se-
quenced
    according to the refined process model.;
Predicate query:
    forall e:**V**{Event}, t:**V**{Task},
        e.type = "START"
        and e -->{SequenceFlow}&{^Task}* -->{SequenceFlow} t @
        count({Event @ thisVertex.type = "START"}&-->{SequenceFlow}&{^Task}*
            -->{SequenceFlow} <--{Refines} t) = 1;
Offending elements query:
    from e:**V**{Event}, t:**V**{Task}
    with e.type = "START"
        and e -->{SequenceFlow}&{^Task}* -->{SequenceFlow} t
        and not count({Event @ thisVertex.type = "START"}&-->{SequenceFlow}
            &{^Task}* -->{SequenceFlow} <--{Refines} t) = 1
    report t **end**

229

Message:

    Some Task and the directly sequenced end Event in a refining

     process model cause an inconsistent refinement, i.e., they may not be sequenced

quenced

    according to the refined process model.;

Predicate query:

    forall e:**V**{Event}, t:**V**{Task},

        e.type = "END"

            and t -->{SequenceFlow}&{^Task}* -->{SequenceFlow} e @

        count(t -->{Refines} -->{SequenceFlow}&{^Task}*

            -->{SequenceFlow}&{Event @ thisVertex.type = "END"}) = 1;

Offending elements query:

    from e:**V**{Event}, t:**V**{Task}

    with e.type = "END"

        and e -->{SequenceFlow}&{^Task}* -->{SequenceFlow} t

        and not count(t -->{Refines} -->{SequenceFlow}

            &{^Task}* -->{SequenceFlow}&{Event @ thisVertex.type = "END"}) = 1

    report t **end**

Message:

    The entry Event and the end Event in a refining process model

    cause an inconsistent refinement, i.e., they may not be directly sequenced

    according to the refined process model.;

Predicate query:

    forall e,f:**V**{Event}, r:**E**{Refines},

        e.type = "END"

        and startVertex(r) <--{Has}-->{Has}&{Event @ thisVertex.type = "START"}

            -->{SequenceFlow}&{^Task}* -->{SequenceFlow} e @

        f.type = "END"

        and endVertex(r) <--{Has}-->{Has}&{Event @ thisVertex.type = "START"}

            -->{SequenceFlow}&{^Task}* -->{SequenceFlow} f;

Offending elements query:

    from e,f:**V**{Event}, r:**E**{Refines}

    with e.type = "END"

        and startVertex(r) <--{Has}-->{Has}&{Event @ thisVertex.type = "START"}

            -->{SequenceFlow}&{^Task}* -->{SequenceFlow} e @

        and not (f.type = "END"

            and endVertex(r) <--{Has}-->{Has}&{Event @ thisVertex.type = "START"}

                -->{SequenceFlow}&{^Task}* -->{SequenceFlow} f)

    report e **end**

Examples	*see Figure 12.1*

TRTT instantiation for GroundsOn.

Property	Value
Name	GroundsOn
Description	A GroundsOn relationship maps a Task in a process model in a refinement chain to the component model Task it is grounded on.
Schema fragment	*see Figure A.3*

Constraints	*Message:*
	Every Task in a process model of a refinement chain may only be grounded on at most one Task in a component model.;
	Predicate query:
	forall t:V{Task},
	    count(t <--{Has}&{ @ isComponentModel = false}) = 1 @
	    outDegree{GroundsOn}(t) < 2;
	Offending elements query:
	from t:V{Task}
	with count(t <--{Has}&{ @ isComponentModel = false}) = 1
	    and not outDegree{GroundsOn}(t) < 2
	report t **end**
	
	Message:
	Every GroundsOn relationship must lead from a Task belonging to a process model to a Task belonging to a component model.;
	Predicate query:
	forall r:E{GroundsOn} @
	    count(startVertex(r) <--{Has}&{ @ isComponentModel = false}) = 1
	    and count(endVertex(r) <--{Has}&{ @ isComponentModel = true}) = 1;
	Offending elements query:
	from t:E{GroundsOn}
	with not (count(startVertex(r) <--{Has}&{ @ isComponentModel = false}) = 1
	    and count(endVertex(r) <--{Has}&{ @ isComponentModel = true}) = 1)
	report r **end**
	
	Message:
	Two successive Tasks in a grounded process model cause an inconsistent grounding, i.e., they may not be directly sequenced according to the grounded on component model.;
	Predicate query:
	forall s,t:V{Task},
	    s -->{GroundsOn}<--{Has}-->{Has}<--{GroundsOn} t
	    and s -->{SequenceFlow}&{^Task}* -->{SequenceFlow} t @
	    s -->{GroundsOn} -->{SequenceFlow}&{^Task}*
	        -->{SequenceFlow} <--{GroundsOn} t
	    or (**exists** f:V{FlowElement}, f -->{SequenceFlow}* <--{Refines} s @
	        f <--{SequenceFlow}&{Gateway @ thisVertex.type = "PARALLEL"}
	            -->{SequenceFlow}&{ @ thisVertex <> f} -->{SequenceFlow}*
	            <--{Refines} t
	        and not s -->{GroundsOn} -->{SequenceFlow}+ <--{GroundsOn} t
	        and not s -->{GroundsOn} <--{SequenceFlow}+ <--{GroundsOn} t);

Offending elements query:
    from s,t:**V**{Task}
    with s -->{GroundsOn}<--{Has}-->{Has}<--{GroundsOn} t
        and s -->{SequenceFlow}&{^Task}* -->{SequenceFlow} t
        and not (s -->{GroundsOn} -->{SequenceFlow}&{^Task}*
            -->{SequenceFlow} <--{Refines} t
        or ((**exists** f:**V**{FlowElement}, f -->{SequenceFlow}* <--{Refines} s @
            f <--{SequenceFlow}&{Gateway @ thisVertex.type = "PARALLEL"}
                -->{SequenceFlow}&{ @ thisVertex <> f}
                -->{SequenceFlow}* <--{Refines} t)
            and not s -->{GroundsOn} -->{SequenceFlow}+ <--{GroundsOn} t
            and not s -->{GroundsOn} <--{SequenceFlow}+ <--{GroundsOn} t)
)
    report s, t **end**

Message:
    Two parallel Tasks in a grounded process model cause an inconsistent
    grounding, i.e., they may not be parallelized according to the grounded on
    component model.;
Predicate query:
    forall s,t:**V**{Task},
        s -->{GroundsOn}<--{Has}-->{Has}<--{GroundsOn} t
        and exists g:**V**{FlowElement}, g -->{SequenceFlow}* s @
            g <--{SequenceFlow}&{Gateway @ thisVertex.type = "PARALLEL"}
                -->{SequenceFlow}&{ @ thisVertex <> g} -->{SequenceFlow}* t @
        (**exists** f:**V**{FlowElement}, f -->{SequenceFlow}* <--{GroundsOn} s @
            f <--{SequenceFlow}&{Gateway @ thisVertex.type = "PARALLEL"}
                -->{SequenceFlow}&{ @ thisVertex <> f} -->{SequenceFlow}*
                <--{GroundsOn} t)
            and not s -->{GroundsOn} -->{SequenceFlow}+ <--{GroundsOn} t
            and not s -->{GroundsOn} <--{SequenceFlow}+ <--{GroundsOn} t;
Offending elements query:
    from s,t:**V**{Task}
    with s -->{GroundsOn}<--{Has}-->{Has}<--{GroundsOn} t
        and (**exists** g:**V**{FlowElement}, g -->{SequenceFlow}* s @
            g <--{SequenceFlow}&{Gateway @ thisVertex.type = "PARALLEL"}
                -->{SequenceFlow}&{ @ thisVertex <> g} -->{SequenceFlow}* t)
        and not (s -->{GroundsOn} -->{SequenceFlow}&{^Task}*
            -->{SequenceFlow} <--{GroundsOn} t
        or ((**exists** f:**V**{FlowElement}, f -->{SequenceFlow}* s @
            f <--{SequenceFlow}&{Gateway @ thisVertex.type = "PARALLEL"}
                -->{SequenceFlow}&{ @ thisVertex <> f}
                -->{SequenceFlow}* t)
            and not s -->{GroundsOn} -->{SequenceFlow}+ <--{GroundsOn} t
            and not s -->{GroundsOn} <--{SequenceFlow}+ <--{GroundsOn} t)
)
    report s,t **end**

Message:
  Some Task in a component model is not grounded on, although another
  Task which can be executed in parallel is.;
Predicate query:
  forall s,t:V{Task},
      exists f:V{FlowElement} @
          s -->{GroundsOn} <--{SequenceFlow}* f <--{SequenceFlow}
              &{Gateway @ thisVertex.type = "PARALLEL"}*
              -->{SequenceFlow}&{ @ thisVertex <> v} -->{SequenceFlow}* t @
          s <--{Has}-->{Has}-->{GroundsOn} t;
Offending elements query:
  from s,t:V{Task},
  with (**exists** f:V{FlowElement} @
          s -->{GroundsOn} <--{SequenceFlow}* f <--{SequenceFlow}
              &{Gateway @ thisVertex.type = "PARALLEL"}*
              -->{SequenceFlow}&{ @ thisVertex <> v} -->{SequenceFlow}* t)
      and not s <--{Has}-->{Has}-->{GroundsOn} t
  report t **end**

Examples	*see Figure 12.2*

A.3 Traceability Relationship Types used in OntoRT

This section lists the OWL-based traceability relationship types provided by the OntoRT Eclipse plug-in introduced in Chapter 13. Listing A.1, showing the ABox of an
Requirements Ontology instantiation, serves as common example.

Listing A.1: Excerpt of an Requirements Ontology instantiation.

```
Prefix( ro:=<http://purl.org/ro/ont#> )
Prefix( rdfs:=<http://www.w3.org/2000/01/rdf−schema#> )
Prefix( xsd:=<http://www.w3.org/2001/XMLSchema#> )
Ontology( <http://purl.org/ro/ont>

# TBox axioms
...

# ABox axioms

# Requirements

ClassAssertion( ro:Requirement ro:LoginToAccess )
AnnotationAssertion( rdfs:comment ro:LoginToAccess "Users must log in to access the system." )

ClassAssertion( ro:Requirement ro:LoginToAccessNew )
AnnotationAssertion( rdfs:comment ro:LoginToAccessNew
```

"Users must log in to access the reservation system.")

ClassAssertion(ro:Requirement ro:UsernameAndPassword)
AnnotationAssertion(rdfs:comment ro:UsernameAndPassword
            "Users must enter user name and password to access the reservation system.")

ClassAssertion(ro:Requirement ro:GuestAccess)
AnnotationAssertion(rdfs:comment ro:LoginToAccess
            "The reservation system shall provide guest access without requiring to enter user
            credentials (for demonstration purposes).")

ClassAssertion(ro:Requirement ro:Tutorial)
AnnotationAssertion(rdfs:comment ro:Tutorial
            "A guided tutorial shall instruct new users on the reservation system.")

ClassAssertion(ro:Requirement ro:OnlineReservations)
AnnotationAssertion(rdfs:comment ro:OnlineReservations
            "Customers must be able to make online reservations.")

ClassAssertion(ro:Requirement ro:WebInterface)
AnnotationAssertion(rdfs:comment ro:WebInterface "The reservation system must provide a web interface.")

ClassAssertion(ro:Challenge ro:DecliningSatisfaction)
AnnotationAssertion(rdfs:comment ro:DecliningSatisfaction "Customer satisfaction is on the decline.")
ClassAssertion(ro:Goal ro:SatisfactionOver70Percent)
AnnotationAssertion(rdfs:comment ro:SatisfactionOver70Percent
            "Customer satisfaction shall rise over the level of 70%.")
ClassAssertion(ro:Obstacle ro:LegacySystem)
AnnotationAssertion(rdfs:comment ro:LegacySystem
            "Customers already registered by the old reservation system to be replaced must be
            registered anew.")
ClassAssertion(ro:Risk ro:SecurityRisk)
AnnotationAssertion(rdfs:comment ro:SecurityRisk
            "Connecting the reservation system to the Internet allows for criminal cyber attacks.")

ClassAssertion(ro:Stakeholder ro:IsabelleDupont)
AnnotationAssertion(rdfs:comment ro:IsabelleDupont "Isabelle Dupont, Software Developer")

ObjectPropertyAssertion(ro:isAlternativeTo ro:GuestAccess ro:Tutorial)
ObjectPropertyAssertion(ro:isInConflictWith ro:LoginToAccessNew ro:GuestAccess)
ObjectPropertyAssertion(ro:isDependentOn ro:OnlineReservations ro:WebInterface)
ObjectPropertyAssertion(ro:isRefinementOf ro:UsernameAndPassword ro:LoginToAccessNew)
ObjectPropertyAssertion(ro:isRevisionOf ro:LoginToAccessNew ro:LoginToAccess)

ObjectPropertyAssertion(ro:hasChallenge ro:LoginToAccessNew ro:DecliningSatisfaction)
ObjectPropertyAssertion(ro:hasGoal ro:LoginToAccessNew ro:SatisfactionOver70Percent)
ObjectPropertyAssertion(ro:hasObstacle ro:WebInterface ro:LegacySystem)
ObjectPropertyAssertion(ro:hasRisk ro:WebInterface ro:SecurityRisk)

ObjectPropertyAssertion(ro:isAuthoredBy ro:WebInterface ro:IsabelleDupont)

```
# Source code

ClassAssertion( ro:Method ro:login )
AnnotationAssertion( rdfs:comment ro:login "public void login(String username, String password)" )

ClassAssertion( ro:Method ro:verify )
AnnotationAssertion( rdfs:comment ro:verify "private void verify(User user)" )

ClassAssertion( ro:Type ro:User )
ClassAssertion( ro:Field ro:Status )
ClassAssertion( ro:Field ro:Rights )

ClassAssertion( ro:Type ro:Reservation )

ObjectPropertyAssertion( ro:calls ro:login ro:verify )
ObjectPropertyAssertion( ro:creates ro:login ro:User )
ObjectPropertyAssertion( ro:derivesFrom ro:Rights ro:Status )
ObjectPropertyAssertion( ro:uses ro:verify ro:User )

# Inter−level relationships

ObjectPropertyAssertion( ro:fulfills ro:Reservation ro:OnlineReservations )

)
```

TRTT instantiation for ro:calls.

Property	Value
Name	ro:calls
Description	An ro:calls relationship states that the source ro:Method invokes the target ro:Method.
Supertypes	ro:hasDesignOrCodeRelationship
Schema fragment	**Declaration(ObjectProperty(ro:calls))**
	ObjectPropertyDomain(ro:calls ro:Method)
	ObjectPropertyRange(ro:calls Method)
Attributes	ro:creationDate, ro:rationale (*modeled as annotations*)
Examples	*see Listing A.1*

TRTT instantiation for ro:creates.

Property	Value
Name	ro:creates
Description	An ro:creates relationship states that the source ro:Method or ro:Type cause the instantiation of the target ro:Type.
Supertypes	ro:hasDesignOrCodeRelationship

235

Schema fragment	**Declaration(ObjectProperty(** ro:creates **))** **ObjectPropertyDomain(** ro:creates **ObjectUnionOf(** ro:Method ro:Type **))** **ObjectPropertyRange(** ro:creates Type **)**
Attributes	ro:creationDate, ro:rationale (*modeled as annotations*)
Examples	*see Listing A.1*

TRTT instantiation for ro:derivesFrom.

Property	Value
Name	ro:derivesFrom
Description	An ro:derivesFrom relationship indicates that the value of the source ro:Field is computed on the basis of the target ro:CodeElement or ro:Resource.
Supertypes	ro:hasDesignOrCodeRelationship
Schema fragment	**Declaration(ObjectProperty(** ro:derivesFrom **))** **ObjectPropertyDomain(** ro:derivesFrom ro:Field **)** **ObjectPropertyRange(** ro:derivesFrom **ObjectUnionOf(** ro:CodeElement ro:Resource **))**
Attributes	ro:creationDate, ro:rationale (*modeled as annotations*)
Examples	*see Listing A.1*

TRTT instantiation for ro:hasChallenge.

Property	Value
Name	ro:hasChallenge
Description	An ro:hasChallenge relationship states that the source ro:Requirement has been formulated to meet the target ro:Challenge.
Schema fragment	**Declaration(ObjectProperty(** ro:hasChallenge **))** **ObjectPropertyDomain(** ro:hasChallenge ro:Requirement **)** **ObjectPropertyRange(** ro:hasChallenge ro:Challenge **)**
Attributes	ro:creationDate, ro:rationale (*modeled as annotations*)
Examples	*see Listing A.1*

TRTT instantiation for ro:hasGoal.

Property	Value
Name	ro:hasGoal
Description	An ro:hasGoal relationship expresses that the source ro:Requirement has been formulated to achieve the target ro:Goal.
Schema fragment	**Declaration(ObjectProperty(** ro:hasGoal **))** **ObjectPropertyDomain(** ro:hasGoal ro:Requirement **)** **ObjectPropertyRange(** ro:hasGoal ro:Goal **)**
Attributes	ro:creationDate, ro:rationale (*modeled as annotations*)
Examples	*see Listing A.1*

TRTT instantiation for ro:hasObstacle.

Property	Value
Name	ro:hasObstacle
Description	An ro:hasObstacle relationship describes that the fulfillment of the source ro:Requirement is threatened by the target ro:Obstacle.
Schema fragment	**Declaration(ObjectProperty(** ro:hasObstacle **))** **ObjectPropertyDomain(** ro:hasObstacle ro:Requirement **)** **ObjectPropertyRange(** ro:hasObstacle ro:Obstacle **)**
Attributes	ro:creationDate, ro:rationale (*modeled as annotations*)
Examples	*see Listing A.1*

TRTT instantiation for ro:hasRisk.

Property	Value
Name	ro:hasRisk
Description	An ro:hasRisk relationship states that the fulfillment of the source ro:Requirement is threatened by the target ro:Risk.
Schema fragment	**Declaration(ObjectProperty(** ro:hasRisk **))** **ObjectPropertyDomain(** ro:hasRisk ro:Requirement **)** **ObjectPropertyRange(** ro:hasRisk ro:Risk **)**
Attributes	ro:creationDate, ro:rationale (*modeled as annotations*)
Examples	*see Listing A.1*

TRTT instantiation for ro:isAlternativeTo.

Property	Value
Name	ro:isAlternativeTo
Description	An ro:isAlternativeTo relationship between two ro:Requirements specifies that only one of them has to be fulfilled.
Supertypes	ro:hasRequirementRelationship
Schema fragment	**Declaration(ObjectProperty(** ro:isAlternativeTo **))** **ObjectPropertyDomain(** ro:isAlternativeTo ro:Requirement **)** **ObjectPropertyRange(** ro:isAlternativeTo ro:Requirement **)**
Attributes	ro:creationDate, ro:rationale (*modeled as annotations*)
Relational properties	symmetric
Constraints	Any two ro:Requirements that are connected by an ro:isAlternativeTo relationship may not be connected by an ro:isDependentOn, ro:isRefinementOf, or ro:isRevisionOf relationship. **DisjointObjectProperties(** ro:isAlternativeTo ro:isDependentOn **)** **DisjointObjectProperties(** ro:isAlternativeTo ro:isRefinementOf **)** **DisjointObjectProperties(** ro:isAlternativeTo ro:isRevisionOf **)**
Examples	*see Listing A.1*

TRTT instantiation for ro:isAuthoredBy.

Property	Value
Name	ro:isAuthoredBy
Description	An ro:isAuthoredBy relationship expresses that the source ro:Artifact was created by the target ro:Stakeholder.
Schema fragment	**Declaration(ObjectProperty(** ro:isAuthoredBy **))** **ObjectPropertyDomain(** ro:isAuthoredBy ro:Artifact **)** **ObjectPropertyRange(** ro:isAuthoredBy ro:Stakeholder **)**
Attributes	ro:creationDate, ro:rationale (*modeled as annotations*)

Impact Designators	If an ro:Requirement individual has two or more ro:isAuthoredBy relationships, it is considered to be an instance of ro:HighPriority.
	
	    SubClassOf(
	        ObjectMinCardinality(2 ro:isAuthoredBy **)**
	        ro:HighPriority
	    )

Examples	*see Listing A.1*

TRTT instantiation for ro:isDependentOn.

Property	Value
Name	ro:isDependentOn
Description	An ro:isDependentOn relationship between two ro:Requirements expresses that the fulfillment of the target ro:Requirement is a prerequisite for the fulfillment of the source ro:Requirement.
Supertypes	ro:hasRequirementRelationship
Schema fragment	**Declaration(ObjectProperty(** ro:isDependentOn **))** **ObjectPropertyDomain(** ro:isDependentOn ro:Requirement **)** **ObjectPropertyRange(** ro:isDependentOn ro:Requirement **)**
Attributes	ro:creationDate, ro:rationale (*modeled as annotations*)
Relational properties	transitive

Constraints	Any two ro:Requirements that are connected by an ro:isDependentOn relationship may not be connected by an ro:isAlternativeTo or ro:isInConflictWith relationship.
	
	    DisjointObjectProperties(ro:isDependentOn ro:isAlternativeTo **)**
	    DisjointObjectProperties(ro:isDependentOn ro:isInConflictWith **)**

Examples	*see Listing A.1*

TRTT instantiation for ro:isInConflictWith.

Property	Value
Name	ro:isInConflictWith
Description	An ro:isInConflictWith relationship between two ro:Requirements specifies that only one of them can be fulfilled, but not both.
Supertypes	ro:hasRequirementRelationship

Schema fragment	**Declaration(ObjectProperty(** ro:isInConflictWith **))** **ObjectPropertyDomain(** ro:isInConflictWith ro:Requirement **)** **ObjectPropertyRange(** ro:isInConflictWith ro:Requirement **)**
Attributes	ro:creationDate, ro:rationale (*modeled as annotations*)
Relational properties	symmetric

Constraints	Any two ro:Requirements that are connected by an ro:isInConflictWith relationship may not be connected by an ro:isDependentOn, ro:isRefinementOf, or ro:isRevisionOf relationship.
	
	  DisjointObjectProperties(ro:isInConflictWith ro:isDependentOn **)**
	  DisjointObjectProperties(ro:isInConflictWith ro:isRefinementOf **)**
	  DisjointObjectProperties(ro:isInConflictWith ro:isRevisionOf **)**

Impact designators	If an ro:isRefinementOf relationship exists from ro:Requirement r_1 to ro:Requirement r_2, and r_2 is connected to another ro:Requirement r_3 via an ro:isInConflictWith relationship, then an ro:isInConflictWith relationship is added between r_1 and r_3.
	
	  SubObjectPropertyOf(
	    ObjectPropertyChain(ro:isRefinementOf ro:isInConflictWith **)**
	    ro:isInConflictWith
	  )

Examples	*see Listing A.1*

TRTT instantiation for ro:isRefinementOf.

Property	Value
Name	ro:isRefinementOf
Description	An ro:isRefinementOf relationship between two ro:Requirements specifies that the source ro:Requirement offers a more detailed description of the target ro:Requirement.
Supertypes	ro:hasRequirementRelationship
Schema fragment	**Declaration(ObjectProperty(** ro:isRefinementOf **))** **ObjectPropertyDomain(** ro:isRefinementOf ro:Requirement **)** **ObjectPropertyRange(** ro:isRefinementOf ro:Requirement **)**
Attributes	ro:creationDate, ro:rationale (*modeled as annotations*)
Relational properties	asymmetric

Constraints	Any two ro:Requirements that are connected by an ro:isRefinementOf relationship may not be connected by an ro:isAlternativeTo or ro:isInConflictWith relationship.
	
	  DisjointObjectProperties(ro:isDependentOn ro:isAlternativeTo **)**
	  DisjointObjectProperties(ro:isDependentOn ro:isInConflictWith **)**

Examples	*see Listing A.1*

TRTT instantiation for ro:isRevisionOf.

Property	Value
Name	ro:isRevisionOf
Description	An ro:isRevisionOf relationship between two ro:Requirements specifies that the source ro:Requirement is a newer version of the target ro:Requirement.
Supertypes	ro:hasRequirementRelationship
Schema fragment	**Declaration(ObjectProperty(** ro:isRevisionOf)) **ObjectPropertyDomain(** ro:isRevisionOf ro:Requirement) **ObjectPropertyRange(** ro:isRevisionOf ro:Requirement)
Attributes	ro:creationDate, ro:rationale (*modeled as annotations*)
Relational properties	transitive
Constraints	Any two ro:Requirements that are connected by an ro:isRevisionOf relationship may not be connected by an ro:isAlternativeTo or ro:isInConflictWith relationship. **DisjointObjectProperties(** ro:isRevisionOf ro:isAlternativeTo) **DisjointObjectProperties(** ro:isRevisionOf ro:isInConflictWith)
Examples	*see Listing A.1*

TRTT instantiation for ro:uses.

Property	Value
Name	ro:uses
Description	An ro:uses relationship specifies that the semantics of the source ro:Resource or ro:CodeEntity depend on the semantics of the target ro:Resource or ro:CodeEntity.
Supertypes	ro:hasDesignOrCodeRelationship
Schema fragment	**Declaration(ObjectProperty(** ro:uses)) **ObjectPropertyDomain(** ro:uses **ObjectUnionOf(** ro:Resource ro:CodeEntity)) **ObjectPropertyRange(** ro:uses **ObjectUnionOf(** ro:Resource ro:CodeEntity))
Attributes	ro:creationDate, ro:rationale (*modeled as annotations*)
Examples	*see Listing A.1*

TRTT instantiation for ro:fulfills.

Property	Value
Name	ro:fulfills
Description	An ro:fulfills relationship indicates that the source ro:Resource or ro:CodeEntity realizes the functionality or constraint specified by the target ro:Requirement.
Supertypes	ro:hasInterLevelRelationship
Schema fragment	**Declaration(ObjectProperty(** ro:fulfills)) **ObjectPropertyDomain(** ro:fulfills **ObjectUnionOf(** ro:ResourceCodeEntity)) **ObjectPropertyRange(** ro:fulfills Requirement)
Attributes	ro:creationDate, ro:rationale (*modeled as annotations*)
Examples	*see Listing A.1*

List of Figures

List of Tables

List of Listings

Bibliography

[Aam94]   Agnar Aamodt and Enric Plaza. Case-Based Reasoning: Foundational Is-
          sues, Methodological Variations, and System Approaches. *Artificial Intelli-
          gence Communications of the ACM*, 7(1):39–59, 1994.

[Aiz05]   Netta Aizenbud-Reshef, Richard F. Paige, Julia Rubin, Yael Shaham-Gafni,
          and Dimitrios S. Kolovos. Operational Semantics for Traceability. In Jon Old-
          evik and Jan Aagedal, editors, *ECMDA Traceability Workshop (ECMDA-TW)
          2005 Proceedings, November 8th 2005, Nuremberg, Germany*, SINTEF Report,
          pages 7–14, Trondheim, Norway, 2005. SINTEF ICT.

[Aiz06]   N. Aizenbud-Reshef, B. T. Nolan, J. Rubin, and Y. Shaham-Gafni. Model
          traceability. *IBM Systems Journal*, 45(3):515–526, 2006.

[Ale08]   Markus Aleksy, Tobias Hildenbrand, Claudia Obergfell, and Michael
          Schwind. A Pragmatic Approach to Traceability in Model-Driven Develop-
          ment. In Armin Heinzl, Hans-Jürgen Appelrath, and Elmar J. Sinz, editors,
          *Process Innovation with Business Software, Proceedings of the PRIMIUM Sub-
          conference at the Multikonferenz Wirtschaftsinformatik 2008 (MKWI), Garching,
          Germany, February 26 - 28, 2008*, volume 328 of *CEUR Workshop Proceedings*.
          CEUR-WS.org, 2008. `http://sunsite.informatik.rwth-aachen.`
          `de/Publications/CEUR-WS/Vol-328/paper1.pdf`.

[Alf77]   Mack W. Alford. A Requirements Engineering Methodology for Real-Time
          Processing Requirements. *IEEE Transactions on Software Engineering*, SE-
          3(1):60–69, 1977.

[Ama08]   Bastien Amar, Hervé Leblanc, and Bernard Coulette. A Traceability Engine
          Dedicated to Model Transformation for Software Engineering. In Jon Olde-
          vik, Gøran K. Olsen, Tor Neple, and Richard Paige, editors, *ECMDA Trace-
          ability Workshop (ECMDA-TW) 2008 Proceedings, June 12th 2008, Berlin, Ger-
          many*, SINTEF Report, pages 7–16, Trondheim, Norway, 2008. SINTEF ICT.

[Amb08]   Albert Ambroziewicz, Jacek Bojarski, Wiktor Nowakowski, and Tomasz
          Straszak. Can Precise Requirements Models Drive Software Case Reuse?
          In Michał Śmiałek, Kizito Mukasa, Markus Nick, and Jürgen Falb, editors,

Proceedings of the 2nd International Workshop on Model Reuse Strategies (MoRSe 2008), pages 27–34, Stuttgart, Germany, 2008. Fraunhofer IRB Verlag.

[Anq08] Nicolas Anquetil, Birgit Grammel, Ismênia Galvão, Joost Noppen, Safoora Shakil Khan, Hugo Arboleda, Awais Rashid, and Alessandro Garcia. Traceability for Model Driven, Software Product Line Engineering. In Jon Oldevik, Gøran K. Olsen, Tor Neple, and Richard Paige, editors, *ECMDA Traceability Workshop (ECMDA-TW) 2008 Proceedings, June 12th 2008, Berlin, Germany*, SINTEF Report, pages 77–86, Trondheim, Norway, 2008. SINTEF ICT.

[Anq10] Nicolas Anquetil, Uirá Kulesza, Ralf Mitschke, Ana Moreira, Jean-Claude Royer, Andreas Rummler, and André Sousa. A model-driven traceability framework for software product lines. *Software and Systems Modeling*, 9(4):427–451, 2010.

[ANS84] ANSI/IEEE. *IEEE Guide to Software Requirements Specifications, ANSI/IEEE Std 830-1984*, 1984.

[Ant01] G. Antoniol, G. Canfora, G. Casazza, and A. De Lucia. Maintaining traceability links during object-oriented software evolution. *Software – Practice and Experience*, 31(4):331–355, 2001.

[Ant02] Giuliano Antoniol, Gerardo Canfora, Gerardo Casazza, Andrea De Lucia, and Ettore Merlo. Recovering Traceability Links between Code and Documentation. *IEEE Transactions on Software Engineering*, 28(10):970–983, 2002.

[Ant06] Giuliano Antoniol, Brian Berenbach, Alex Eyged, Stephanie Ferguson, Jonathan Maletic, and Andrea Zisman. Problem Statements and Grand Challenges. Technical Report COET-GCT-06-01-0.9, Center of Excellence of Traceability, September 2006. Draft Version.

[Ark02] Paul Arkley, Paul Mason, and Steve Riddle. Position Paper: Enabling Traceability. In *Proceedings of the 1st International Workshop on Traceability in Emerging Forms of Software Engineering, September 28th 2002, Edinburgh, U.K.*, 2002. http://www.soi.city.ac.uk/~zisman/traceworkshop.html.

[Ark05] Paul Arkley and Steve Riddle. Overcoming the Traceability Benefit Problem. In *Proceedings: 13th IEEE International Conference on Requirements Engineering, RE 2005, Paris, France, 29 August - 2 September 2005*, pages 385–389, Los Alamitos, CA, USA, 2005. IEEE Computer Society.

[Ass11] Namfon Assawamekin, Thanwadee Sunetnanta, and Charnyote Pluempitiwiriyawej. Ontology-based multiperspective requirements traceability framework. *Knowledge and Information Systems*, 25(3):493–522, 2011.

[Asu07]   Hazeline U. Asuncion, Frédéric François, and Richard N. Taylor. An End-To-End Industrial Software Traceability Tool. In *ESEC/FSE 2007 Proceedings: The 6th Joint Meeting of the European Software Engineering Conference and the ACM SIGSOFT Symposium on the Foundations of Software Engineering, Dubrovnik, Croatia, September 3 – 7, 2007*, pages 115–124, New York, NY, USA, 2007. ACM.

[Aze11]   Paulo José Azevedo Vianna Ferreira and Márcio de Oliveira Barros. Traceability between Function Point and Source Code. In *Sixth International Workshop on Traceability in Emerging Forms of Software Engineering (TEFSE 2011), Proceedings, May 23, 2011, Waikiki, Honolulu, HI, USA*, pages 10–16, New York, NY, USA, 2011. ACM.

[Baa03]   Franz Baader, Diego Calvanese, Deborah L. McGuinness, Daniele Nardi, and Peter F. Patel-Schneider, editors. *The Description Logic Handbook: Theory, Implementation and Applications*. Cambridge University Press, Cambridge, United Kingdom, 2003.

[Bae10]   Ricardo Baeza-Yates and Berthier Ribeiro-Neto. *Modern Information Retrieval*. Addison-Wesley, Reading, MA, USA, 2010.

[Bar07]   Mikaël Barbero, Marcos Didonet Del Fabro, and Jean Bézivin. Traceability and Provenance Issues in Global Model Management. In Jon Oldevik, Gøran K. Olsen, and Tor Neple, editors, *ECMDA Traceability Workshop (ECMDA-TW) 2007 Proceedings, June 12th 2007, Haifa, Israel*, SINTEF Report, pages 47–55, Trondheim, Norway, 2007. SINTEF ICT.

[Bar08]   Andreas Bartho, Harald Kühn, Stefano Tinella, Wilfried Utz, and Srdjan Zivkovic. Requirements definition of ontology-driven software process guidance system. Project Deliverable ICT216691/BOC/WP2-D1/D/PU/b1.00, MOST Project, August 2008. `http://www.most-project.eu`.

[Bar09]   Andreas Bartho. Creating and maintaining tutorials with DEFT. In *Proceedings of the 2009 IEEE 17th International Conference on Program Comprehension, May 17–19, 2009, Vancouver, Canada*, pages 309–310. IEEE, 2009.

[Bar11]   Andreas Bartho, Gerd Gröner, Tirdad Rahmani, Yuting Zhao, and Srdjan Zivkovic. Guidance in Business Process Modelling. In Schahram Dustdar and Fei Li, editors, *Service Engineering – European Research Results*, pages 201–231. Springer-Verlag, Wien, New York, 2011.

[Bec04]   Dave Beckett (ed.). RDF/XML Syntax Specification (Revised) – W3C Recommendation 10 February 2004. `http://www.w3.org/TR/2004/REC-rdf-syntax-grammar-20040210`, February 2004.

[Bec11] David Beckett and Tim Berners-Lee. Turtle – Terse RDF Triple Language – W3C Team Submission 28 March 2011. `http://www.w3.org/TeamSubmission/2011/SUBM-turtle-20110328`, March 2011.

[Ber05] T. Berners-Lee, R. Fielding, and L. Masinter. Uniform Resource Identifier (URI): Generic Syntax. `http://www.ietf.org/rfc/rfc3986.txt`, January 2005. Internet Engineering Task Force Network Working Group, Request for Comments: 3987.

[Ber07] Anders Berglund, Scott Boag, Don Chamberlin, Mary F. Fernández, Michael Kay, Jonathan Robie, and Jérôme Siméon (eds.). XML Path Language (XPath) 2.0 – W3C Recommendation 23 January 2007. `http://www.w3.org/TR/2007/REC-xpath20-20070123`, January 2007.

[Bil07] Daniel Bildhauer, Jürgen Ebert, Volker Riediger, Katharina Wolter, Markus Nick, Andreas Jedlitschka, Sebastian Weber, Hannes Schwarz, Albert Ambroziewicz, Jacek Bojarski, Tomasz Straszak, Sevan Kavaldjian, Roman Popp, and Alexander Szep. Software Case Marking Language Definition. Project Deliverable D4.3, ReDSeeDS Project, 2007. `http://www.redseeds.eu`.

[Bil08] Daniel Bildhauer, Jürgen Ebert, Volker Riediger, and Hannes Schwarz. Using the TGraph Approach for Model Fact Repositories. In Michał Śmiałek, Kizito Mukasa, Markus Nick, and Jürgen Falb, editors, *Proceedings of the Second International Workshop MoRSe 2008: Model Reuse Strategies – Can requirements drive reuse of software models?*, pages 9–18, Stuttgart, Germany, 2008. Fraunhofer IRB Verlag.

[Bil09a] Daniel Bildhauer, Jürgen Ebert, Tassilo Horn, Lothar Hotz, Stephanie Knab, Volker Riediger, and Katharina Wolter. Definition of a software case query language - second iteration. Project Deliverable D4.5, ReDSeeDS Project, 2009. `http://www.redseeds.eu`.

[Bil09b] Daniel Bildhauer, Tassilo Horn, and Jürgen Ebert. Similarity-driven software reuse. In *CVSM '09: Proceedings of the 2009 ICSE Workshop on Comparison and Versioning of Software Models*, pages 31–36, Los Alamitos, CA, USA, 2009. IEEE Computer Society.

[Bil11a] Daniel Bildhauer. Associations as First-Class Elements. In Janis Barzdins and Marite Kirikova, editors, *Databases and Information Systems VI: Selected Papers from the Ninth International Baltic Conference, DB&IS 2010, Riga, Latvia*, Frontiers in Artificial Intelligence and Applications. IOS Press, Amsterdam, Netherlands, 2011.

[Bil11b] Daniel Bildhauer and Jürgen Ebert. DHHTGraphs – Modeling Beyond Plain Graphs. In *Proceedings of the 2011 IEEE 27th International Conference on Data Engineering Workshops, April 11–16, 2011, Hannover, Germany*, pages 100–105. IEEE Computer Society, 2011.

[Bir01] Paul V. Biron and Ashok Malhotra (eds.). XML Schema Part 2: Datatypes – W3C Recommendation 02 May 2001. http://www.w3.org/TR/2001/REC-xmlschema-2-20010502, May 2001.

[Ble03] David M. Blei, Andrew Y. Ng, and Michael I. Jordan. Latent Dirichlet Allocation. *Journal of Machine Learning Research*, 3:993–1022, 2003.

[Boa07] Scott Boag, Don Chamberlin, Mary F. Fernández, Daniela Florescu, Jonathan Robie, and Jérôme Siméon (eds.). XQuery 1.0: An XML Query Language – W3C Recommendation 23 January 2007. http://www.w3.org/TR/2007/REC-xquery-20070123, January 2007.

[Boh91] Shawn A. Bohner. Software Change Impact Analysis for Design Evolution. In *Proceedings of the 8th International Conference on Software Maintenance and Re-engineering, Washington, DC, USA, August 1991*, pages 292–301, 1991.

[Bol10a] Harold Boley, Gary Hallmark, Michael Kifer, Adrian Paschke, Axel Polleres, and Dave Reynolds (eds.). RIF Core Dialect – W3C Recommendation 22 June 2010. http://www.w3.org/TR/2010/REC-rif-core-20100622, June 2010.

[Bol10b] Harold Boley and Michael Kifer (eds.). RIF Basic Logic Dialect – W3C Recommendation 22 June 2010. http://www.w3.org/TR/2010/REC-rif-bld-20100622, June 2010.

[Bra08] Tim Bray, Jean Paoli, C. M. Sperberg-McQueen, Eve Maler, and François Yergeau (eds.). Extensible Markup Language (XML) 1.0 (Fifth Edition) – W3C Recommendation 26 November 2008. http://www.w3.org/TR/2008/REC-xml-20081126, November 2008.

[Brc08] Robert Brcina and Matthias Riebisch. Defining a Traceability Link Semantics for Design Decision Support. In Jon Oldevik, Gøran K. Olsen, Tor Neple, and Richard Paige, editors, *ECMDA Traceability Workshop (ECMDA-TW) 2008 Proceedings, June 12th 2008, Berlin, Germany*, SINTEF Report, pages 39–48, Trondheim, Norway, 2008. SINTEF ICT.

[Bri04] Dan Brickley and R.V. Guha (eds.). RDF Vocabulary Description Language 1.0: RDF Schema – W3C Recommendation 10 February 2004. http://www.w3.org/TR/2004/REC-rdf-schema-20040210, February 2004.

[Bro02]   Jeen Broekstra, Arjohn Kampman, and Frank van Harmelen. Sesame: A Generic Architecture for Storing and Querying RDF and RDF Schema. In Ian Horrocks and James Hendler, editors, *The Semantic Web – ISWC 2002: First International Semantic Web Conference, Sardinia, Italy, June 9–12, 2002, Proceedings*, volume 2342 of *Lecture Notes in Computer Science*, pages 54–68, Berlin, Heidelberg, 2002. Springer-Verlag.

[Bru10]   Jos de Bruijn (ed.). RIF RDF and OWL Compatibility – W3C Recommendation 22 June 2010. http://www.w3.org/TR/2010/REC-rif-rdf-owl-20100622, June 2010.

[Buc11]   Georg Buchgeher and Rainer Weinreich. Automatic Tracing of Decisions to Architecture and Implementation. In *Proceedings: Ninth Working IEEE/IFIP Conference on Software Architecture, WICSA 2011, 20–24 June 2011, Boulder, Colorado, USA*, pages 46–55, Los Alamitos, CA, USA, 2011. IEEE Computer Society.

[Cam11]   Franklin Camacho and Ramón Pino Pérez. Leximax Relations in Decision Making through the Dominanc Plausible Rule. In Weiru Liu, editor, *Symbolic and Quantitative Approaches to Reasoning with Uncertainty, 11th European Conference, ECSQARU 2011, Belfast, UK, June/July 2011, Proceedings*, volume 6717 of *Lecture Notes in Artificial Intelligence*, pages 569–581, Heidelberg, Dordrecht, London, New York, 2011. Springer.

[Car01]   Pär Carlshamre, Kristian Sandahl, Mikael Lindvall, Björn Regnell, and Johan Natt och Dag. An Industrial Survey of Requirements Interdependencies in Software Product Release Planning. In *Proceedings: Fifth IEEE International Symposium on Requirements Engineering, August 27–31,2001, Royal York Hotel, Toronto, Canada*, pages 84–92, Los Alamitos, CA, USA, 2001. IEEE Computer Society.

[Car03]   Jeremy J. Carroll, Ian Dickinson, Chris Dollin, Dave Reynolds, Andy Seaborne, and Kevin Wilkinson. Jena: Implementing the Semantic Web Recommendations. Technical Report HPL-2003-146, Digital Media Systems Laboratory, HP Laboratories Bristol, December 2003.

[Cer05]   Humberto Cervantes and Richard S. Hall. Technical Concepts of Service Orientation. In Zoran Stojanović and Ajantha Dahanayake, editors, *Service-Oriented Software System Engineering: Challenges and Practices*, chapter 1, pages 1–26. Idea Group Inc. (IGI), Hershey, PA, USA, 2005.

[Cha74]   Donald D. Chamberlin and Raymond F. Boyce. Sequel: A Structured English Query Language. In *SIGFIDET '74: Proceedings of the 1974 ACM SIGFIDET (now SIGMOD) Workshop on Data Description, Access and Control, Ann Arbor, Michigan, USA*, pages 249–264, New York, NY, USA, 1974. ACM.

[Che76]   Peter Pin-Shan Chen. The Entity-Relationship Model—Toward a Unified View of Data. *ACM Transactions on Database Systems*, 1(1):9–36, 1976.

[Che10]   Xiaofan Chen. Extraction and Visualization of Traceability Relationships between Documents and Source Code. In *ASE'10: Proceedings of the IEEE/ACM International Conference on Automated Software Engineering, September 20–24, 2010, Antwerp, Belgium*, pages 505–509, New York, NY, USA, 2010. ACM.

[Cle03a]   Jane Cleland-Huang, Carl K. Chang, and Mark Christensen. Event-Based Traceability for Managing Evolutionary Change. *IEEE Transactions on Software Engineering*, 29(9):796–810, 2003.

[Cle03b]   Jane Cleland-Huang and David Schmelzer. Dynamically Tracing Non-Functional Requirements through Design Pattern Invariants. In *Proceedings of the 2nd International Workshop on Traceability in Emerging Forms of Software Engineering (TEFSE 2003), October 7th 2003, Montreal, Canada*, 2003.

[Cle06]   Jane Cleland-Huang. Just Enough Requirements Traceability. In *Proceedings: 30th Annual International Computer Software and Applications Conference, COMPSAC 2006, 17–21 September 2006, Chicago, Illinois, Volume I: Regular Papers/Panels*, pages 41–42, Los Alamitos, CA, USA, 2006. IEEE Computer Society.

[Cle07a]   Jane Cleland-Huang, Brian Berenbach, Stephen Clark, Raffaella Settimi, and Eli Romanova. Best Practices for Automated Traceability. *Computer*, 40(6):27–35, 2007.

[Cle07b]   Jane Cleland-Huang and Rafal Habrat. Visual Support In Automated Tracing. In *Proceedings of the Second International Workshop on Requirements Engineering Visualization, REV 2007*, Los Alamitos, CA, USA, 2007. IEEE Computer Society.

[Con95]   Panos Constantopoulos, Matthias Jarke, John Mylopoulos, and Yannis Vassiliou. The Software Information Base: A Server for Reuse. *The VLDB Journal – The International Journal on Very Large Data Bases*, 4(1):1–43, 1995.

[Cor96]   Jean-Pierre Corriveau. Traceability Process For Large OO Projects. *Computer*, 29(9):63–68, 1996.

[Cor01]   Thomas H. Cormen, Charles E. Leiserson, Ronald L. Rivest, and Clifford Stein. *Introduction to Algorithms*. The MIT Press, 2001.

[Cos07]   Marco Costa and Alberto Rodrigues da Silva. RT-MDD Framework – A
          Practical Approach. In Jon Oldevik, Gøran K. Olsen, and Tor Neple, edi-
          tors, *ECMDA Traceability Workshop (ECMDA-TW) 2007 Proceedings, June 12th
          2007, Haifa, Israel*, SINTEF Report, pages 17–26, Trondheim, Norway, 2007.
          SINTEF ICT.

[Cys08]   Gilberto Cysneiros and Andrea Zisman. Traceability and Completeness
          Checking for Agent-Oriented Systems. In *The 23rd Annual ACM Symposium
          on Applied Computing, Fortaleza, Ceará, Brazil, March 16–20, 2008x*, pages 71–
          77, New York, NY, USA, 2008. ACM.

[Cza06]   K. Czarnecki and S. Helsen. Feature-based survey of model transformation
          approaches. *IBM Systems Journal*, 45(3):621–645, 2006.

[Dah03]   Åsa G. Dahlstedt and Anne Persson. Requirements Interdependencies -
          Moulding the State of Research into a Research Agenda. In *REFSQ'03: Ninth
          International Workshop on Requirements Engineering: Foundation for Software
          Quality. In conjunction with CAiSE '03, Klagenfurt/Velden, Austria*, pages 71–
          80, 2003.

[Das01]   Eric M. Dashofy, André van der Hoek, and Richard N. Taylor. A Highly-
          Extensible, XML-Based Architecture Description Language. In *Proceedings
          of the Working IEEE/IFIP Conference on Software Architecture (WISCA'01), Ams-
          terdam, Netherlands, August 28–August 31, 2001*, pages 103–112, Los Alamitos,
          CA, USA, 2001. IEEE Computer Society.

[DeL06a] Andrea De Lucia, Fausto Fasano, Rocco Oliveto, and Genoveffa Tortora.
          ADAMS: ADvanced Artefact Management System. In *Proceedings: 10th Euro-
          pean Conference on Software Maintenance and Reengineering, 22–24 March 2006,
          Bari, Italy*, pages 349–350, Los Alamitos, CA, USA, 2006. IEEE Computer So-
          ciety.

[DeL06b] Andrea De Lucia, Rocco Oliveto, and Paola Sgueglia. Incremental Approach
          and User Feedbacks: a Silver Bullet for Traceability Recovery. In *ICSM
          2006 Proceedings, 22nd IEEE International Conference on Software Maintenance,
          Philadelphia, Pennsylvania, September 24–27, 2006*, pages 299–309, Los Alami-
          tos, CA, USA, 2006. IEEE Computer Society.

[DeL08]   Andrea De Lucia, Rocco Oliveto, and Genoveffa Tortora. ADAMS Re-
          Trace: Traceability Link Recovery via Latent Semantic Indexing. In *ICSE'08:
          Proceedings of the Thirtieth International Conference on Software Engineering,
          Leipzig, Germany, May 10–18, 2008*, pages 839–842, New York, NY, USA, 2008.
          ACM.

[DeL09]   Andrea De Lucia, Rocco Oliveto, and Genoveffa Tortora. Assessing IR-based traceability recovery tools through controlled experiments. *Empirical Software Engineering*, 14(1):57–92, 2009.

[DeL11]   Andrea De Lucia, Massimiliano Di Penta, Rocco Oliveto, Annibale Panichella, and Sebastiano Panichella. Improving IR-based Traceability Recovery Using Smoothing Filters. In *Proceedings: 2011 IEEE 19th International Conference on Program Comprehension, ICPC 2011, 22–24 June 2011, Kingston, Canada*, pages 21–30, Los Alamitos, CA, USA, 2011. IEEE Computer Society.

[DeR10]   Steve DeRose, Eve Maler, David Orchard, and Norman Walsh (eds.). XML Linking Language (XLink) Version 1.1 – W3C Recommendation 06 May 2010. `http://www.w3.org/TR/2010/REC-xlink11-20100506`, May 2010.

[Dic02]   Jeremy Dick. Rich Traceability. In *Proceedings of the 1st International Workshop on Traceability in Emerging Forms of Software Engineering, September 28th 2002, Edinburgh, U.K.*, 2002. `http://www.soi.city.ac.uk/~zisman/traceworkshop.html`.

[Döm98]   Ralf Dömges and Klaus Pohl. Adapting Traceability Environments to Project-Specific Needs. *Communications of the ACM*, 41(12):54–62, 1998.

[Dri08]   Nikolaos Drivalos, Dimitrios S. Kolovos, Richard F. Paige, and Kiran J. Fernandes. Engineering a DSL for Software Traceability. In Dragan Gašević, Ralf Lämmel, and Eric Van Wyk, editors, *Software Language Engineering: First International Conference, SLE 2008, Toulouse, France, September 29–30, 2008, Revised Selected Papers*, volume 5452 of *Lecture Notes in Computer Science*, pages 151–167. Springer-Verlag, Berlin, Heidelberg, 2008.

[Dri10]   Nikolaos Drivalos-Matragkas, Dimitrios S. Kolovos, Richard F. Paige, and Kiran J. Fernandes. A State-Based Approach to Traceability Maintenance. In Jon Oldevik, Gøran K. Olsen, and Dimitrios S. Kolovos, editors, *Proceedings of the 6th ECMFA Traceability Workshop 2010 (ECMFA-TW), June 15th 2010, Paris, France*, ACM International Conference Proceedings Series, pages 23–30, New York, NY, USA, 2010. ACM Press.

[Dua06]   Chuan Duan and Jane Cleland-Huang. Visualization and Analysis in Automated Trace Retrieval. In *Proceedings of the 1st International Workshop on Requirements Engineering Visualization, REV 2006*, Los Alamitos, CA, USA, 2006. IEEE Computer Society.

[Due05]   M. Duerst and M. Suignard. Internationalized Resource Identifiers (IRIs). `http://www.ietf.org/rfc/rfc3987.txt`, January 2005. Internet Engineering Task Force Network Working Group, Request for Comments: 3987.

[Dut01]   Allen H. Dutoit and Barbara Paech. Rationale Management in Software En-
            gineering. In S. K. Chang, editor, *Handbook of Software Engineering & Knowl-
            edge Engineering, Fundamentals*, volume 1, pages 787–816. World Scientific
            Publishing Company, Singapore, 2001.

[Ebe95]   Jürgen Ebert and Angelika Franzke. A Declarative Approach to Graph Based
            Modeling. In Ernst W. Mayr, Gunther Schmidt, and Gottfried Tinhofer, ed-
            itors, *Graph-Theoretic Concepts in Computer Science, 20th International Work-
            shop. WG '94, Herrsching, Germany, June 16–18, 1994, Proceedings*, volume 903
            of *Lecture Notes in Computer Science*, pages 38–50, Berlin, Heidelberg, 1995.
            Springer-Verlag.

[Ebe97]   Jürgen Ebert, Roger Süttenbach, and Ingar Uhe. Meta-CASE in Practice: a
            Case for KOGGE. In Antoni Olivé and Joan Antoni Pastor, editors, *Ad-
            vanced Information Systems Engineering, 9th International Conference, CAiSE'97,
            Barcelona, Catalonia, Spain, June 16–20, 1997, Proceedings*, volume 1250 of
            Lecture Notes in Computer Science, pages 203–216, Berlin, Heidelberg, 1997.
            Springer-Verlag.

[Ebe02]   Jürgen Ebert, Bernt Kullbach, Volker Riediger, and Andreas Winter. GUPRO.
            Generic Understanding of Programs - An Overview. *Electronic Notes in The-
            oretical Computer Science*, 72(2), 2002.

[Ebe08]   Jürgen Ebert, Volker Riediger, and Andreas Winter. Graph Technology in Re-
            verse Engineering, The TGraph Approach. In Rainer Gimnich, Uwe Kaiser,
            Jochen Quante, and Andreas Winter, editors, *10th Workshop Software Reengi-
            neering (WSR 2008), 5-7 May 2008, Bad Honnef, Germany*, volume 126 of *Lec-
            ture Notes in Informatics*, pages 67–81, Bonn, Germany, 2008. GI.

[Ebe10]   Jürgen Ebert and Daniel Bildhauer. Reverse Engineering Using Graph
            Queries. In Andy Schürr, Claus Lewerentz, Gregor Engels, Wilhelm Schäfer,
            and Bernhard Westfechtel, editors, *Graph Transformations and Model Driven
            Engineering*, volume 5765 of *Lecture Notes in Computer Science*, pages 335–362.
            Springer-Verlag, Berlin, Heidelberg, 2010.

[Ebe11]   Jürgen Ebert and Tobias Walter. Interoperability Services for Models and
            Ontologies. In Janis Barzdins and Marite Kirikova, editors, *Databases and
            Information Systems VI: Selected Papers from the Ninth International Baltic Con-
            ference, DB&IS 2010, Riga, Latvia*, Frontiers in Artificial Intelligence and Ap-
            plications. IOS Press, Amsterdam, Netherlands, 2011.

[Ebn02]   Gerald Ebner and Hermann Kaindl. Tracing All Around in Reengineering.
            IEEE Software, 19(3):70–77, 2002.

[Egy01]   Alexander Egyed. A Scenario-Driven Approach to Traceability. In *ICSE '01: Proceedings of the 23rd International Conference on Software Engineering, Toronto, Ontario, Canada*, pages 123–132, Los Alamitos, CA, USA, 2001. IEEE Computer Society.

[Esp06]   Angelina Espinoza, Pedro P. Alarcón, and Juan Garbajosa. Analyzing and Systematizing Current Traceability Schemas. In *Proceedings: 30th Annual IEEE/NASA Software Engineering Workshop, SEW-30, 24–28 April 2006, Columbia, Maryland*, pages 21–32, Los Alamitos, CA, USA, 2006. IEEE Computer Society.

[Esp11]   Angelina Espinoza and Juan Garbajosa. A study to support agile methods more effectively through traceability. *Innovations in Systems and Software Engineering*, 7(1):53–69, 2011.

[Fal09]   Kerstin Falkowski and Jürgen Ebert. Graph-based Urban Object Model Processing. In Uwe Stilla, Franz Rottensteiner, and Nicolas Paparoditis, editors, *CMRT09: Object Extraction for 3D City Models, Road Databases and Traffic Monitoring – Concepts, Algorithms and Evaluation CMRT, Paris, France, September 3 – 4, 2009*, volume 38, pages 115–120. International Society for Photogrammetry and Remote Sensing, 2009.

[Far03]   Scott Farrar and Terry Langendoen. A linguistic ontology for the semantic web. *GLOT International*, 7(3):97–100, 2003.

[Fel98]   Christiane Fellbaum, editor. *WordNet: An Electronic Lexical Database*. MIT Press, Cambridge, MA, USA, 1998.

[Fon02]   Frederico T. Fonseca, Max J. Egenhofer, Peggy Agouris, and Gilberto Câmara. Using Ontologies for Integrated Geographic Information Systems. *Transactions in GIS*, 6(3):231–257, 2002.

[Gam94]   Erich Gamma, Richard Helm, Ralph Johnson, and John Vlissides. *Design Patterns – Elements of Reusable Object-Oriented Software*. Addison-Wesley, 1994.

[Gei07]   Michael Geisser, Tobias Hildenbrand, and Norman Riegel. Evaluating the Applicability of Requirements Engineering Tools for Distributed Software Development. Working Paper 2/2007, University of Mannheim, Mannheim, Germany, January 2007.

[Gli08]   Flori Glitia, Anne Etien, and Cédric Demoulin. Fine Grained Traceability for an MDE Approach of Embedded System Conception. In Jon Oldevik, Gøran K. Olsen, Tor Neple, and Richard Paige, editors, *ECMDA Traceability Workshop (ECMDA-TW) 2008 Proceedings, June 12th 2008, Berlin, Germany*, SINTEF Report, pages 27–37, Trondheim, Norway, 2008. SINTEF ICT.

[Gok11]   Arda Goknil, Ivan Kurtev, Klaas van den Berg, and Jan-Willem Veldhuis. Semantics of trace relations in requirements models for consistency checking and inferencing. *Software and Systems Modeling*, 10(1):31–54, 2011.

[Gor02]   Tony Gorschek and Kaarina Tejle. A Method for Assessing Requirements Engineering Process Maturity in Software Projects. Master's thesis, Blekinge Institute of Technology, June 2002.

[Got94]   Orlena C. Z. Gotel and Anthony C. W. Finkelstein. An Analysis of the Requirements Traceability Problem. In *Proceedings of the First International Conference on Requirements Engineering, Colorado Springs, CO, USA*, pages 94–102, Los Alamitos, CA, USA, 1994. IEEE Computer Society.

[Got95]   Orlena Gotel and Anthony Finkelstein. Contribution Structures. In *Proceedings of the Second IEEE International Symposium on Requirements Engineering*, pages 100–107, Los Alamitos, CA, USA, 1995. IEEE Computer Society.

[Gra10]   Birgit Grammel and Stefan Kastenholz. A Generic Traceability Framework for Facet-based Traceability Data Extraction in Model-driven Software Development. In Jon Oldevik, Gøran K. Olsen, and Dimitrios S. Kolovos, editors, *Proceedings of the 6th ECMFA Traceability Workshop 2010 (ECMFA-TW)*, pages 7–14, 2010.

[Gre78]   S. Greenspan and C. McGowan. Structuring Software Development for Reliability. *Microelectronics and Reliability*, 17(1):75–83, 1978.

[Gre07]   Mark Grechanik, Kathryn S. McKinley, and Dewayne E. Perry. Recovering And Using Use-Case-Diagram-To-Source-Code Traceability Links. In *ESEC/FSE 2007 Proceedings: The 6th Joint Meeting of the European Software Engineering Conference and the ACM SIGSOFT Symposium on the Foundations of Software Engineering, Dubrovnik, Croatia, September 3 – 7, 2007*, pages 95–104, New York, NY, USA, 2007. ACM.

[Gus97]   Dan Gusfield. *Algorithms on Strings, Trees, and Sequences: Computer Science and Computational Biology*. Cambridge University Press, Cambridge, New York, Melbourne, 1997.

[Haa04]   Volker Haarslev, Ralf Möller, and Michael Wessel. Querying the Semantic Web with Racer + nRQL. In *Proceedings of the KI-2004 International Workshop on Applications of Description Logics (ADL'04), 2004*, 2004.

[Hal11]   Matthew Hale, Noah Jorgenson, and Rose Gamble. Analyzing the Role of Tags as Lightweight Traceability Links. In *Sixth International Workshop on*

Traceability in Emerging Forms of Software Engineering (TEFSE 2011), Proceedings, May 23, 2011, Waikiki, Honolulu, HI, USA, pages 71–74, New York, NY, USA, 2011. ACM.

[Har11] Steve Harris and Andy Seaborne (eds.). SPARQL 1.1 Query Language – W3C Working Draft 12 May 2011. `http://www.w3.org/TR/2011/WD-sparql11-query-20110512/`, May 2011.

[Hay04] Patrick Hayes (ed.). RDF Semantics – W3C Recommendation 10 February 2004. `http://www.w3.org/TR/2004/REC-rdf-mt-20040210`, February 2004.

[Hoo08] Colin Hood, Simon Wiedemann, Stefan Fichtinger, and Urte Pautz. *Requirements Management: The Interface Between Requirements Development and All Other Systems Engineering Processes*. Springer-Verlag, Berlin, Heidelberg, 2008.

[Hor04] Ian Horrocks, Peter F. Patel-Schneider, Harold Boley, Said Tabet, Benjamin Grosof, and Mike Dean. SWRL: A Semantic Web Rule Language – Combining OWL and RuleML – W3C Member Submission 21 May 2004. `http://www.w3.org/Submission/2004/SUBM-SWRL-20040521`, May 2004.

[Hor09] Matthew Horridge and Peter F. Patel-Schneider. OWL 2 Web Ontology Language Manchester Syntax – W3C Working Draft 21 April 2009. `http://www.w3.org/TR/2009/WD-owl2-manchester-syntax-20090421`, April 2009.

[Hor11] Tassilo Horn and Jürgen Ebert. The GReTL Transformation Language. In Jordi Cabot and Eelco Visser, editors, *Theory and Practice of Model Transformations – International Conference, ICMT 2011, Zurich, Switzerland, June 2011, Proceedings*, volume 6707 of *Lecture Notes in Computer Science*, pages 183–197, Berlin, Heidelberg, 2011. Springer-Verlag.

[Hot09] Lothar Hotz, Katharina Wolter, Stephanie Knab, and Arved Solth. Ontology-based similarity of software cases. In *KEOD 2009 – Proceedings of the International Conference on Know ledge Engineering and Ontology Development*, pages 183–191. INSTICC Press, 2009.

[Hov09] David ten Hove, Arda Goknil, Ivan Kurtev, Klaas van den Berg, and Koos de Goede. Change Impact Analysis for SysML Requirements Models based on Semantics of Trace Relations. In Jon Oldevik, Gøran K. Olsen, Tor Neple, and Dimitrios Kolovos, editors, *ECMDA Traceability Workshop (ECMDA-TW) 2009 Proceedings, June 23rd 2009, Twente, Netherlands*, CTIT Workshop Proceedings Series, pages 17–28, Enschede, Netherlands, 2009. CTIT.

[Huf06]   Jane Huffman Hayes, Alex Dekhtyar, and Senthil Karthikeyan Sundaram. Advancing Candidate Link Generation for Requirements Tracing: The Study of Methods. *IEEE Transactions ON Software Engineering*, 32(1):4–19, 2006.

[Ins90]   The Institute of Electrical and Electronics Engineers, Inc., New York, NY, USA. *IEEE Standard Glossary of Software Engineering Terminology, IEEE Std 610.12-1990(R2002)*, 1990.

[Iva10]   V.I. Ivanenko. *Decision Systems and Nonstochastic Randomness.* Springer Science+Business Media, New York, Dordrecht, Heidelberg, London, 2010.

[Jar98]   Matthias Jarke.   Requirements Tracing.   *Communications of the ACM,* 41(12):32–36, 1998.

[Jir09]   Waraporn Jirapanthong and Andrea Zisman. XTraQue: traceability for product line systems. *Software and Systems Modeling*, 8(1):117–144, 2009.

[Jou05]   Frédéric Jouault. Loosely Coupled Traceability for ATL. In Jon Oldevik and Jan Aagedal, editors, *ECMDA Traceability Workshop (ECMDA-TW) 2005 Proceedings, November 8th 2005, Nuremberg, Germany*, SINTEF Report, pages 29–37, Trondheim, Norway, 2005. SINTEF ICT.

[Jou06]   Frédéric Jouault and Ivan Kurtev. Transforming Models with ATL. In Jean-Michel Bruel, editor, *Satellite Events at the MoDELS 2005 Conference: MoDELS 2005 International Workshops, Doctoral Symposium, Educators Symposium, Montego Bay, Jamaica, October 2–7, 2005, Revised Selected Papers*, volume 3844 of *Lecture Notes in Computer Science*, pages 128–138. Springer-Verlag, Berlin, Heidelberg, 2006.

[Jun00]   Stefan Junginger, Harald Kühn, Robert Strobl, and Dimitris Karagiannis. Ein Geschäftsprozessmanagement-Werkzeug der nächsten Generation – ADONIS: Konzeption und Anwendungen. *Wirtschaftsinformatik*, 42(5):392–401, 2000.

[Kai93]   Hermann Kaindl. The Missing Link in Requirements Engineering. *SIGSOFT Software Engineering Notes*, 18(2):30–39, 1993.

[Kai99]   Hermann Kaindl, Stefan Kramer, and Papa Samba Niang Diallo. Semiautomatic Generation of Glossary Links: A Practical Solution. In *HYPERTEXT '99: Proceedings of the Tenth ACM Conference on Hypertext and Hypermedia: Returning to our Diverse Roots, Darmstadt, Germany*, pages 3–12, New York, NY, USA, 1999. ACM.

[Kal04]   Audris Kalnins, Janis Barzdins, and Edgars Celms. Model Transformation Language MOLA. In Uwe Aßmann, Mehmet Aksit, and Arend Rensink, editors, *Model Driven Architecture, European MDA Workshops: Foundations and Applications, MDAFA 2003 and MDAFA 2004, Twente, The Netherlands, June 26–27, 2003 and Linköping, Sweden, June 10–11, 2004, Revised Selected Papers*, volume 3599 of *Lecture Notes in Computer Science*, pages 62–76, Berlin, Heidelberg, 2004. Springer-Verlag.

[Kal07a]   Audris Kalnins, Elina Kalnina, Edgars Celms, Agris Sostaks, Hannes Schwarz, Albert Ambroziewicz, Jacek Bojarski, Wiktor Nowakowski, Tomasz Straszak, Sevan Kavaldjian, and Jürgen Falb. Reusable Case Transformation Rule Specification. Project Deliverable D3.3, ReDSeeDS Project, 2007. http://www.redseeds.eu.

[Kal07b]   Audris Kalnins, Agris Sostaks, Edgars Celms, Elina Kalnina, Albert Ambroziewicz, Jacek Bojarski, Wiktor Nowakowski, Tomasz Straszak, Volker Riediger, Hannes Schwarz, Daniel Bildhauer, Sevan Kavaldjian, Roman Popp, and Jürgen Falb. Reuse-Oriented Modelling and Transformation Language Definition. Project Deliverable D3.2.1, ReDSeeDS Project, 2007. http://www.redseeds.eu.

[Kam98]   Manfred Kamp. Managing a Multi-File, Multi-Language Software Repository for Program Comprehension Tools — A Generic Approach. Fachbericht Informatik 1/98, Institut für Informatik, Universität Koblenz-Landau, Koblenz, Germany, 1998.

[Kli09]   Lars Klimpke and Tobias Hildenbrand. Towards End-to-End Traceability – Insights and Implications from Five Case Studies. In *Proceedings: The Fourth International Conference on Software Engineering Advances, ICSEA 2009, 20–25 September 2009, Porto, Portugal*, pages 465–470, Los Alamitos, CA, USA, 2009. IEEE Computer Society.

[Klo11]   Samuel Klock, Malcom Gethers, Bogdan Dit, and Denys Poshyvanyk. Traceclipse: An Eclipse Plug-in for Traceability Link Recovery and Management. In *Sixth International Workshop on Traceability in Emerging Forms of Software Engineering (TEFSE 2011), Proceedings, May 23, 2011, Waikiki, Honolulu, HI, USA*, pages 24–30, New York, NY, USA, 2011. ACM.

[Kly04]   Graham Klyne and Jeremy J. Carroll (eds.). Resource Description Framework (RDF): Concepts and Abstract Syntax – W3C Recommendation 10 February 2004. http://www.w3.org/TR/2004/REC-rdf-concepts-20040210, February 2004.

261

[Kne02] Antje von Knethen and Barbara Paech. A Survey on Tracing Approaches in Theory and Practice. Requirements Engineering and the Semantic Web: Part II. Representation, Management, and Validation of Requirements and System-Level Architectures 095.01/E, Fraunhofer IESE, Kaiserslautern, Germany, January 2002.

[Kol06] Dimitrios S. Kolovos, Richard F. Paige, and Fiona A.C. Polack. On-Demand Merging of Traceability Links with Models. In Jan Aagedal, Tor Neple, and Jon Oldevik, editors, *ECMDA Traceability Workshop (ECMDA-TW) 2006 Proceedings, July 10th 2006, Bilbao, Spain*, SINTEF Report, Trondheim, Norway, 2006. SINTEF ICT.

[Kom06] Péter Komjáth and Vilmos Totik. *Problems and Theorems in Classical Set Theory.* Springer Science+Business Media, New York, NY, USA, 2006.

[Kul99] Bernt Kullbach and Andreas Winter. Querying as an Enabling Technology in Software Reengineering. In Paolo Nesi and Chris Verhoef, editors, *Proceedings of the Third European Conference on Software Maintenance and Reengineering, Chapel of St. Agnes, University of Amsterdam, The Netherlands, March 3 – 5, 1999*, pages 42–50, Los Alamitos, CA, USA, 1999. IEEE Computer Society.

[Kur02] Ivan Kurtev, Jean Bézivin, and Mehmet Aksit. Technological Spaces: an Initial Appraisal. In Robert Meersman and Zahir Tari et al., editors, *International Symposium on Distributed Objects and Applications, DOA 2002, 30 October – 1 November 2002, Irvine, USA*, volume 2519 of *Lecture Notes on Computer Science*, pages 1–6, Berlin, Heidelberg, 2002. Springer-Verlag.

[Lam11] Luis C. Lamb, Waraporn Jirapanthong, and Andrea Zisman. Formalizing Traceability Relations for Product Lines. In *Sixth International Workshop on Traceability in Emerging Forms of Software Engineering (TEFSE 2011), Proceedings, May 23, 2011, Waikiki, Honolulu, HI, USA*, pages 42–45, New York, NY, USA, 2011. ACM.

[Leh04] Ingmar Lehmann and Wolfgang Schulz. *Mengen, Relationen, Funktionen – Eine anschauliche Einführung.* Teubner, Stuttgart, Leipzig, Wiesbaden, 2 edition, 2004.

[Let02] Patricio Letelier. A Framework for Requirements Traceability in UML-based Projects. In *Proceedings of the 1st International Workshop on Traceability in Emerging Forms of Software Engineering, September 28th 2002, Edinburgh, U.K.*, 2002. http://www.soi.city.ac.uk/~zisman/traceworkshop.html.

[Lin94] Mikael Lindvall. *A study of traceability in object-oriented systems development.* Licentiate thesis, Linköping University, 1994.

[Lin06]   Jun Lin, Chan Chou Lin, Jane Cleland-Huang, Raffaella Settimi, Joseph
            Amaya, Grace Bedford, Brian Berenbach, Oussama Ben Khadra, Chuan
            Duan, and Xuchang Zou. Poirot: A Distributed Tool Supporting Enterprise-
            Wide Automated Traceability. In Martin Glinz and Robyn Lutz, editors, *Pro-
            ceedings: 14th IEEE International Requirements Engineering Conference, RE'06,
            Minneapolis/St. Paul, Minnesota, USA, September 11–15, 2006*, pages 356–357,
            Los Alamitos, CA, USA, 2006. IEEE Computer Society.

[Lis87]   Barbara Liskov. Data Abstraction and Hierarchy. In *OOPSLA '87: Adden-
            dum to the Proceedings on Object-Oriented Programming Systems, Languages and
            Applications (Addendum)*, pages 17–34, New York, NY, USA, 1987. ACM.

[Mäd07]   Patrick Mäder, Ilka Philippow, and Matthias Riebisch. Customizing Trace-
            ability Links for the Unified Process. In Sven Overhage, Clemens A. Szyper-
            ski, Ralf Reussner, and Judith A. Stafford, editors, *Software Architectures,
            Components, and Applications: Third International Conference on Quality of Soft-
            ware Architectures, QoSA2007 Medford, MA, USA, July 11–13, 2007, Revised Se-
            lected Papers*, volume 4880 of *Lecture Notes in Computer Science*, pages 53–71.
            Springer-Verlag, Berlin, Heidelberg, 2007.

[Mäd08a]   Patrick Mäder, Orlena Gotel, Tobias Kuschke, and Ilka Philippow. *trace-
            Maintainer* - Automated Traceability Maintenance. In *Proceedings of the 16th
            IEEE International Requirements Engineering Conference, September 8 – 12, 2008,
            Barcelona, Catalunya, Spain*, pages 329–330, Los Alamitos, CA, USA, 2008.
            IEEE Computer Society.

[Mäd08b]   Patrick Mäder, Orlena Gotel, and Ilka Philippow. Rule-Based Maintenance
            of Post-Requirements Traceability Relations. In *Proceedings of the 16th IEEE
            International Requirements Engineering Conference, September 8 – 12, 2008,
            Barcelona, Catalunya, Spain*, pages 23–32, Los Alamitos, CA, USA, 2008. IEEE
            Computer Society.

[Mäd10]   Patrick Mäder and Jane Cleland-Huang. A Visual Traceability Modeling
            Language. In Dorina C. Petriu, Nicolas Rouquette, and Øystein Haugen,
            editors, *Model Driven Engineering Languages and Systems, 13th International
            Conference, MODELS 2010, Oslo, Norway, October 3–8, 2010, Proceedings, Part
            I*, volume 6394 of *Lecture Notes in Computer Science*, pages 226–240, Berlin,
            Heidelberg, 2010. Springer-Verlag.

[Mal05]   Jonathan I. Maletic, Michael L. Collard, and Bonita Simoes. An XML Based
            Approach to Support the Evolution of Model-to-Model Traceability Links.
            In Jonathan I. Maletic, Jane Cleland-Huang, Jane Huffman Hayes, and Giu-
            liano Antoniol, editors, *Proceedings: The 3rd ACM International Workshop on*

Traceability in Emerging Forms of Software Engineering, TEFSE 2005, 8 November 2005, Long Beach California, USA, pages 67–72, New York, NY, USA, 2005. ACM.

[Mal07]   Ashok Malhotra, Jim Melton, and Norman Walsh (eds.).   XQuery 1.0 and XPath 2.0 Functions and Operators – W3C Recommendation 23 January 2007.   `http://www.w3.org/TR/2007/` `REC-xpath-functions-20070123`, January 2007.

[Mal09]   Jonathan I. Maletic and Michael L. Collard. TQL: A Query Language to Support Traceability. In *TEFSE 2009 Proceedings, 2009 ICSE Workshop on Traceability in Emerging Forms of Software Engineering, May 18, 2009, Vancouver, Canada*, pages 16–20, 2009.

[Man04]   Frank Manola and Eric Miller (eds.).   RDF Primer – W3C Recommendation 10 February 2004.   `http://www.w3.org/TR/2004/` `REC-rdf-primer-20040210`, February 2004.

[Mar05a] Andrian Marcus, Jonathan I. Maletic, and Andrey Sergeyev. Recovery of Traceability Links Between Software Documentation and Source Code. *International Journal of Software Engineering and Knowledge Engineering*, 15(4):811–836, 2005.

[Mar05b] Andrian Marcus, Xinrong Xie, and Denys Poshyvanyk. When and How to Visualize Traceability Links? In Jonathan I. Maletic, Jane Cleland-Huang, Jane Huffman Hayes, and Giuliano Antoniol, editors, *Proceedings: The 3rd ACM International Workshop on Traceability in Emerging Forms of Software Engineering, TEFSE 2005, 8 November 2005, Long Beach California, USA*, pages 56–61, New York, NY, USA, 2005. ACM.

[McA10]   Jeff McAffer, Jean-Michel Lemieux, and Chris Aniszczyk. *Eclipse Rich Client Platform*. Addison-Wesley, 2 edition, 2010.

[Mer05]   Marjan Mernik, Jan Heering, and Anthony M. Sloane. When and How to Develop Domain-Specific Languages. *ACM Computing Surveys*, 37(4):316–344, 2005.

[Mir11]   Mehdi Mirakhorli and Jane Cleland-Huang. Transforming Trace Information in Architectural Documents into Re-usable and Effective Traceability Links. In *Workshop on SHAring and Reusing architectural Knowledge (SHARK 2011), Proceedings, May 24, 2011, Waikiki, Honolulu, HI, USA*, pages 45–52, New York, NY, USA, 2011. ACM.

[Moo07]   Mikyeong Moon, Heung Seok Chae, Taewoo Nam, and Keunhyuk Yeom. A Metamodeling Approach to Tracing Variability between Requirements and Architecture in Software Product Lines. In *Proceedings: 7th IEEE International Conference on Computer and Information Technology (CIT 2007), 16–19 October 2007, Aiku-Wakamatsu City, Fukushima, Japan*, pages 927–933, Los Alamitos, CA, USA, 2007. IEEE Computer Society.

[Mot09a]   Boris Motik, Peter F. Patel-Schneider, and Bernardo Cuenca Grau (eds.). OWL 2 Web Ontology Language Direct Semantics – W3C Recommendation 27 October 2009. http://www.w3.org/TR/2009/REC-owl2-direct-semantics-20091027, October 2009.

[Mot09b]   Boris Motik, Peter F. Patel-Schneider, and Bijan Parsia (eds.). OWL 2 Web Ontology Language Structural Specification and Functional-Style Syntax – W3C Recommendation 27 October 2009. http://www.w3.org/TR/2009/REC-owl2-syntax-20091027, October 2009.

[Müh06]   Susanne Mühlbauer. Werkzeuge im Anforderungsmanagement. *OBJEKT-spektrum – Online-Ausgabe: Requirements Engineering*, RE/2006, 2006.

[Mun05]   Ethan V. Munson and Tien N. Nguyen. Concordance, Conformance, Versions, and Traceability. In Jonathan I. Maletic, Jane Cleland-Huang, Jane Huffman Hayes, and Giuliano Antoniol, editors, *Proceedings: The 3rd ACM International Workshop on Traceability in Emerging Forms of Software Engineering, TEFSE 2005, 8 November 2005, Long Beach California, USA*, pages 62–66, New York, NY, USA, 2005. ACM.

[Mur95]   Gail C. Murphy, David Notkin, and Kevin Sullivan. Software Reflexion Models: Bridging the Gap between Source and High-Level Models. In Gail E. Kaiser, editor, *SIGSOFT '95: Proceedings of the 3rd ACM SIGSOFT Symposium on Foundations of Software Engineering, Washington, D.C., USA*, pages 18–28. ACM Press, 1995.

[Mur08]   Leonardo G. P. Murta, André van der Hoek, and Cláudia M. L. Werner. Continuous and Automated Evolution of Architecture-to-Implementation Traceability Links. *Automated Software Engineering*, 15(1):75–107, 2008.

[Myl90]   John Mylopoulos, Alex Borgida, Matthias Jarke, and Manolis Koubarakis. Telos: Representing Knowledge About Information Systems. *ACM Transactions on Information Systems*, 8(4):325–362, 1990.

[Ngu03]   Tien N. Nguyen and Ethan V. Munson. A Model for Conformance Analysis of Software Documents. In *Proceedings: Sixth International Workshop on Principles of Software Evolution, 1–2 September 2003, Helsinki, Finland*, pages 24–35, Los Alamitos, CA, USA, 2003. IEEE Computer Society.

[Obj06]   Object Management Group. *Meta Object Facility (MOF) Core Specification,*
           OMG Available Specification, Version 2.0, January 2006. `http://www.omg.`
           `org/spec/MOF/2.0`.

[Obj10a]   Object Management Group. *Object Constraint Language, Version 2.2,* February
           2010. `http://www.omg.org/spec/OCL/2.2`.

[Obj10b]   Object Management Group. *OMG Systems Modeling Language (OMG*
           SysML^{TM}), Version 1.2, June 2010. `http://www.omg.org/spec/SysML/`
           `1.2`.

[Obj10c]   Object Management Group. *OMG Unified Modeling Language^{TM} (OMG*
           UML), Superstructure, Version 2.3, May 2010. `http://www.omg.org/`
           `spec/UML/2.3`.

[Obj11]   Object Management Group. *Business Process Model and Notation (BPMN),*
           Version 2.0, January 2011. `http://www.omg.org/spec/BPMN/2.0`.

[Old06]   Jon Oldevik and Tor Neple. Traceability in Model to Text Transformations.
           In Jan Aagedal, Tor Neple, and Jon Oldevik, editors, *ECMDA Traceability*
           Workshop (ECMDA-TW) 2006 Proceedings, July 10th 2006, Bilbao, Spain, SIN-
           TEF Report, Trondheim, Norway, 2006. SINTEF ICT.

[Oli04]   Jos'e Nuno Fonseca de Oliveira and C'esar de Jesus Pereira Cunha Ro-
           drigues. Transposing Relations: From Maybe Functions to Hash Tables. In
           Dexter Kozen, editor, *Mathematics of Program Construction, 7th International*
           Conference, MPC 2004, Stirling, Scotland, UK, July 12-14, 2004, Proceedings, vol-
           ume 3125 of *Lecture Notes in Computer Science,* pages 334–356, Berlin, Heidel-
           berg, 2004. Springer-Verlag.

[Oli10]   Rocco Oliveto, Malcom Gethers, Denys Poshyvanyk, and Andrea De Lu-
           cia. On the Equivalence of Information Retrieval Methods for Automated
           Traceability Link Recovery. In Giuliano Antoniol, Keith Gallagher, and Pe-
           dro Rangel Henriques, editors, *Proceedings: 18th IEEE International Conference*
           on Program Comprehension, ICPC 2010, 30 June–2 July 2010, Braga, Minho, Por-
           tugal, pages 68–71, Los Alamitos, CA, USA, 2010. IEEE Computer Society.

[Ols02]   Thomas Olsson and John Grundy. Supporting Traceability and Inconsis-
           tency Management between Software Artifacts. In *Proceedings of the IASTED*
           International Conference on Software Engineering and Applications (SEA 2002),
           November 4 – 6, 2002, Cambridge, Massachusetts, USA, 2002.

[Ols07]   Gøran K. Olsen and Jon Oldevik. Scenarios of Traceability in Model to Text
           Transformations. In David H. Akehurst, Régis Vogel, and Richard F. Paige,

editors, *Model Driven Architecture – Foundations and Applications, Third European Conference, ECMDA-FA 2007, Haifa, Israel, June 11-15, 2007, Proccedings [sic]*, volume 4530 of *Lecture Notes in Computer Science*, pages 144–156, Berlin, Heidelberg, 2007. Springer-Verlag.

[Pai08]   Richard F. Paige, Goran K. Olsen, Dimitrios S. Kolovos, Steffen Zschaler, and Christopher Power. Building Model-Driven Engineering Traceability Classifications. In Jon Oldevik, Gøran K. Olsen, Tor Neple, and Richard Paige, editors, *ECMDA Traceability Workshop (ECMDA-TW) 2008 Proceedings, June 12th 2008, Berlin, Germany*, SINTEF Report, pages 49–58, Trondheim, Norway, 2008. SINTEF ICT.

[Pat09]   Peter F. Patel-Schneider and Boris Motik (eds.).   OWL 2 Web Ontology Language Mapping to RDF Graphs – W3C Recommendation 27 October 2009.   `http://www.w3.org/TR/2009/REC-owl2-mapping-to-rdf-20091027`, October 2009.

[Pfe10]   Rolf-Helge Pfeiffer and Andrzey Wąsowski. An Aspect-based Traceability Mechanism for Domain Specific Languages. In Jon Oldevik, Gøran K. Olsen, and Dimitrios S. Kolovos, editors, *Proceedings of the 6th ECMFA Traceability Workshop 2010 (ECMFA-TW)*, pages 47–52, 2010.

[Pil08]   Jens von Pilgrim, Bert Vanhooff, Immo Schulz-Gerlach, and Yolande Berbers. Constructing and Visualizing Transformation Chains. In Ina Schieferdecker and Alan Hartman, editors, *Model Driven Architecture – Foundations and Applications, 4th European Conference, ECMDA-FA 2008, Berlin, Germany, June 9–13, 2008, Proceedings*, volume 5095 of *Lecture Notes in Computer Science*, pages 17–32, Berlin, Germany, 2008. Springer-Verlag.

[Pin96a] Francisco A.C. Pinheiro. *Design of a Hyper-Environment for Tracing Object-Oriented Requirements*. Phd thesis, University of Oxford, 1996.

[Pin96b] Francisco A.C. Pinheiro and Joseph A. Goguen. An Object-Oriented Tool for Tracing Requirements. *IEEE Software*, 13(2):52–64, 1996.

[Pin03]   Francisco A.C. Pinheiro. Requirements Traceability. In Julio Cesar Sampaio do Prado Leite and Jorge Horacio Doorn, editors, *Perspectives on Software Requirements*, volume 753 of *The Kluwer International Series in Engineering and Computer Science*, chapter 5, pages 91–113. Kluwer Academic Publishers, Dordrecht, Netherlands, 2003.

[Poh96a] Klaus Pohl. PRO-ART: Enabling Requirements Pre-Traceability. In *Proceedings of the Second International Conference on Requirements Engineering*, pages 76–84, Los Alamitos, CA, USA, 1996. IEEE Computer Society Press.

[Poh96b] Klaus Pohl. *Process-Centered Requirements Engineering*. Research Studies Press Ltd., Taunton, Somerset, England, 1996.

[Por11] Dan Port, Allen Nikora, Jane Huffman Hayes, and LiGuo Huang. Text Mining Support for Software Requirements: Traceability Assurance. In Ralph H. Sprague, Jr., editor, *Proceedings of the 44th Annual Hawaii International Conference on System Sciences, 4–7 January 2011, Koloa, Kauai, Hawaii*, pages 46–55, Los Alamitos, CA, USA, 2011. IEEE Computer Society.

[Pot88] C. Potts and G. Bruns. Recording the Reasons for Design Decisions. In *Proceedings of the 10th International Conference on Software Engineering, Singapore, 1988*, pages 418–427, Los Alamitos, CA, USA, 1988. IEEE Computer Society Press.

[Pru08] Eric Prud'hommeaux and Andy Seaborne (eds.). SPARQL Query Language for RDF – W3C Recommendation 15 January 2008. http://www.w3.org/TR/2008/REC-rdf-sparql-query-20080115, January 2008.

[Qus10] Abdallah Qusef, Rocco Oliveto, and Andrea De Lucia. Recovering Traceability Links between Unit Tests and Classes Under Test: An Improved Method. In *Proceedings: 2010 IEEE International Conference on Software Maintenance, September 12–18, 2010, Timişoara, Romania*, Los Alamitos, CA, USA, 2010. IEEE Computer Society.

[Ram90] C. V. Ramamoorthy, Yutaka Usuda, Atul Prakash, and W. T. Tsai. The Evolution Support Environment System. *IEEE Transactions on Software Engineering*, 16(11):1225–1234, 1990.

[Ram93] Balasubramaniam Ramesh and Michael Edwards. Issues in the Development of a Requirements Traceability Model. In *RE'93: IEEE Symposium on Requirements Engineering, January 4–6, 1993, San Diego, California*, pages 256–259, Los Alamitos, CA, USA, 1993. IEEE Computer Society.

[Ram95] B. Ramesh, T. Powers, C. Stubbs, and M. Edwards. Implementing Requirements Traceability: A Case Study. In *Proceedings of the Second IEEE International Symposium on Requirements Engineering*, pages 89–95, Los Alamitos, CA, USA, 1995. IEEE Computer Society.

[Ram01] Balasubramaniam Ramesh and Matthias Jarke. Toward Reference Models for Requirements Traceability. *IEEE Transactions on Software Engineering*, 27(1):58–93, 2001.

[Rei08] Michał Rein, Albert Ambroziewicz, Jacek Bojarski, Wiktor Nowakowski, Tomasz Straszak, Audris Kalnins, Edgars Celms, Elina Kalnina, Daniel Bildhauer, and Tomasz Szymański. ReDSeeDS Prototype – Implementing the

ReDSeeDS Engine prototype - 1st iteration. Project Deliverable D5.4.2, ReD-SeeDS Project, 2008. http://www.redseeds.eu.

[Ren09]   Yuan Ren, Gerd Gröner, Jens Lemcke, Tirdad Rahmani, Andreas Friesen, Yuting Zhao, Jeff Z. Pan, and Steffen Staab. Validating Process Refinement with Ontologies. In Elisa F. Kendall, Jeff Z. Pan, Marwan Sabbouh, Ljiljana Stojanovic, and Yuting Zhao, editors, *Semantic Web Enabled Software Engineering 2009, Proceedings of the 5th International Workshop on Semantic Web Enabled Software Engineering (SWESE 2009), Washington DC, USA, October 25, 2009,* volume 524 of *CEUR Workshop Proceedings,* pages 1–15. CEUR-WS.org, 2009. http://ceur-ws.org/Vol-524/swese2009_1.pdf.

[Ric03]   Julian Richardson and Jeff Green. Traceability Through Automatic Program Generation. In *Proceedings of the 2nd International Workshop on Traceability in Emerging Forms of Software Engineering (TEFSE 2003), October 7th 2003, Montreal, Canada,* 2003.

[Rie11]   Matthias Riebisch, Stephan Bode, Qurat-Ul-Ann Farooq, and Steffen Lehnert. Towards Comprehensive Modelling by Inter-Model Links Using an Integrating Repository. In *Proceedings: 18th IEEE International Conference and Workshops on Engineering of Computer-Based Systems, Las Vegas, Nevada, 27 – 29 April 2011,* pages 284–291, Los Alamitos, CA, USA, 2011. IEEE Computer Society.

[Ros08]   Cornelius Rosse and José L. V. Mejino Jr. The Foundational Model of Anatomy Ontology. In Albert Burger, Duncan Davidson, and Richard Baldock, editors, *Anatomy Ontologies for Bioinformatics: Principles and Practice,* volume 6, pages 59–117. Springer-Verlag, 2008.

[Sch08]   Hannes Schwarz, Jürgen Ebert, Volker Riediger, and Andreas Winter. Towards Querying of Traceability Information in the Context of Software Evolution. In Rainer Gimnich, Uwe Kaiser, Jochen Quante, and Andreas Winter, editors, *10th Workshop Software Reengineering (WSR 2008), 5-7 May 2008, Bad Honnef, Germany,* volume 126 of *Lecture Notes in Informatics,* pages 144–148, Bonn, Germany, 2008. GI.

[Sch09a] Michael Schneider (ed.). OWL 2 Web Ontology Language RDF-Based Semantics – W3C Recommendation 27 October 2009. http://www.w3.org/TR/2009/REC-owl2-rdf-based-semantics-20091027, October 2009.

[Sch09b] Hannes Schwarz. Report on Extracting and Using Traceability Information During the Development Process. Project Deliverable ICT216691/UoKL/WP4-D2/D/PU/b1, MOST Project, July 2009.

[Sch09c] Hannes Schwarz. Taxonomy and Definition of the Explicit Traceability Information Suppliable for Guiding Model-Driven, Ontology-Supported Development. Project Deliverable ICT216691/UoKL/WP4-D1/D/PU/b1, MOST Project, January 2009.

[Sch10a] Hannes Schwarz and Jürgen Ebert. Bridging Query Languages in Semantic and Graph Technologies. In Uwe Aßmann, Andreas Bartho, and Christian Wende, editors, *Reasoning Web: Semantic Technologies for Software Engineering, 6th International Summer School 2010, Dresden, Germany, August 30 – September 3, 2010, Tutorial Lectures*, volume 6325 of *Lecture Notes in Computer Science*, pages 119–160. Springer-Verlag, Berlin, Heidelberg, 2010.

[Sch10b] Hannes Schwarz, Jürgen Ebert, Jens Lemcke, Tirdad Rahmani, and Srdjan Zivkovic. Using Expressive Traceability Relationships for Ensuring Consistent Process Model Refinement. In Radu Calinescu, Richard Paige, and Marta Kwiatkowska, editors, *Proceedings; 2010 IEEE International Conference on Engineering of Complex Computer Systems, ICECCS 2010, 22–26 March 2010, Oxford, United Kingdom*, pages 183–192, Los Alamitos, CA, USA, 2010. IEEE Computer Society.

[Sch10c] Hannes Schwarz, Jürgen Ebert, and Andreas Winter. Graph-based traceability: a comprehensive approach. *Software and Systems Modeling*, 9(4):473–492, 2010.

[Sei10] Andreas Seibel, Stefan Neumann, and Holger Giese. Dynamic hierarchical mega models: comprehensive traceability and its efficient maintenance. *Software and Systems Modeling*, 9(4):493–528, 2010.

[Set04] Raffaella Settimi, Jane Cleland-Huang, Oussama Ben Khadra, Jigar Mody, Wiktor Lukasik, and Chris DePalma. Supporting Software Evolution through Dynamically Retrieving Traces to UML Artifacts. In Katsuro Inoue, Tsuneo Ajisaka, and Harald Gall, editors, *Proceedings: 7th International Workshop on Principles of Software Evolution, IWPSE 2004. In conjunction with RE 2004. 6-7 September 2004, Kyoto, Japan*, pages 49–54, Los Alamitos, CA, USA, 2004. IEEE Computer Society.

[Sha11] Bonita Sharif and Huzefa Kagdi. On the Use of Eye Tracking in Software Traceability. In *Sixth International Workshop on Traceability in Emerging Forms of Software Engineering (TEFSE 2011), Proceedings, May 23, 2011, Waikiki, Honolulu, HI, USA*, pages 67–70, New York, NY, USA, 2011. ACM.

[She03] Susanne A. Sherba, Kenneth M. Anderson, and Maha Faisal. A Framework for Mapping Traceability Relationships. In *Proceedings of the 2nd International*

Workshop on Traceability in Emerging Forms of Software Engineering (TEFSE 2003), October 7th 2003, Montreal, Canada, 2003.

[Sie11]   Katja Siegemund, Edward J. Thomas, Yuting Zhao, Jeff Pan, and Uwe Assmann.   Towards Ontology-driven Requirements Engineering.   In Kalina Bontcheva, Jeff Z. Pan, and Yuting Zhao, editors, *SWESE2011: The 7th International Workshop on Semantic Web Enabled Software Engineering, Co-located with ISWC2011, Bonn, Germany, 24th October, 2011*, 2011. `http://www.abdn.ac.uk/~csc280/event/workshop/swese2011`.

[Śmi06]   Michał Śmiałek. Towards a requirements driven software development system. Poster presentation at MoDELS, 9th International Conference, Genova, Italy, October 2006.

[Son98]   Xiping Song, William M. Hasling, Gaurav Mangla, and Bill Sherman. Lessons Learned From Building A Web-Based Requirements Tracing System. In *Proceedings: Third International Conference on Requirements Engineering. April 6–10, 1998, Colorado Springs, Colorado, USA*, pages 41–50, Los Alamitos, CA, USA, 1998. IEEE Computer Society.

[Sou08]   André Sousa, Uirá Kulesza, Andreas Rummler, Nicolas Anquetil, Ralf Mitschke, Ana Moreira, Vasco Amaral, and João Araújo. A Model-Driven Traceability Framework to Software Product Line Development. In Jon Oldevik, Gøran K. Olsen, Tor Neple, and Richard Paige, editors, *ECMDA Traceability Workshop (ECMDA-TW) 2008 Proceedings, June 12th 2008, Berlin, Germany*, SINTEF Report, pages 97–109, Trondheim, Norway, 2008. SINTEF ICT.

[Spa04]   George Spanoudakis, Andrea Zisman, Elena Pérez-Miñana, and Paul Krause. Rule-based generation of requirements traceability relations. *Journal of Systems and Software*, 72(2):105–127, 2004.

[Spa05]   George Spanoudakis and Andrea Zisman.   Software Traceability: A Roadmap. In S. K. Chang, editor, *Handbook of Software Engineering & Knowledge Engineering, Recent Advances*, volume 3, pages 395–428. World Scientific Publishing Company, Singapore, 2005.

[Sta10]   Steffen Staab, Tobias Walter, Gerd Gröner, and Fernando Silva Parreiras. Model Driven Engineering with Ontology Technologies. In Uwe Aßmann, Andreas Bartho, and Christian Wende, editors, *Reasoning Web – Semantic Technologies for Software Engineering, 6th International Summer School 2010, Dresden, Germany*, volume 6325 of *Lecture Notes in Computer Science*, pages 62–98. Springer-Verlag, Berlin, Heidelberg, 2010.

[Ste08]   Dave Steinberg, Frank Budinsky, Marcelo Paternostro, and Ed Merks. *EMF: Eclipse Modeling Framework*. The Eclipse Series. Addison-Wesley, 2 edition, 2008.

[Str02]   Darijus Strašunskas. Traceability in Collaborative Systems Development from Lifecycle Perspective – A Position Paper. In *Proceedings of the 1st International Workshop on Traceability in Emerging Forms of Software Engineering, September 28th 2002, Edinburgh, U.K.*, 2002. http://www.soi.city.ac. uk/~zisman/traceworkshop.html.

[Tre07]   Christoph Treude, Stefan Berlik, Sven Wenzel, and Udo Kelter. Difference Computation of Large Models. In *ESEC/FSE 2007 Proceedings: The 6th Joint Meeting of the European Software Engineering Conference and the ACM SIG-SOFT Symposium on the Foundations of Software Engineering, Dubrovnik, Croatia, September 3 – 7, 2007*, pages 295–304, New York, NY, USA, 2007. ACM.

[Try97]   Eirik Tryggeseth and Øystein Nytrø. Dynamic Traceability Links Supported by a System Architecture Description. In *Proceedings: International Conference on Software Maintenance, October 1 - 3, 1997, Bari, Italy*, pages 180–187, Los Alamitos, CA, USA, 1997. IEEE Computer Society.

[Van07]   Bert Vanhooff, Dhouha Ayed, Stefan Van Baelen, Wouter Joosen, and Yolande Berbers. UniTI: A Unified Transformation Infrastructure. In Gregor Engels, Bill Opdyke, Douglas C. Schmidt, and Frank Weil, editors, *Model Driven Engineering Languages and Systems, 10th International Conference, MODELS 2007, Nashville, USA, September 30 - October 5, 2007, Proceedings*, volume 4735 of *Lecture Notes in Computer Science*, pages 31–45, Berlin, Heidelberg, 2007. Springer-Verlag.

[Wal06]   Ståle Walderhaug, Ulrik Johansen, Erlend Stav, and Jan Aagedal. Towards a Generic Solution for Traceability in MDD. In Jan Aagedal, Tor Neple, and Jon Oldevik, editors, *ECMDA Traceability Workshop (ECMDA-TW) 2006 Proceedings, July 10th 2006, Bilbao, Spain*, SINTEF Report, Trondheim, Norway, 2006. SINTEF ICT.

[Wal10]   Tobias Walter, Hannes Schwarz, and Yuan Ren. Establishing a Bridge from Graph-based Modeling Languages to Ontology Languages. In Fernando Silva Parreiras, Jeff Z. Pan, and Uwe Assmann, editors, *TWOMDE-2010: Proceedings of the 3rd Workshop on Transforming and Weaving Ontologies in Model Driven Engineering, Málaga, Spain, June 30, 2010*, volume 604 of *CEUR Workshop Proceedings*. CEUR-WS.org, 2010. http://CEUR-WS.org/Vol-604.

[Wen07]   Sven Wenzel, Hermann Hutter, and Udo Kelter. Tracing Model Elements. In *Proceedings of the 2007 IEEE International Conference on Software Maintenance,*

October 2–5, 2007, Paris, France, pages 104–113, Los Alamitos, CA, USA, 2007.
IEEE Computer Society.

[Wen10]   Christian Wende, Srdjan Zivkovic, Uwe Aßmann, and Harald Kühn.
Feature-based Customisation of MDSD Tool Environments. Technical Report TUD-FI10-05-Juli 2010, Technische Universität Dresden, Fakultät Informatik, Dresden, Germany, July 2010.

[Whi97]   James E. Whitehead Jr. An Architectural Model for Application Integration
in Open Hypermedia Environments. In Mark Bernstein, Kasper Østerbye,
and Leslie Carr, editors, *HYPERTEXT '97: Proceedings of the Eighth ACM Conference on Hypertext,* pages 1–12, New York, NY, USA, 1997. ACM.

[Wie95]   Roel Wieringa. An Introduction to Requirements Traceability. Technical
Report IR-389, Faculty of Mathematics and Computer Science, Amsterdam,
Netherlands, November 1995.

[Wil75]   R. D. Williams. Managing the Development of Reliable Software. In *Proceedings of the International Conference on Reliable Software, Los Angeles, California,*
pages 3–8, New York, NY, USA, 1975. ACM.

[Win00]   Andreas Winter. *Referenz-Metaschema für visuelle Modellierungssprachen.* DUV
Informatik. Deutscher Universitätsverlag, Wiesbaden, Germany, 2000.

[Win10]   Stefan Winkler and Jens von Pilgrim. A survey of traceability in requirements engineering and model-driven development. *Software and Systems
Modeling,* 9(4):529–565, 2010.

[Wit07]   René Witte, Yonggang Zhang, and Juergen Rilling. Empowering Software
Maintainers with Semantic Web Technologies. In Enrico Franconi, Michael
Kifer, and Wolfgang May, editors, *The Semantic Web: Research and Applica-
tions, 4th European Semantic Web Conference, ESWC 2007, Innsbruck, Austria,
June 3-7, 2007, Proceedings,* volume 4519 of *Lecture Notes in Computer Science,*
pages 37–51, Berlin, Heidelberg, 2007. Springer-Verlag.

[Wol07]   Katharina Wolter, Thorsten Krebs, Daniel Bildhauer, Markus Nick, and
Lothar Hotz. Software Case Similarity Measure. Project Deliverable D4.2,
ReDSeeDS Project, 2007. http://www.redseeds.eu.

[Wol08]   Katharina Wolter, Thorsten Krebs, and Lothar Hotz. Determining similarity
of model-based and descriptive requirements by combining different similarity measures. In Michał Śmiałek, Kizito Mukasa, Markus Nick, and Jürgen
Falb, editors, *Model Reuse Strategies – Can requirements drive reuse of software
models?, Proceedings of the Second International Workshop MoRSe 2008, Beijing,*

China, May 2008, pages 1–8, Stuttgart, Germany, 2008. Fraunhofer IRB Verlag.

[Wol09] Katharina Wolter, Michał Śmiałek, Lothar Hotz, Stephanie Knab, Jacek Bojarksi, and Wiktor Nowakowski. Mapping MOF-based requirements representations to ontologies for software reuse. In Fernando Silva Parreiras, Jeff Z. Pan, and Uwe Assmann, editors, *Proceedings of the 2nd International Workshop on Transforming and Weaving Ontologies in Model Driven Engineering (TWOMDE 2009), Denver, Colorado, USA, October 4, 2009*, volume 531 of *CEUR Workshop Proceedings*. CEUR-WS.org, 2009. http://CEUR-WS.org/Vol-531.

[Wyn01] George M. Wyner and Jintae Lee. Defining Specialization for Process Models. Working Paper 216, Center for Coordination Science, Massachusetts Institute of Technology, 2001.

[Yie09] Andrés Yie and Dennis Wagelaar. Advanced Traceability with ATL. In Frédéric Jouault, editor, *Model Transformation with ATL: 1st International Workshop, MtATL 2009, Nantes, France, July 8–9, 2009, Preliminary Proceedings*, pages 78–87, 2009. http://docatlanmod.emn.fr/MtATL2009Presentations/PreliminaryProceedings.pdf.

[Yil11] Levent Yilmaz and David Kent. ACART: An API Compliance and Analysis Report Tool for Discovering Reference Design Traceability. In *Proceedings of the 49th Annual Association for Computing Machinery Southeast Conference, Kennesaw, Georgia, USA, March 24–26, 2011*, pages 243–248, New York, NY, USA, 2011. ACM.

[Yos09] Takashi Yoshikawa, Shinpei Hayashi, and Motoshi Saeki. Recovering Traceability Links between a Simple Natural Language Sentence and Source Code using Domain Ontologies. In *ICSM 2009: 2009 IEEE International Conference on Software Maintenance (ICSM), Proceedings of the Conference, September 20–26, 2009, Edmonton, Alberta, Canada*, pages 551–554, Los Alamitos, CA, USA, 2009. IEEE Computer Society.

[Yus07] Shehnaaz Yusuf, Huzefa Kagdi, and Jonathan I. Maletic. Assessing the Comprehension of UML Class Diagrams via Eye Tracking. In Kenny Wong, Eleni Stroulia, and Paolo Tonella, editors, *Proceedings: ICPC 2007, 15th IEEE International Conference on Program Comprehension, 26–29 June 2007, Banff, Alberta, Canada*, pages 113–122, Los Alamitos, CA, USA, 2007. IEEE Computer Society.

[Zil11] Christian Zillmann, Andreas Winter, Werner Teppe, Axel Herget, Marianne Theurer, Andreas Fuhr, Tassilo Horn, Volker Riediger, Uwe Erdmenger, Uwe

Kaiser, Denis Uhlig, and Yvonne Zimmermann. The SOAMIG Process Model in Industrial Applications. In Tom Mens, Yiannis Kanellopoulos, and Andreas Winter, editors, *Proceedings: 2011 15th European Conference on Software Maintenance and Reengineering (CSMR 2011), 1–4 March 2011, Oldenburg, Germany*, pages 393–342, Los Alamitos, CA, USA, 2011. IEEE Computer Society.

[Ziv10]   Srdjan Zivkovic, Christian Wende, Andreas Bartho, Katja Siegemund, Yuan Ren, Boris Gregorcic, and Krzysztof Miksa. Final prototype of ontology-driven software process guidance system. Project Deliverable ICT216691/BOC/WP2-D4/D/PU/b1.00, MOST Project, August 2010. http://www.most-project.eu.

About the Author

Biography

Hannes Schwarz, born in 1980, received the Abitur in Koblenz, Germany, in 1999. He studied computer science with a focus on information systems at the University of Koblenz-Landau, Germany, where he received his Diplom in 2006. Subsequently, he worked as research assistant at the Institute for Software Technology at the University Koblenz-Landau, Research Group Software Technology. He was involved in the projects "Requirements-Driven Software Development System" (ReDSeeDS) and "Marrying Ontologies and Software Technology" (MOST), which were funded by the European Commission.

His main research interests include traceability, graph technology, metamodeling, and query languages.

Publications

[1] Jürgen Ebert, Daniel Bildhauer, Hannes Schwarz, and Volker Riediger. Using Difference Information to Reuse Software Cases. In *Proceedings of the Workshop "Vergleich und Versionierung von UML-Modellen" (VVUM07), March 27th 2007, Hamburg, Germany*, 2007.

[2] Hannes Schwarz. *Program Slicing - Ein dienstorientiertes Modell*. Vdm Verlag Dr. Müller, 2007.

[3] Daniel Bildhauer, Jürgen Ebert, Volker Riediger, and Hannes Schwarz. Using the TGraph Approach for Model Fact Repositories. In *Proceedings of the Second International Workshop MoRSe 2008: Model Reuse Strategies – Can requirements drive reuse of software models?*, pages 9–18. Fraunhofer IRB Verlag, 2008.

[4] Hannes Schwarz, Jürgen Ebert, Volker Riediger, and Andreas Winter. Towards Querying of Traceability Information in the Context of Software Evolution. In *10th Workshop Software Reengineering (WSR 2008), 5-7 May 2008, Bad Honnef, Germany*, volume 126 of *Lecture Notes in Informatics*, pages 144–148. GI, 2008.

[5] Hannes Schwarz, Jürgen Ebert, and Andreas Winter. Graph-based Traceability - A Comprehensive Approach. Technical Report 04/2009, Institut für Softwaretechnik, Universität Koblenz-Landau, 2009. Arbeitsberichte aus dem Fachbereich Informatik.

[6] Hannes Schwarz. Towards a Comprehensive Traceability Approach in the Context of Software Maintenance. In *Proceedings: 13th European Conference on Software Maintenance and Reengineering, CSMR 2009, 24–27 March 2009, Kaiserslautern, Germany*, pages 339–342. IEEE Computer Society Press, 2009.

[7] Hannes Schwarz and Jürgen Ebert. Bridging Query Languages in Semantic and Graph Technologies. In *Reasoning Web: Semantic Technologies for Software Engineering, 6th International Summer School 2010, Dresden, Germany, August 30 – September 3, 2010, Tutorial Lectures*, volume 6325 of *Lecture Notes in Computer Science*, pages 119–160. Springer-Verlag, 2010.

[8] Hannes Schwarz, Jürgen Ebert, and Andreas Winter. Graph-based traceability: a comprehensive approach. *Software and Systems Modeling*, 9(4):473–492, 2010.

[9] Hannes Schwarz, Jürgen Ebert, Jens Lemcke, Tirdad Rahmani, and Srdjan Zivkovic. Using Expressive Traceability Relationships for Ensuring Consistent Process Model Refinement. In *Proceedings; 2010 IEEE International Conference on Engineering of Complex Computer Systems, ICECCS 2010, 22–26 March 2010, Oxford, United Kingdom*, pages 183–192, Los Alamitos, CA, USA, 2010. IEEE Computer Society.

[10] Tobias Walter, Hannes Schwarz, and Yuan Ren. Establishing a Bridge from Graph-based Modeling Languages to Ontology Languages. In *TWOMDE-2010: Proceedings of the 3rd Workshop on Transforming and Weaving Ontologies in Model Driven Engineering, Málaga, Spain, June 30, 2010*, volume 604 of *CEUR Workshop Proceedings*. CEUR-WS.org, 2010. http://CEUR-WS.org/Vol-604.